To the Eden, Leew & Collin
family
with love from Maria
and special thanks
to Sam

ROCKS, ICE AND DIRTY STONES

For Gisela Ecker,
long-time dear friend and valued colleague

ROCKS, ICE AND DIRTY STONES
DIAMOND HISTORIES

MARCIA POINTON

REAKTION BOOKS

Published by Reaktion Books Ltd
Unit 32, Waterside
44–48 Wharf Road
London N1 7UX, UK

www.reaktionbooks.co.uk

First published 2017

Printed and bound in China
by 1010 Printing International Ltd

A catalogue record for this book is available from the British Library

ISBN 978 1 78023 752 7

CONTENTS

1 'Udachnaya' diamond pipe, Sakha Republic, Russia, 2010.

INTRODUCTION

AS EVERY ELEMENTARY CHEMISTRY student knows, diamonds are constituted of pure carbon (C) formed at conditions of high pressures and temperatures within the Earth's mantle at depths of approximately 140 km and below; they are brought to the surface by eruptions of ancient volcanoes, which probably destroy the vast majority of them. Natural diamonds extracted from mines (illus. 1) are, therefore, geological survivors. This knowledge of diamonds' chemical properties is, however, relatively recent. For centuries savants baked, boiled and plunged precious stones into acid in an attempt to discover what they were made of. But in any case, to know that coal and diamonds are constituted of identical atoms is to say rather little. It is the idea that something deemed so beautiful and precious is identical to a substance that is dirty, black and, until the Clean Air Act of 1956, used to heat homes and produce energy throughout Britain, that is startling and that grips the imagination (illus. 2). Since the early nineteenth century, the blackness of coal might be said perpetually to cloud the fabled luminosity of the diamond, casting a sinister shadow and fostering superstitions that have made readers of novels and spectators of films tense with anticipation. Most recent among these is Anthony Doerr's Pulitzer Prize-winning novel *All the Light We Cannot See*. For, while De Beers and other jewellers, not least high street companies, work hard and largely effectively to persuade customers that the gift of a diamond is a prerequisite to a successful relationship, or to its continuation, the idea that diamonds are cursed, bring bad luck and engender destruction of individuals and nations underpins a swathe of fiction and film.

In this book I explore significant landmarks in the economic and cultural history of diamonds. Although my emphasis is post-medieval, the origins of gem lore in antiquity and the Middle Ages are also brought into focus. I take a look at the history of diamond mining and the ways in which diamonds were a crucial part of early modern mercantilism, as well as the role they have played in the history of empire and the conflicts that have ensued since independence. I examine the processes through which rough diamonds are brought to consumers, whether the singular celebrated stone like the Koh-i-noor or the modestly priced small stone in a young couple's engagement ring. Diamonds have been set in jewellery at least since Roman times (illus. 3) and readers will be introduced along the way to some jewellers and their work. However, this is neither a history of jewellery nor a technical treatise: up-to-date information about scientific and gemmological aspects of diamonds is readily available elsewhere and books on the history of jewellers like Cartier and Tiffany abound.[1] My interest lies with how and why people have acquired diamonds, whether to wear or as financial capital, as well as with questions that are ineradicably connected with precious stones – desire, ambition, theft, fraud and other forms of criminality. Why did, and do, diamonds matter? The extraordinary history of diamonds as objects of desire and materials of fantasy runs through this book like a seam of coal. The notion that diamonds are more than merely a mineral, the supply of which has been artificially controlled,

2 Alicja Kwade, *Lucy*, 2004, pressed black coal and adhesive agent, 14 × 14 × 18 cm.

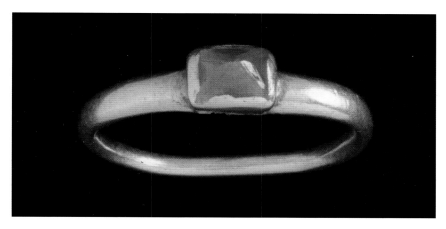

3 Roman ring set with a diamond.

and that possession of a diamond can profoundly affect a life, is compelling
and substantiated. At the same time, the characteristic crystalline structure of
a diamond has given its name to a four-sided motif that overlaps conceptually
with the lozenge and the rhombus and that proves to be a significant device
in architectural and other forms of ornament. The unparalleled hardness of
diamonds means that they have always been not only decorative but useful;
they have long been employed to engrave a design or an inscription onto glass
or to cut glass.[2] So-called 'scribbling rings' survive, and records of court cases
from the Old Bailey in the early modern period indicate that the removal of
a pane of window glass by cutting it with a diamond was a common means
of breaking and entering.[3]

Pliny the Elder was born in late 23 or early 24 CE and died in the eruption of Vesuvius in 79 CE. Along with the Greek Theophrastus (*c.* 371–*c.* 287
BCE) he is the most significant recorder and analyst of minerals prior to the
Renaissance, and the observations and definitions in his chapters on stones
in the *Natural History* not only formed the foundation of medieval writing
on minerals and precious stones but are found underpinning lapidary studies
as late as the eighteenth century.[4] The word 'adamas', generally understood
to mean diamond in these texts has, as J. F. Healy points out, a long pedigree
in the ancient world, being used to describe any unusually hard substance.[5]
Roman trade with the East flourished during the Roman Empire and Pliny
describes several kinds of diamonds including those that come from India; he

SOME OF THE OUTSTANDING PROPERTIES OF DIAMOND

Extreme mechanical hardness ($\sim$90 GPa).
Strongest known material, highest bulk modulus (1.2×10^{12} N/m^2), lowest compressibility (8.3×10^{-13} m^2/ N).
Highest known value of thermal conductivity at room temperature (2×10^3 W / m / K).
Thermal expansion coefficient at room temperature (0.8×10^{-6} K) is comparable with that of invar.
Broad optical transparency from the deep UV to the far IR region of the electromagnetic spectrum.
Good electrical insulator (room temperature resistivity is $\sim$10^{16} Ω cm).
Diamond can be doped to change its resistivity over the range 10-10^6 Ω cm, so becoming a semiconductor with a wide bad gap of 5.4 eV.
Very resistant to chemical corrosion.
Biologically compatible.
Exhibits low or 'negative' electron affinity.

also accurately describes the crystal system of the diamond and notices that it resembles rock crystal, which, in later centuries, was often used as a cheaper substitute in artefacts. As with subsequent writers right up until the eighteenth century, Pliny recognizes the diamond's unique hardness but fails to understand how its cleavage makes it extremely brittle. The pioneering French naturalist Georges-Louis Leclerc, Comte de Buffon, in *L'Histoire naturelle des minéraux* (1783–8) recognized that diamonds were relatively ancient in geological terms without realizing the truth; he remarked that it must have taken perhaps centuries for the crystallization of a diamond to occur whereas salt crystallized in a few minutes.[6] It is now recognized that there are differing degrees of hardness to a diamond in different directions – hard faces and soft faces – and each face has a grain. At first diamonds could only be polished; as technical knowledge increased it became closely guarded within guilds. The trade of diamond polishing, the earliest form of which involved rounding off the sharp angles to produce what is known as a cabochon, was already registered in Nuremberg in 1373 and there were certainly polishers in Paris by 1477.[7]

4 Diamond in its matrix, Kimberley, 1890.

Like other gemstones, diamonds were understood by medieval and early modern scholars as microcosmic and therefore as capable of interacting with the human body. Pigments were (and still are) made from gems like lapis lazuli and they provide the measure and much of the vocabulary for colour: think of 'emerald green' and 'ruby red'. Stones had symbolic qualities and virtues; they were valued for their medicinal and prophylactic properties. Impurities in a diamond can turn it into a blue or pink stone but generally diamonds are colourless. On the other hand, as well as being harder than any other known material, they give off light and refracted colour even in their natural state (illus. 4); when polished they give off a lustre. As Thomas Nichols wrote in 1659:

> The true *Diamond* is the hardest of all other stones, without colour, like unto pure water transparent: and if it have any yellowness or black-nesse, it is a fault in it. This property it hath, that it will snatch colour and apply it and unite it to itself; and thus will it cast forth at a great distance its lively shining rayes, so no other jewell can sparkle as it will.[8]

These light-giving properties made diamond imagery central to Christian symbolism and teaching. In a homily on Jeremiah written around 240 CE, the Christian Father of the Church Origen wrote of the similarity between a diamond (an incorruptible stone) and a saint or a martyr resisting temptation. Simultaneously for Origen the diamond is the truth of the Word of God that is revealed in Christ. The inner illumination of the diamond – the way it shines without intervention – heals medical conditions at the same time as it reveals the invincibility of the Almighty.[9] One of the most famous and widely circulated lapidaries was the poem written by Marbodus (or Marboeuf), bishop of Rennes, in the eleventh century, known through manuscript copies and then published in Fribourg in 1531.[10]

Lapidaries depended heavily on Pliny and over the ages the same truths and myths are repeated. The idea that diamond's invincibility yields to soaking in the warm blood of a goat, as reported by Pliny, is reiterated by Marbodus and repeated by Camillus Leonardus (or Camillo Leonardo) in 1502 in *Speculum lapidum*, translated as *The Mirror of Stones* in 1750.[11] Remy Belleau includes diamond in his philosophical suite of poems, each devoted to a separate stone, first published in 1576.[12] For all its brilliance and 'fire', the diamond is hard and cold, states Belleau, and therefore associated with Saturn, a planet that is believed to be cold and dry. But its perfection brings it close to the perfection of death and it is therefore to be taken as a powder by a person wishing to commit suicide.[13] Its benefits, however, are psycho-physiological and it can therefore protect the wearer (or consumer) from superstition and madness, nightmares, mania, fears and delusions.[14] These are all conditions that were thought in the early modern period to derive from a humoral disequilibrium. Diamond had long been thought to warn the wearer of infidelity by growing pale,[15] but equally, we learn from Belleau that whoever wears this stone in a ring of gold or silver need not fear the anguish of love or the charms that affect the brain. Experiments with stones were fundamental to early modern science. Francis Bacon's technical interest in gems focused on his conviction that Cornish diamonds (rock crystal) and rock rubies were 'Exudations of stone', just as gum comes from trees, and he experimented with pearls, corals and turquoises in a six-week trial in which he buried them to see if their colour would be affected.[16] A belief in the medicinal efficacy of precious stones like diamonds was enduring (and not without foundation, given the chemical composition of certain common remedies in today's pharmacy).

The physical properties of the diamond, as well as its outward form, have been a source of great fascination. Europe's expansion of trade, its development of mining and its discovery of new sources of mineral wealth was accompanied by, and stimulated through, new knowledge about minerals and their extraction. Anselmus Boëtius de Boodt, a Bruges-born doctor who was medical adviser to the Habsburg court of Rudolf II and who therefore had access to the precious stones in the Habsburg treasury, introduces a note of scientific scepticism into his many times reprinted and copied book *Gemmarum et lapidum historia* (1609); he suspected but could not prove that diamonds might be destroyed by extreme heat. A famous historical experiment was carried out in 1694 in the presence of Cosimo III, Grand Duke of Tuscany. Using a powerful burning glass, the Florentine academicians managed to obtain a high enough temperature to burn away a diamond. Experiments on diamonds by natural philosophers like Robert Boyle, who published his *Essay about the Origin and Virtues of Gems* in 1672, were concerned with establishing their physical properties and their medicinal qualities. Boyle, who was intrigued by the phosphorus that a diamond produced when rubbed, causing it to glow in the dark, suspended judgement on the powers of stones as prophylactic amulets.[17] Phosphorescence is a property not only of diamonds; before his death in 1642, Galileo had demonstrated phosphorescence in the so-called Bologna stone (baryte).[18]

Recent work on papers Charles Dufay (1698–1739) delivered to the French Académie des Sciences in the 1720s highlights the connection between those who sought to understand luminosity and electricity by submitting precious stones to various tests and those who were concerned with singularities and wonders. There are, we learn, continuities between seventeenth- and eighteenth-century attitudes to the wonderful or marvellous, and many of Dufay's fellow chemists were also alchemists.[19] How, we may ask, did these early experimental scientists get the materials for their experiments? Doubtless the Grand Duke of Tuscany had plenty of diamonds but what of a thirty-year-old Parisian chemist? From his laboratory 'Notes sur l'électricité' we learn that Dufay has in his possession a 'beau diamant bleu' that produces a little electricity when rubbed on wool. We do not know who lent Dufay the blue diamond, but he had others to work on: that lent him by M. Philippe became luminous in darkness while 'le diamant jaune de Mr. Bigones' left for four minutes in the shade also became luminous. It seems that Dufay may have thought that the colour of a diamond determined the degree to which it became luminescent. How to measure this luminosity was a problem and Dufay resorted to the refraction and reflection of a brilliant-cut diamond as the ultimate measure. After the diamonds had demonstrated their luminosity he plunged them into ink.[20]

In 1768, when the French chemist Jean Darcet (1725–1801) conducted experiments in connection with furnaces for producing porcelain, there was great astonishment when academicians learned that such an apparently 'incorruptible' body as the diamond could, like a drop of water, disappear under intense heat. The question of the destruction of the diamond was widely discussed. Antoine-Laurent Lavoisier (1743–1794) presented the definitive demonstration that a diamond would burn by means of oxygen in a closed container to the Académie des Sciences in 1772.[21] But it was Smithson Tennant in 1797 who concluded that a diamond decomposed into soot after he had

5 Marble being cut with the most up-to-date Dazzini diamond-strengthened wire cutter, at a Carrara quarry, 2015.

burnt it mixed with nitre (nitrogen) in a gold container closed at one end but
with a glass tube at the other to admit the gas. Fascination with a mineral so
hard, valuable and beautiful and yet so readily destroyed or, later, artificially
produced, provokes philosophical questions that lie at the heart of works by
some contemporary conceptual artists (see illus. 2), some of which I examine
in Chapter Three.

Darcet's experiments were initiated as part of an enquiry into industrial
production and it is in this context that diamonds played, and still play – not
least in an age of increasingly sophisticated laboratory-produced diamonds
– a major role in technology and industry.[22] Diamonds have been used for
cutting since the Middle Ages, but with increasing demand for drilling in
road building and mining from the late nineteenth century, they took on a
central importance. Combined with nickel, for example, they have provided
the technology used to cut marble in the great quarries of Carrara, where day
after day a diamond- and nickel-strengthened cord slowly cuts its way through
the thousands-of-years-old blocks of marble (illus. 5). On extraction from the
mine, diamonds are sorted into those that are gem quality (a tiny proportion)
and those that are small, flawed and of poor colour. These are industrial diamonds, whose super-abrasive properties and extreme hardness have made
them essential components in precision tools and instruments. The Industrial
Diamond Association was formed in 1946 and research began in the 1950s in
the United States, Sweden and the Soviet Union into the possibility of creating
diamonds in laboratories through high-pressure, high-temperature techniques

that produce small crystals suitable for industrial use. The diamonds thus produced need to be differentiated from so-called 'simulant diamonds' as used in the jewellery trade, which when mounted often look as sparkly as real diamonds (illus. 6); the most popular are cubic zirconia (CZ) and the artificially produced moissanite. As prices of mined-gem-quality diamonds have soared alongside publicity about the often devastating effects of diamond extraction on the environment and on the communities affected by the global hyper-valuation of natural diamonds, it has become more acceptable to purchase lookalike diamonds in jewellery. And there is nothing new about this. Just as alchemists searched for ways of turning dross into gold, so jewellers described ways of making paste stones: the reputable jeweller David Jeffries included a section in his eminently worthy *Treatise on Diamonds and Pearls* on the 'True Method of manufacturing DIAMONDS'.[23] A jeweller named Christopher Pinchbeck had particular success in this regard, lending his name not only to affordable 'diamonds' that were sold countrywide but generically to anything that was fake.[24]

7 Table showing the relative weight of precious stones in (Spanish) quelatos, (French) grains and (Italian) ducats from Juan de Arfe y Villafañe, *Quiltador, de la plata, oro, y piedras, conforme a las leyes reales, y para declaracion de ellas* (1598).

Supply and demand of natural diamonds has always been an issue, as with any commodity that is costly to extract. Consequent on this was the need to establish comparative measures for stones and their values that could be recognized across global frontiers. Juan de Arfe y Villafañe, a jeweller like Jeffries, published in 1572 his system for regulating the sale and purchase of precious stones (illus. 7). In the 1730s there was great concern about the cheapness of diamonds imported from Brazil via Lisbon. David Jeffries was provoked by this to try to establish his own rational system for the valuation of any stone. He dedicated his work to the king because, he argued, these jewels 'constitute so large a part of publick wealth' and are 'the chief ornaments of great and distinguished personages, in most parts of the world'.[25] Jeffries described the consternation among dealers who believed that diamonds 'were likely to become as plenty [sic] as transparent pebbles'.[26] His system, which did not work, is a notable early example of attempts to set up guidelines to regulate the diamond trade which culminated in the (only partially successful) Kimberley Process, an intergovernmental scheme set up in 2003 to prevent 'conflict diamonds' from entering the rough diamond exchange system through which internecine wars were being funded, especially in Africa.[27] Despite endeavours to subvert the monopoly by, among others, Russia, which has significant mines in Siberia (see illus. 1), De Beers still controls the supply of most of the world's raw diamonds. Sales of diamond jewellery by De Beers in 2013 totalled $79 billion and demand was expected to grow by 4.5 per cent in 2014, largely because of a growth of 6 per cent in the United States, an indication presumably of the ever-increasing wealth of those whom we now know as the super-rich.[28]

Recognition that the rarity and value of diamonds were artificially controlled is also not new, though modern-day media has ensured wider debate on the subject. Long before De Beers's South African monopoly, there were accusations of conspiracy to keep prices high and of a failure to recognize the aesthetic qualities of other minerals. Thus in 1785, R. E. Raspe pointed out that Captain Cook possessed a polished jade of the type used as ornaments:

> Its fine colour is between the emerald and chrysolite, and its uncommon clearness and transparency make it, in its kind, and in the eyes of the naturalists, as inestimable as any uncommonly large and clear

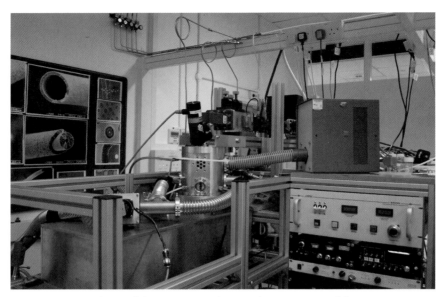

8 CVD diamonds being grown in the Bristol University CVD lab, 2014,
with photos of diamond-coated wire in the background.

diamond possibly can be in the interested opinion of the East India
companies, the Portuguese, and their drudges the merchants and
lapidaries, who, in that mercenary quality, have done the business of
their employers, and, by exaggerated praises of the diamond above
many finer stones, have raised it to an unconscionable price, even
beyond what it cost an hundred years ago in the times of *Tavernier*.[29]

In this book, I shall draw attention to some things that have changed
very little, like the way in which diamond cutters go about their business,
the desire for diamonds as ornamental and symbolic, and the value placed
on diamonds as an exchange currency that maintains its value and can move
invisibly in a global market. Other things have changed dramatically, including
the locations in which diamonds are extracted. The long list of areas within
which diamond super-abrasives are now used include the aerospace and
automotive industries. Diamonds provide the drill bits in oil and gas explor-
ation while electronics manufacturers use diamond to texture disk drives
for memory. The most significant development of the past twenty years has
been in polycrystalline diamond films, made by chemical vapour deposition

(CVD), a technique pioneered in Russia in the 1970s and then optimized by groups in America and Japan in the late 1980s. In CVD, a gas-phase chemical reaction involving hydrogen and a carbon-containing gas (such as methane, acetylene or even ethanol) above a solid surface results in deposition of the carbon atoms onto that surface in the form of a thin coating of diamond (illus. 8). Various materials can be used as a substrate, including a silicon wafer (for electronic applications), different metals (to make wear-resistant mechanical components), tungsten carbide (for cutting tools), or a natural or industrial diamond stone (to make a larger diamond gemstone) and onto that is grown a diamond film (or layer) that can be of a thickness ranging from nanometres to millimetres.[30] These films are often polycrystalline (a continuous film composed of many different crystals in different orientations bonded together into a solid layer), or single crystal, as in gemstones. CVD diamond films exhibit many of the properties that have been so valued in natural diamonds from time immemorial, but because they are lab-grown their properties can be altered depending on their required application. Natural diamonds come in a great range of sizes and are expensive but they also contain a range of unique and irreproducible defects, meaning that no two natural diamonds are identical. In contrast, CVD diamonds have far fewer defects. Moreover, diamonds can be produced in which impurities have deliberately been included to alter the diamond's properties. And this can be done repeatedly and reproducibly – an essential requirement for electronic applications where starting materials need to be identical and well characterized. One such impurity is boron, which when incorporated into the diamond structure at a few parts per million (a few boron atoms for every million carbons), enables the diamond to conduct electricity. This is what makes the Hope diamond discussed below blue and uncharacteristically electrically conductive.

Conversely, by eliminating virtually all impurities from the CVD process, extremely pure lab-grown diamond gemstones can now be made that far exceed natural diamonds in purity and perfection. These lab-grown diamonds are now beginning to emerge into the gemstone market competing directly against mined diamonds. The fact that an absolutely pure diamond can now be produced has impacted on the advertising of natural gem diamonds; whereas before a stone as clean as possible was the ultimate desirable acquisition, the notion of a pure stone now suggests something artificially produced. Indeed, the emerging industry of CVD diamond gemstones prefers to call their diamonds 'lab-grown diamonds' or 'CVD diamonds', rather than 'synthetic' or 'artificial', as those latter two terms, although technically accurate, are analogous to a poor-quality copy in the minds of the public, who are very aware that cubic zirconia and moissanite gems were previously called 'synthetic diamonds'. De Beers have been involved in synthetic diamond research and manufacture since the 1950s for high-pressure, high-temperature 'industrial' diamonds, and then since the mid-1990s for CVD diamonds. In 2002 they set up a separately named company called Element Six under the De Beers umbrella and in 2013 opened in Oxfordshire the largest centre for research into and production of what they term 'supermaterials'.[31]

The uses to which CVD – an extraordinarily innovative and multi-use high-tech material – may be put can scarcely be overstated and would have seemed miraculous to alchemists and lapidaries of centuries past. For example, in information technology, diamond films may be key to the fabrication of quantum computers, which use light to store and transmit data far faster than conventional silicon computers. In theory, this could also lead to uncrackable computer codes. A further example of the application of CVD diamond is in work on brain-computer interfaces (BCI). Here the standard method of attaching

9 Cartier diamond and platinum tiara, 1906, Salzburg.

20

electrodes to nerve cells employs metal probes and/or silicon computing. But these materials are detected by the body's immune system, which then attacks them, causing scarring and inflammation. Diamond is bioinert (the body doesn't recognize it as a foreign object) and so there is no immune response. By using diamond, an electrode can be permanently implanted in the brain, central nervous system or peripheral nerves, allowing signals to be passed to and from the nerves to an external computer. The illegal concealment of diamonds within body cavities and orifices is a theme that is explored in this book in relation to miners in the early years of South African diamond extraction. It is the ability to visualize the body's interior, first through X-ray and then through sophisticated methods of scanning, that made possible these non-covert pathological insertions. Implanted diamonds could lead to treatments for paralysis and many neurodegenerative diseases (Parkinson's, Alzheimer's, epilepsy, stroke), as well as the exciting (or scary) idea of thought-controlled computers, cars, toys and so on. It seems that diamonds really are forever, and are beautiful in ways far more meaningful than a Cartier tiara might lead us to believe (illus. 9).

Diamond importers have always searched for diamonds without flaws; today stones can be scanned and inclusions invisible to the eye on the diamond's surface can be detected, as I describe in Chapter Two. Importers of diamonds from India in the seventeenth century bemoaned the existence of inclusions that only showed up once a large and expensive stone was cleaved: 'The great stone I showd you of 60 carat has since cut but answers not Expectation a great flaw or two remaining on the sides, & a black small point or Two yet have wasted near Two Thirds . . . when a customer will present for them God knows,' wrote one diamond importer in 1683 to an associate in India.[32] For today's geologists (or more accurately petrologists) conducting research into the earth's interior at depths of 300 to 600 km or so, it is precisely these flaws or inclusions that are of interest. Essentially the diamonds act as impervious bottles that trap minerals (and in some cases fluid species) which can be inspected in the laboratory. In some cases the minerals garnered from diamond inclusions can be dated using isotopes produced by radioactive decay. For example, the sulphides can be dated using lead isotopes produced by the decay of uranium. Sometimes ages greater than three thousand million years have been measured, much older than the eruption ages. An unusual type of diamond, sometimes referred to as a 'coated stone' or 'Zaire cube', has a dark coating which is composed of large numbers of ultra-microscopic inclusions. The composition of these inclusions indicates high quantities of chlorine, sodium and potassium, a combination indicating the presence in the diamond-forming region of a brine. In 2014 a small 'ugly brown' alluvial diamond was discovered in Brazil containing the mineral ringwoodite, a high-pressure polymorph of the magnesium silicate olivine found in meteorites. The presence of ringwoodite at the greatest depths is a feature of theoretical models of the deep earth. The presence of water in its structure appears to imply large quantities of water stored in the earth's interior.[33] These are highly specialized areas of research by chemists, geologists and physicists that are challenging for the layperson. They are mentioned here as they lend an insight into the aim of this book, which is to spread a net sufficiently wide to capture in essence the extraordinary material, economic and cultural history of the king of stones in all its global relevance, richness and multifaceted variety.

Diamonds may, as we have seen, give us important clues to the history of our environment and may help to keep us alive and well, even if not in the way early lapidaries envisaged. However, thinking about these extraordinary minerals conjures perhaps above all a history of emotions. Extremely small in volume but equally very high in financial value, diamonds were from earliest times – and still are when smuggled – the most convenient form of portable wealth. In diasporas, in the movement of peoples displaced by war or other forms of hardship, jewels play a crucial role: they have exchange value and so can facilitate a new life elsewhere, and they have associative value – they may work as repositories for memories of the old life or for the fabrication of comforting myths. A case in point is Vladimir Nabokov and his family who fled the Bolshevik Revolution. In his many-times-rewritten autobiography, he tells how his family paid their living expenses in London with the 'handful of jewels' which Natasha, a far-sighted old chambermaid, just before his mother's departure from St Petersburg, had swept off a dresser into a '*nécessaire* de voyage of pigskin', which had been bought 'in 1897 for my mother's wedding trip to Florence'.[34] The memory of this white Russian family's escape from persecution and death is evoked by one singular object – a jewel case. We travel with luggage that contains our prized possessions; nothing more pathetic than an

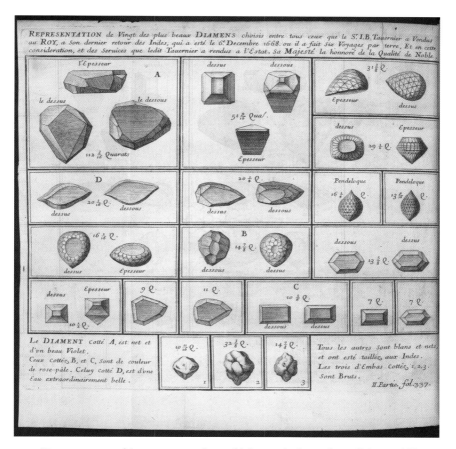

10 'Representation of the twenty most beautiful diamonds chosen from all those sold by M. Tavernier to the King', illustration from *Les Six voyages de Jean-Baptiste Tavernier, ecuyer Baron d'Aubonne en Turquie, en Perse et aux Indes* (Paris, 1676).

empty suitcase, nothing sadder than the memory of things that were dear and are now lost. The family of Gary Shteyngart were by contrast poor Russian Jews who emigrated to the USA in 1979 when U.S. President Carter made a deal with President Khrushchev to supply grain after the USSR harvest had failed, in return for exit visas for Russian Jews who wanted to emigrate. In his memoir Shteyngart describes how a customs agent at Leningrad airport, prior to their departure, took off his child's fur hat and poked around in the lining, looking for diamonds that his parents might have concealed there.[35]

Diamonds go missing. If they possessed DNA, life would be a great deal easier for those who have custody of them or deal in them. As it is, the theft of

11 The Hope blue diamond, Smithsonian Museum, Washington, DC.

a diamond or a piece of diamond jewellery means that the gems are generally never recovered – once recut they are unrecognizable. Controversy over the identity of famous historic diamonds has given rise to debate and fantasy, not least in the case of the Koh-i-noor discussed in Chapter One. One example will suffice here to indicate how problematic it has been, and remains, to track diamonds. Among the stones brought back to Europe by the merchant Jean-Baptiste Tavernier was an exceptional 112-carat diamond he sold to Louis XIV in 1668.[36] Tavernier illustrated it in his book (illus. 10) showing (top left) the stone from above, below and from the side, which makes it clear that the diamond was, as he states, cut in the Indian manner (a lasque – in which the minimum was lost and the stone's asymmetry maintained). Tavernier describes the diamond, to which he gives pride of place in this collection, as 'clear and of a beautiful violet'.[37]

At the time little was understood of coloured diamonds and this was the first such diamond to enter the French royal collection. After the sequestration of the crown jewels by the revolutionary government, a large quantity of precious stones including Tavernier's diamond, by now universally described as blue, were looted from the badly protected Garderobe in the Tuileries in September 1792. Although many of the gems were recovered, what became known as 'the French blue' was not. In 1812 a deep blue diamond of unknown origin was in the possession of a London diamond merchant called Daniel Eliason; John Francillon, a Huguenot lapidary and natural historian, made a note of this blue diamond, including a drawing of the exact size and shape having traced round the diamond with a pencil 'by leave of Mr Eliason'.[38] Speculation tended to favour the view that this reappeared stone was a section cut from Tavernier's purloined 'blue' diamond. After 1812 this diamond disappeared again from view, possibly into the possession of George IV. A diamond that was *apparently* the same as Eliason's reappeared in the collection of an Englishman, Henry Philip Hope, in 1839, though nobody knew from whom he had bought it. It was exhibited in 1851 at the Great Exhibition and eventually, after many years and many changes of hands, was acquired by Harry Winston Inc., who in 1958 donated it to the Smithsonian Museum, Washington, DC, where it is on permanent display as one of the nation's greatest treasures (illus. 11). Recently the discovery of a lead cast of Tavernier's diamond and the application of new research methodologies has resulted in a rethink.[39] Not only have the French royal archives been meticulously trawled, but 3D printing and photorealist simulations have been used and all the evidence on colour (taking into account historical linguistics and how cutting changes a diamond's colour) has been evaluated. It is proposed not only that this stone in its gold setting had special allegorical significance for the *roi soleil*, but also that the Smithsonian blue diamond is one of a number of 'avatars' of Tavernier's diamond. This is an example of how historical research and the use of modern computers and sophisticated software make it possible 'to recreate and understand the optical properties of a forgotten seventeenth-century masterpiece that served the image and power of the King of France'.[40]

JEAN BAPTISTE TAVERNIER,
Baron d'Aubone,
en habit Persien, qui lui fut donné en 1665.
par le Roy de Perse.

12 Portrait of Jean-Baptiste Tavernier, from *Les Six voyages de Jean-Baptiste Tavernier* . . .
(Paris, 1676).

ONE

DIAMONDS AND EMPIRE

India

BY FAR THE MOST READILY PORTABLE form of wealth, diamonds have oiled the machinery of empires as well as forming a significant element in its spoils. The building of empire is predicated on the expectation of riches, as is evident in the pre-twentieth-century history of diamond exploitation in India, Brazil and South Africa. There is nowhere better to start than with Jean-Baptiste Tavernier, the celebrated French merchant who travelled extensively in the seventeenth century through Persia, Turkey and India (illus. 12). His account of rulers, their courts and their treasuries fuelled Western desire for Indian diamonds. Tavernier tells of the diamond mines near Golconda in the Hyderabad district of India that had already been famed for centuries as the source of some of the most mythic diamonds.[1] He claims to have opened up a road for the French 'to these mines, which are the only places on earth where one finds diamonds'. Tavernier doubtless embroiders his autobiography – Asia was the fictional site of excessive power and unbelievable personal riches, and Tavernier was not one to disappoint his audience, which rapidly became international. Nonetheless, there is a precision and pragmatism in his account that makes it valuable as historical evidence, as, for example, his description of the Indian miners who lack iron wheels to polish the stones they mine, and the merchants who purchase the miners' finds, having weighed them and valued them. He himself buys diamonds in exchange for gold coins minted either in Holland or in England, but the miners prefer the former as they are better certified.[2]

13 Gustave Doré, *Sinbad amongst the Serpents in the Valley of Diamonds*, 1870, colour engraving.

By Tavernier's time Indian diamonds were regularly exported to the West. Alexander the Great in 327 BCE is thought to have been the first to bring diamonds from India to Europe, and in the thirteenth century Marco Polo left an account of diamond mining:

> In this kingdom [of Masulipatam], you must know, is found the diamond; there are several mountains, among which during rain, water flows with great turbulence, and through wide caverns; and when the shower ceases, men search through the ground previously inundated, and find the gems. In summer there is not a drop of water, and the heat can scarcely be endured, while fierce and venomous serpents inspire great fear; yet those who venture thither discover valuable diamonds.[3]

Until the discovery between 1726 and 1729 of diamonds in the area of Brazil now called Minas Gerais (the name means General Mines), India was the sole source of this desired mineral apart from minor deposits in Borneo, for which the East India Company was in competition with the Dutch.[4] The French, Dutch and English competed in India for access to the best stones, with the EIC aggressively seeking a monopoly. Marco Polo's description of alluvial diamond mining is one of the earliest: stones are retrieved after being washed to the surface by the agency of water, whether in rivers or, as happens today, by artificial flooding. While this passage rings true, it is followed immediately by an account of a long, deep and totally inaccessible valley of diamonds. Merchants throw down pieces of flesh, to which the diamonds adhere, whereupon eagles swoop down and seize the chunks of meat and fly away; once frightened by the shouts of onlookers, the birds drop the meat and the men then retrieve the diamonds. Even if the birds have swallowed the meat, they can be caught and the stones retrieved from their excrement.

In *One Thousand and One Nights*, known in English as *The Arabian Nights* (first English edition 1706), Sinbad the Sailor, on his second voyage, is stranded on a desert island; he escapes by tying himself to a monstrous bird, which then flies away and deposits him in the valley of diamonds described by Marco Polo (illus. 13):

As I walked through this valley, I perceived it was strewed with diamonds some of which were of surprising bigness. I took a great deal
of pleasure to look upon them, but speedily saw at a distance such
objects as very much diminished my satisfaction and which I could
not look upon without terror.[5]

These objects were the huge serpents. Then he also notices the meat. By
using his turban to tie himself to the largest piece he can find and lying on
the ground face down with a bag of the biggest diamonds he has been able
to collect, Sinbad is lifted out of the valley in the claws of an eagle, to the
astonishment of the merchants who are waiting above for their spoils.

This fantastic story of diamonds and serpents has a powerful hold on the
Western imagination – John Ruskin, for example, drew on it in the first lecture
of *The Ethics of the Dust*.[6] I have lingered over it because it encapsulates many
of the themes generated by the actual extraction of diamonds: the melding of
something beautiful and desirable with something utterly loathsome and
destructive, the impossibility of attaining diamonds without extreme danger
to the person, the association of diamonds with enormous intrepidity, the
ingenious means devised by merchants to secure precious stones and the idea
that there are places where large diamonds lie for the picking. Even the story
of retrieving diamonds from the excrement of birds has unpleasant echoes
of the exploitation of slave labourers in diamond mines suspected of secreting
diamonds, who were subjected to body searches; as workers were naked in
the heat, human orifices were the only possible hiding places. The mineralogist John Mawe, who claimed to be the first foreigner to visit the mines of
Serro do Frio in Brazil in the early nineteenth century, describes the many
precautions taken to prevent 'Negroes' embezzling diamonds. They change
troughs frequently to prevent diamonds being secreted and anyone suspected
of swallowing a stone is confined to the strong room 'until the fact can be
ascertained'.[7]

Diamond deposits also exist in Panna in the northeast of India and,
though the gems extracted there tend to be smaller, some mining continues
today. Known since antiquity (Ptolemy's 'La Pannassa'), Panna was visited
in the nineteenth century by Louis Rousselet, a French photographer whose

14 'A Diamond Mine at Pannah', drawn by E. Bayard after a sketch, engraved J. Gauchard, from Louis Rousselet, *L'Inde des Rajahs: Voyage dans l'Inde Centrale* (Paris, 1877).

records of his tour of India formed the basis of a volume describing his travels, illustrated with over three hundred wood engravings; where photography was impractical a drawing was made (illus. 14).[8] One of these shows how the miners, overseen by guards, worked naked knee-deep in water at the bottom of a well of around 12 to 15 m wide and 20 m deep that was sunk to reach the thin layer of sedimentary diamond conglomerate. Some break up the ground with pickaxes while others are shovelling the gravel into baskets, which are then hauled to the surface where other miners will sift the gravel. At the right can be seen the rope ladders providing access to the mine. In alluvial mining vast amounts of gravel will be sifted in the chance of one modest stone. The effort involved is a vivid illustration of the economic value of diamonds, but the image of the tiny gleaming stone in a heap of rubble is also one that has perennial currency in alluding to extreme contrasts between objects of desire and waste. The diamond stands for what is irreducible – it is uncontaminated by the filth in which it is found. By this time there were cutters at Panna working on stones; Rousselet describes these as of superb quality and great purity, but he doubted that the cutters could compete in skill with those of Holland, though their cut stones were not to be dismissed.[9] He also claimed it was very rare for these stones to reach Europe and that what people were buying as Indian diamonds had in fact come from Brazil.[10]

Brazil

Diamonds were discovered in the Portuguese colony of Brazil at the very time when Indian production was in pronounced decline. The shift in fashions in European jewellery from pearls in the seventeenth century to diamonds in the eighteenth was partly owing to the more immediate availability of good-quality stones. Other factors were connected to the development of cutting techniques that brought out the refractive qualities of the stone and the enhancement of artificial lighting that allowed for maximum glitter. While panning for gold, some *garimpeiros* (small-scale and often extremely poor miners) noticed that there were shiny pebbles in their sieves but having never seen diamonds they failed to recognize them until – allegedly – in the mid-1720s a *faiscador* (prospector) named Bernardo Fonseca Lobo recognized that what he had found among the gold washings at a place called Morrinhos in the Serro do Frio were diamonds, but he told only a few friends.[11] Under pressure from a judge, Fonseca was forced to sell his site. As a consequence he made a trip in 1727 to Vila Rica and informed the governor of what had occurred. The latter waited two years before reporting the news to Portugal and then only did so after learning that a priest, António Xavier de Sousa, was sailing for Lisbon and would inform the king of the discovery. The governor had lived in Goa and undoubtedly knew the value of the pebbles he had been shown but claimed that only jewellers in Lisbon had the authority to decide. Meanwhile he suspended gold washing and mining in the Serro do Frio and cancelled allotments that had been granted.[12] The news of discovery of diamonds provoked enormous celebration in Lisbon with fêtes, *Te Deums* and processions.[13] The government offered the pope the first diamonds to arrive back in Portugal, and the discovery became a talking point throughout European high society. This was the era when men as well as women were described as 'covered in diamonds' and when women amassed quantities of diamonds as part of their personal wealth.[14]

In the seventeenth century Portugal had regarded the coastal areas of Brazil, with their plantations of sugar and tobacco, as the main source of their wealth. Gold mining brought Portuguese speculators to its colony but it also threatened to depopulate the coastal areas, creating fears of possible foreign invasion. The gold rush brought, it has been calculated, nearly 600,000 Portuguese to Brazil in the first sixty years of the eighteenth century; people of all kinds – small merchants, proprietors, prostitutes, priests and all sorts of adventurers.[15] Migration to the interior was prohibited, roads were closed, numerous permits were required, foreigners were expelled and newly imported slaves were distributed in a manner disadvantageous to the mining regions.[16] But in the early eighteenth century the importance of mineral extraction was recognized and strict laws were enacted to control this. The initial code (*regimento*) for diamond mining was therefore based on these existing models but was considerably harsher. A head tax was payable on each miner or slave, a judge decided all issues concerning claims, no one was allowed to purchase diamonds from a slave and any friar found in the district was to be expelled (the clergy were practised in smuggling).

Once large stones were found, the regulations became draconian: anyone not active in washing for diamonds was threatened with expulsion (meaning families in well-established gold-mining camps were left homeless) and free 'Negroes' and 'mulattoes' were prohibited from searching for diamonds.[17] Thus in the early 1730s officially demarcated areas became the diamond district, headed by a colonial governor (*intendente*). Slaves were at the base of society; their continuous importation kept the economy going as they were only worked for seven to ten years, it has been estimated.[18] In 1734 diamond mining was prohibited for several years as a result of a glut in the European market and when it was renewed it was under even tighter supervision, following the granting of a monopoly to Portuguese merchant João Fernandes.[19] No more than six hundred slaves could be used in working the sites, though it is clear that this was not observed and there was a substantial head tax payable to the crown on each 'Negro'. The communities of the Portuguese owners of land and representatives of the crown flourished and large houses were built, many of which survive today. The population data of Minas Gerais indicates that in 1776, of the 320,000 inhabitants, 50 per cent were black, 26 per cent 'mulatto' and 22 per cent white. By 1787 manumitted slaves were 41 per cent of the population; they were freed as the mines petered out.[20]

The Diamond Code, promulgated in 1771 at the time the mining monopoly ended and diamond mining became 'royal extraction', centralized all diamond sales in the Royal Treasury, setting up in Lisbon an office – the Conta da Minha – headed by the Marquis of Pombal and three directors who in turn appointed the administrators to carry out their orders supervising the

15 *Final Washing, M. Schubert's Mine, Brazil*, heliograph after Dujardin, Henri Jacobs et Nicolas Chatrian, *Le Diamant* (Paris, 1884).

diamond district in Brazil.[21] João v of Portugal (1689–1750) had been able to exploit the wealth of gold and diamonds in the colony of Brazil to make himself absolute monarch and the owner of unimaginable wealth, much of which was spent on building projects, works of art and a lifestyle of luxurious excess. Of all that was extracted – by slaves imported from Africa – 20 per cent (the *quinto*, or one-fifth) was crown property. Gold and diamonds enabled Portugal to recover economic stability after its wars with Spain and the Netherlands but it was at the price of terrible repression: the fiscal administration in Portugal more than 7,000 km away was incapable of grasping the punishment meted out to those alleged to have attempted to extract diamonds or gold illicitly, with the army brought in to suppress rebellions. Culprits were sent in galleys to Angola. When much of Lisbon was destroyed by the Great Earthquake and tsunami of 1755, it was perceived in Brazil as divine punishment. In 1801 France and Spain declared war on Portugal and the crown pledged diamonds to the banks of Amsterdam and London to raise money for troops. After the treaty of Madrid, Napoleon acquired through his brother Lucien considerable quantities of Brazilian diamonds which, it has been suggested, contributed not only to his personal passion for diamonds but to the growth of French jewellery design and manufacture.[22] Diamantina (originally Tijuco), where it all began, is now a world heritage site and a city of fine Baroque architecture. Some alluvial diamond mining continued in the nineteenth century (illus. 15) and today *garimpeiros* still try to scratch a living in Brazil panning for gold or diamonds. The mercury used in processing gold has caused untold damage to the environment and to the miners, whose hands and feet are permanently affected and among whom malaria is endemic.

South Africa

In 1917 the following description of life in the diamond-digging fields of the Orange River, South Africa, was published by the Diamond Fields Advertiser Company, whose newspaper, founded in Kimberley in 1878, is still in print:

> the two great boons which digging offers are an almost ideally healthy life, and personal independence. It is usually said that nobody ever

dies on the River except of old age or pneumonia – the latter being a somewhat comprehensive term . . . The children in the different camps grow up in the open air sturdy and almost aggressively vigorous. Even the frequent dust-storms which are the most objectionable feature of the climate, do not seem to have any ill effect on the inhabitants. It is no uncommon thing to see men of seventy and upwards at their claims regularly.[23]

It is hard to reconcile this cheerfully optimistic description with the history of German and British colonialism and the extraction of diamonds in South Africa. Underlying this description, with its glib dismissal of sickness and old age, lies a history of desperation, ruination, mental and physical suffering and sudden death. It is perhaps fitting that the most tangible and vivid memorial to this history is a huge hole (illus. 16). A gigantic 463 m in width and originally 240 m in depth (though it was partly infilled with debris and now is also partly filled with water), the Kimberley Big Hole is testimony to the labour of around fifty thousand miners with picks and shovels between 1871 and 1914. It was from these and subsequent excavations, under the control of De Beers, that some of the most famous diamonds in the world have been

16 Kimberley Big Hole, open pit and underground mine, South Africa, 2015.

extracted: the Great Star of Africa, the Cullinan, the Centenary, the Tiffany (see illus. 34).[24] The discovery of diamonds triggered by a child playing with shiny stones on a farm by the Orange River in 1866 led to the recognition of the volcanic pipe, allowing identification of the type of potassic volcanic rock (now named kimberlite) within which diamond formations might be found (see illus. 4). This permitted the discovery of diamonds in other areas of Africa, in Siberia (see illus. 1) and in Canada, and made possible the development of dry diggings as opposed to the river panning that had gone on in India and Brazil. In short, it is from the game of Daniel Jacobs, son of a poor Boer farmer, that modern-day diamond mining evolved.

Kimberlite occurs in the earth's crust in vertical structures known as pipes and these are now the most important source of diamonds today, in mines like the great Premier Mine in Pretoria, opened in 1902. It is believed that kimberlites are formed at depths of between 150 and 450 km from the earth's surface and are erupted violently from depths greater than any other igneous rock;[25] they are carriers of diamonds and garnets but are also of great interest to scientists. The Premier Mine was renamed the Cullinan after the manager when a 3,106.75-carat gem was found there on 26 January 1905 by an unnamed black labourer. This was the largest rough gem-quality diamond ever found (described as 'the mightiest and most magnificent of all diamonds').[26] The second largest, discovered in Botswana in November 2015 (1,111 carat), is described as only slightly smaller than a tennis ball.[27] It was impossible to find a buyer for a stone the size of the Cullinan and in 1907 General Botha, prime minister of the Transvaal and a former Boer commando, introduced a motion authorizing the government to acquire the Cullinan diamond and present it to Edward VII as an expression of the colony's loyalty following the Boer war and in commemoration of the grant of responsible government that had been awarded the year before.[28]

The transfer of diamonds is a highly symbolic public event so it was not surprising that this proposed 'gift' aroused controversy in London, where *The Times* reported concern that it might be better if His Majesty's subjects in the colony, many of whom proved their loyalty during the recent war, and who were suffering material deprivation, unemployment and hunger, were provided for before a glamorous gift was made to the crown.[29] However, the Cabinet thought it unwise to refuse the gift and the Cullinan arrived in London where it was cleaved into two by a team of three members of the famous Amsterdam diamond-cutting family of I. J. Asscher, who allegedly took eight months working fourteen hours a day to complete the work. Altogether nine gems were derived from the single rough diamond. Of these the Great Star of Africa (or Cullinan I) and Cullinan II are crown jewels and can be viewed in the Tower of London. Most of the rest also reached the royal family as personal jewels as they were bought back from Asscher's (to whom they had been given as payment for their work) as gifts.[30]

The diamond rush began immediately after the discovery of the diamond at the Jacobs farm in the South African veld, when experienced gold prospectors descended on Cape Town, Durban and Port Elizabeth and then set off across the mountains and desert in mule carts, on horseback or on foot heading for the Orange River. It was not until 1869 that more diamonds were found but by 1875 there were ten thousand diggers in the small town of Kimberley, where the pit was now a patchwork of small claims, 31 sq. ft dug to a depth of 20, 50 or even 100 ft, part of which was left standing for the carts and across which thousands of pulleys were stretched to haul buckets containing the blue soil to the surface (illus. 17). By 1889 the sections left standing had caved in; the work was extraordinarily hazardous and many died.[31] The poor Boer farmers gradually – and sometimes belatedly – recognized that the value of the land for which they had trekked, which they had settled, and on which they had laboured, lay not in what they could cultivate therein but in what sum they could sell it for. It was thus in 1871 that a name with which diamond would henceforth be seemingly forever imbricated became known, when diamonds were discovered on the land of Johannes and Diederik De Beer, near the banks of the Orange River in the independent Orange Free State (later a British colony) in the Transvaal area of South Africa. The farmers sold off the parcels of land. According to the rules, nobody could have more than two of these concessions and if any claim was left unworked for seven days it could be appropriated. The law required that any diamond found must immediately be taken to the registrar on threat of punishment by fifteen years of penal servitude.[32] Attention has been drawn to the almost complete lack of understanding of the geological realties of the area and the lack of any

17 C. Evans, *De Beer's Mine* in the Northern Cape province of South Africa, 1873, photograph.

form of modern machinery.[33] The situation was violent and anarchic. Even the optimistic language of the *Diamond Fields Advertiser* is unable to varnish the harsh realities:

> One of the chief drawbacks to digging is the constant leakage caused by the theft of diamonds by native labourers. . . . in spite of the strictest supervision, it is almost impossible to prevent a smart 'boy' from getting away with the stones if he is determined to do so. . . . It is felt, too, that there is too easy channel at hand [sic] for the disposal of stolen diamonds in the presence of the native licensed digger, who may be the thief's father, uncle, brother or other relation.[34]

In 1877, of the sites in the area, Kimberley's claims were officially valued at over £1 million, De Beers's £200,000, Dutoitspan £76,000 and Bultfontein £30,000, but the De Beers mine was only a quarter of the depth of Kimberley and cheaper to dig. Anthony Trollope, visiting Kimberley, wrote: 'There are places to which men are attracted by the desire of gain which seem to be so repulsive that no gain can compensate for the miseries incidental to such an habitation.'[35] When Lord Randolph Churchill arrived in Africa in 1891 as correspondent to the *Daily Telegraph*, he remarked with the utmost distaste – and misogyny – that since diamonds are extracted solely for the wealthy classes, it is 'females' who are ultimately responsible for the dreadful sights he saw, as they display 'a lust for personal adornment essentially barbaric if not altogether savage'; if only diamonds 'adorned the beautiful, the virtuous and the young'. But, he concludes, because 'this is unhappily far from being the case . . . a review of the South African diamond mines brings me coldly to the conclusion that, whatever may be the origin of man, woman is descended from an ape'.[36]

From 1876 onwards, necessity turned the era of small claims into one of organized companies. De Beers Consolidated Mines Ltd. was formed by Cecil Rhodes (still in his thirties) in March 1888. By 1890 the company controlled 90 per cent of the world's diamond production. It was estimated that every load (weighing about 1,600 lb) of blue ground from the Kimberley Mine yielded at that time on average from 1¼ to 1¼ carats of diamonds, from De Beer's Mine 1⅕ to 1⅓ carats, from Dutoitspan ⅙ to ⅕ carats, and from Bultfontein only ⅕ to ⅓ of a carat.[37] These were the four sites and the figures demonstrate what an extraordinary amount of ground had to be moved in order to find a single diamond. By 1889 Rhodes had achieved a complete monopoly of all the South African mines now generally known as Kimberley – 90 per cent of the world's diamond production at that time (illus. 18). Then, ready to bribe at any stage, he set out to achieve a monopoly of all diamond trade. By 1891 virtually all of Kimberley's output was channelled to members of a syndicate based in London that controlled the system. Rhodes used his power base to pursue his political white supremacist and imperialist ideals. De Beers Consolidated Mines, moreover, had ambitions far beyond mining; like the East India Company in the seventeenth century, it sought the right not only to control the world's diamond trade but also to engage in other business enterprises, maintain a standing army and annexe land.[38] The British government was complicit in these aims, with Rand millionaires buying properties in London, which may resonate with the experience of Londoners watching the property market in recent years.

In 1926 the majority stakeholder of De Beers was the Anglo American Corporation, a gold mining company founded in 1917 by Ernest Oppenheimer

(1880–1957). The Diamond Trading Company (DTC) was established in London in 1934 as the sole distributor of rough diamonds for De Beers, for whom it remains today its sales and marketing subsidiary and the world's largest distributor of rough diamonds. Here the rough stones were allocated through the traditional annual distribution ritual to sight-holders (authorized bulk diamond buyers) who could either accept or reject what they were allocated. The business was immensely secretive but accounts of people in the know affirm that anyone who rejected their bulse (the name traditionally given to a small bag of rough diamonds) would be henceforth excluded. The same system – employed throughout the history of diamond dealing and practised already in London in the eighteenth century – remains in use today, but De Beers has been compelled by adverse publicity and the global communications revolution to become more open.[39] You can now consult a sight-holders directory on the web; it contains the names of eighty firms but does not include that of Harry Winston who, allegedly, refused his 'sight'.[40] Of the listed sight-holders virtually all are now based, according to the information supplied, in India, Israel and Antwerp, with a small number in places as far afield as New York and Dubai. This configuration reflects both the history of

18 Diamond fields, Kimberley, with Cecil Rhodes (fifth from left), 1870–75.

diamond mining and the commodity chain that ensures that cut and polished gem-quality stones reach jewellers and then consumers in the wealthy capital cities of the developed world. India, for centuries the only diamond producer, is now the major processor of precious stones – often those that are so small others are unwilling to try to facet them.

When in 1927 Ernest Oppenheimer took over De Beers and proceeded to consolidate the monopoly of the company, it was involved in a number of controversies, including the allegation that it refused to release industrial-quality diamonds for the U.S. war effort.[41] Because of its large market share, De Beers was (and allegedly still is) able to manipulate prices by adjusting the large stockpile it had accumulated to serve the purpose of reacting to market shifts.[42] The company was convicted in 1994 under the Sherman Act for fixing the prices of industrial diamonds and was therefore unable to operate in the USA. However, it paid a $10 million fine in 2005 and now operates there legally.[43] The Harrow-educated Nicky Oppenheimer, grandson of Ernest, sold his 40 per cent stake in De Beers to Anglo American, allegedly for $5.1 billion cash, in 2012, meaning that Anglo American owns 85 per cent of the company, with Botswana owning the remaining 15 per cent.[44] Anglo American has major interests in South African mining and was mired in controversy in 2012–13 about its safety record and the working conditions in its mines.[45] De Beers, whose chair is now Anglo American CEO Mark Cutifani, remains at the heart of issues about diamond mining and trading but competition from the opening up of diamond mines in Russia and other countries in the second half of the twentieth century forced it into cooperation with producers and organizations worldwide. Outrage over the impact of diamond extraction by Western companies on the lives of impoverished people, and the effects of the information highways that render difficult the kind of secrecy with which the company operated for several generations, have also played their part. The industry – and none in it as adept as De Beers – have learned to play the knowledge game. The World Diamond Council was set up in 2000 to represent the diamond industry in the development and implementation of regulatory and voluntary systems to control the trade in diamonds embargoed by the United Nations.[46] Andrew Bone, until 2015 Director of International Relations at De Beers Group, is Vice President of the organization and the

'Ethics' page of the De Beers Group website claims, albeit without substantiation, that '100% of De Beers' diamonds are certified conflict-free.'[47]

The history of conflict diamonds and the effectiveness of the Kimberley Process Certification Scheme (KPCS) that was endorsed initially by 37 states plus the European Commission, growing to 74 states plus the EC in 2009, is extremely complex and open to interpretation. What is clear is that KPCS requires each state to implement national legislation regulating trade in rough diamonds in accordance with the minimal standards set by KPCS. Practically, this means that each KP country must devise a national chain of custody, export and import laws and rough diamond certificates. Non-state actors are involved in the decision-making and implementation aspects of the agreement; these include non-governmental organizations such as Global Witness and Partnership Africa Canada (PAC).[48] Canada's Arctic diamond mines in the Northwest Territories where modern technology allows mining during two months of the year is, like Western Australia, among many remote areas of the world where diamonds are mined today.[49] The principle is that there should be what Franziska Bieri calls a 'chain of custody' that records each diamond's journey from the mine to the office where a Kimberley certificate is issued.[50] But KPCS is a voluntary agreement and not a treaty, and the degree to which it works to protect civilian populations as well as miners depends on how effective governments are at ensuring, for example, that diamonds are handled in sealed containers.[51] Moreover, the definition of 'conflict diamonds' under the protocol refers only to gemstones sold to fund a rebel movement attempting to overthrow the state. Thus, when in 2008 the Zimbabwean army seized a major diamond deposit and massacred more than two hundred miners, it was not considered a breach of Kimberley Process protocols.[52]

The apologists for KPCS point out that countries which do not sign up or, having signed up, do not ensure that the requirements are observed effectively, will be frozen out of the market. So what operates here, albeit on a large scale, is exactly the same principal as that which keeps diamond dealing in the Antwerp bourse in good odour and (so we are invited to believe) free of scandal. If you don't observe the rules we won't work with you. At the time of writing PAC has four countries on its watchlist. The first of these is the Central African Republic; this is one of the poorest countries in the world, where exports have been suspended since 23 May 2013, when the KPCS intervened after the government was overthrown by a rebel group that took control of diamond trade and production. There has been a focus on this region since June 2010 when rebels established control over mining areas and concerns arose that illicit diamonds were being smuggled between the Central African Republic (ranked twelfth among the world's producers of rough diamonds by value) and Sudan, which is not a signatory to KPCS.[53] However, a United Nations panel of experts estimates that 140,000 carats of diamonds have been smuggled out of the country since it was suspended, probably across the border to the Congo, where they are given Kimberley Process certificates before being traded internationally.[54] This perhaps illustrates both the success and the limitations of KPCS, which can do little more than advise neighbouring countries and trading centres (Belgium and the United Arab Emirates) to be vigilant as to the sources of diamond imports. However, the United Arab Emirates is also on the watchlist, as are Lebanon and Venezuela.[55] Global Witness continues to assert that the global trade in diamonds and precious stones remains associated with conflict and human rights abuse, and to claim that concerns about these issues in countries such as Afghanistan and Zimbabwe demonstrate that existing responsible sourcing initiatives are failing adequately to address the problems. In other words KPCS is not working, or at least not working sufficiently to protect people.[56] Much depends on the will and determination of the chair of the organization, an honorary post that therefore involves the post-holder's country in expense. The current chair is Bin Sulayem (UAE), who, in his welcome letter to the KPC's 'family', promised to work for the resumption of the supply of rough diamonds from the Central African Republic.[57]

Diamond dealing was often, though not exclusively, the preserve of Jewish merchant families whose ethnic networks crossed geopolitical boundaries and whose informal communal arrangements based on reputation and trust were well suited to dealing in minerals of very small dimensions and very high financial value. Thus it is unsurprising to find Israeli companies high on the list of sight-holders. Antwerp has been a diamond cutting and polishing centre since the sixteenth century and New York was the chosen destination for many Jewish families escaping Nazi persecution. What we should remark

19 Antwerp diamond bourse, *c.* 1960s.

on here is how these stones move around the world – and have always more or less done so. From the Diamond Trading Company (DTC) rough diamonds go to cleavers, sawyers, cutters and polishers and from these highly skilled workers they return to middlemen who then dispose of them on the diamond bourses, thirty of which are officially listed around the world from Australia and Singapore to Shanghai and Vienna. Antwerp has four (illus. 19); there, the stones are evaluated and sold again by professional middlemen to jewellers.[58] And throughout, the process of mining, transporting, selling and modifying is structured by states, national movements and conflicts, and by tense international relations.[59] Russia is notably absent from the DTC list of sight-holders but in 2014 Israel, under political pressure from the EU over its obstructions to any meaningful Middle East peace process, was reported to have begun talks on a new free trade agreement with Russia, with whom Israel already trades $2 billion a year's worth of diamonds.[60]

The Kimberley Searching System

The history of South African apartheid is directly linked to the exploitation of its mineral wealth. Cape Town was founded around 1650 by Dutch settlers and was invaded in 1795 and again in 1806 by the British. It was ceded to them by treaty in 1815, at which time slavery was abolished. From the 1890s, De Beers organized compounds for their black workers who lived away from their homes for long periods – sometimes for years – and whose contracts were not renewed unless they complied. While not technically forced labour, the conditions of employment of the 'kaffirs' ('boys' or indigenous workers) were hugely exploitative. In the 1960s labourers were recruited from Lesotho, Botswana, Zambia and Angola in order to avoid having to pay the rates that urban-employed Africans were earning; one black photojournalist managed to get into a mine and found conditions of abject misery, worse than the slums of Johannesburg.[61]

In his monumental history of black mineworkers in South Africa, V. L. Allen explains how in the 1870s black migrant workers behaved like a free market and either only worked for a few months to be able to purchase a gun and then returned to their tribal lands, or moved employers if the pay was not enough or the food poor, or if they regarded a mine as unsafe. Initially there was no discrimination between black and white workers: diggers and labourers lived alongside each other in mining camps.[62] By the 1880s a closed compound system had been established with institutionalized recruitment and labour touts who, owing to the constant demand for labour, attained a powerful position. Political and economic forces drove the ever-increasing control of the black population so that by the mid-1880s 80 per cent of Kimberley's mine labour came from areas under white control. However, the price of diamonds was unstable and, as profits fell, a search for scapegoats led to an obsession with what were seen as the stealing tendencies of black workers, creating a mythology that spread beyond the borders of South Africa (illus. 20). As Allen points out, the very notion of private property was alien to the Zulu migrant workers. By the early 1880s it has been estimated that 25 to 40 per cent of all finds were disposed of illicitly; the many lengthy stages which the blue ground went through before it reached the washing machine, and the lengths to which white diamond touts and dealers went to secure stones secreted by black labourers, made illicit diamond buying rife across the diamond fields.[63]

Ordinance 11 of 1880 gave the employers the legal right to strip-search all workers, black and white, but white workers soon objected that they were being treated like 'common kaffirs'. After a joint strike in 1884 (during which six white strikers were killed) unity crumbled and thereafter only black workers were searched. As we have seen, body searching took place a century earlier in Brazilian mines where slave labour was used but it was in South Africa that the strip-searching, combined with closed compounds to control African labourers and facilitate searching, became institutionalized.[64] It also became increasingly invasive: in April 1887 black miners went on strike over the use of the speculum for detecting diamonds hidden in the rectum.[65] Cecil Rhodes (see illus. 18) was aware of the Brazilian precedent when he proposed in 1882 an amalgamation plan for all black workers to be confined to barracks. In 1884 De Beers negotiated with the Cape Colony government for free service from men in local jails, resulting in many young men being arrested and

The diamond thief is suspended in a cage and left there until his sentence is served.

20 *Punishment of a Diamond Thief*, unidentified book/magazine illustration, late 19th century, from the personal scrapbook of Charles M. Field (1860–1940).

21 Robert Harris, *Searching System, Kimberley*, c. 1880.

jailed on minor or trumped-up charges. These tools of labour control, it has
been argued, included the pass laws that became so notoriously central to
apartheid.[66]

Robert Harris was a photographer known to have had a studio in Port
Elizabeth in 1880–90.[67] He exhibited at one of the nineteenth century's
great exhibitions of trade and industry, the Colonial and Indian Exhibition
in London in 1886, and produced albums containing 'permanent photographs' (Woodburytypes) of views of various South African landscapes and
townscapes.[68] Harris's works were sometime signed with his full name and
sometimes with his initials. It seems indisputable that he was responsible for
a series of eight frank and deeply disturbing photographs of the Kimberley
searching system, photographic copies of which are now in Yale University
Library.[69] In one of these (illus. 21) a black overseer, seen full-length in profile
and wearing a cap but otherwise naked apart from a shirt tied round his waist
like an apron, peers into the open mouth of a naked Zulu worker, tipping up
the worker's chin with his left hand while, in his right, he holds up a lighted
candle. This light would not illuminate fully the inside of the man's mouth
but any diamond secreted therein would glitter when caught in the light

from the candle's flame. The search is taking place outside against the wall of a corrugated iron shed, in which is a closed door, while in the background piled-up sacks suggest a sandbag-protected area, perhaps part of a mine. The dehumanizing nature of this moment of humiliation is echoed in the out-of-focus dog that is cleaning itself at the overseer's feet, while the desolate sense of this being a non-place is conveyed in the sharply focused slab of stone and abandoned tin cup lying between the figures and the wall of the shed.

The photograph is signed 'R.H.' The entire series must have been photographed in the same location and probably at roughly the same time. But contemporary accounts make clear that when a worker reached the end of his contract he was subjected to confinement and every inch of his body critically examined to see that none of the coveted gems were concealed in his hair, nose, mouth, ears or any other orifice. Everything removed from the building was subject to the same scrutiny.[70] With this image of an invasive act, the camera that had been used to secure faithful representations of colonial buildings and landscapes homes in on the exposed body of the colonized subject. Through the search – which is not just random but part of a system, as the title tells us – the Zulu labourer's body becomes no more or less than the kimberlite ground of the mine in which the telltale glitter of a diamond might be perceived in the dross of the mine; the orifice stands in relation to the aperture of the mine itself, and the non-life of the mineral is (whether in actuality or imagination) a part of that body. Harris's work bears testimony to the way in which, through this humiliation, the black worker was subsumed into the organization of the mining corporation. That the process is named and photographed indicates just how proud its organizers were of what they had achieved. By the 1920s X-ray machines had been introduced at Kimberley, allowing what geographer Gareth Hoskins sees as a new form of visualization that might enable us not only to understand surveillance techniques but to recognize the de-animation of the miner through these techniques.[71]

The idea of the South African Cape as a treasure house at the disposal of Britain's industry, a faraway place whose native inhabitants were a source of cheap labour, had been institutionalized from the start at the heart of British government and is revealed dramatically in the cultural representations that appeared in established British media at the end of the nineteenth century. Dipti Bhagat has studied the 'Cape Court' at the Colonial and Indian Exhibition, held in South Kensington in 1886, at which Harris also exhibited. The organization had a subcommittee with a section responsible for collecting indigenous living subjects and artefacts to populate the Cape display. The 'kaffirs' were induced to make the long journey to London by the promise of payment of cattle.[72] Another subcommittee, for minerals, planned the construction of a model mine over a pyramid of diamonds (actually to be made of wood and covered with crystals) as a way of demonstrating the importance of diamond mining to the Cape economy. The Court displayed 'the entire process of diamond mining, sorting, cutting and polishing, from the diamond-rich ore to the setting of a diamond'. Diamonds in the rough and polished were shown and the whole ensemble was regarded as a success, especially the diamond-washing machine, which was operated by 'the kafirs and bushmen', who were 'generally well conducted, and had great interest taken in them by the British public'.[73] According to one review in the London press:

> There is a beautiful model of the Bultfontein mine, with all the machinery in working order . . . a large diamond washing machine, in which real blue [kimberlite] ground from various mines is washed and sorted daily, and in which several good sized diamonds have already been found . . .[74]

This clinical demonstration – a very far cry from the squalid conditions in which the miners actually worked – served to endorse Britain's unquestioning claim to colonial wealth and the ingenuity of her government in manipulating public opinion so that benevolence and industrial progress appeared to drive production. Sir Ernest Oppenheimer used the notion of enlightened self-interest to justify his employment policies, arguing that improved living conditions for natives should 'make for healthy, efficient, law-abiding service'.[75] Today, groups of extinct volcanic pipes that yield diamonds as well as diamond-bearing rock are found not only in South Africa but in neighbouring Namibia, Lesotho, Zimbabwe and Botswana and, further away, in Angola, the Central African Republic and Sierra Leone (illus. 22). There are also, as earlier indicated, diamond mines in Siberia and in Australia and Canada, but it is in

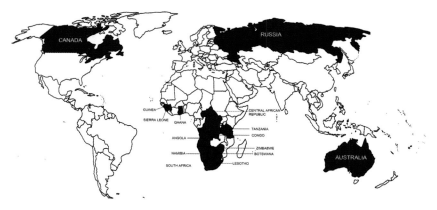

22 Map showing areas of the world where major producers of gem-quality diamonds are located, 2008–13.

connection with many of these African nations that members of the public for whom purchasing diamonds is either financially impossible or morally repugnant have learned about the extraction of diamonds and the political destabilization that has all too often ensued.

India and London: The Koh-i-noor Diamond

To conclude, I return to India, where we began, and to the period in which Britain's overseas empire had encompassed a large part of the Indian subcontinent, to focus on one particular diamond. Even the identity of the celebrated Koh-i-noor, now set in what is known as the 'consort crown' among the British crown jewels (illus. 23), has been disputed. Worn by Queen Elizabeth the Queen Mother for the coronation of her husband George VI in 1937, at her funeral in 2002 it lay on her coffin on a purple cushion. The crown jewels are on public view in the Tower of London but the reappearance of the Koh-i-noor on a state occasion invariably provokes critical and sometimes hostile reactions, so much is it seen as a symbol of colonial oppression. A comment piece in *The Times* described its appearance at the Queen Mother's funeral as '108 carats of blood stained jewellery, fought over by Afghan, Persian, Indian and Sikh [and] recently claimed by the Taliban'. It was remarked that the diamond is a 'priceless reminder of the furious historical feuding in central Asia, of murder, treachery and skulduggery, and the complex political legacy

23 The Koh-i-noor diamond in the consort crown.

of empire in that region'.[76] The extremely large diamond was removed by Garrard & Co., the crown-jeweller responsible for cleaning the crown, in 1988, and weighed on a modern certified electric balance in the presence of witnesses. It was found to be 105.60 metric carats as opposed to the previously published 108.93.[77]

Weight is one of the ways diamonds are identified, along with cut, colour and clarity and any imperfections in the stone. Early accounts of a diamond that may have been the Koh-i-noor date from the fourteenth century, but its existence is fairly securely traceable only over the past two and a half centuries. Large diamonds are named, often with the owner's patronym; in this way the prestige of purchase is symbolically anchored in the stone. The mystery attaching to the ownership and whereabouts of notable gems still fascinates: they are seen briefly and disappear again from sight, in all probability these days into a bank vault. Laurence Graff of Graff Diamonds bought a pink diamond for U.S.$46 million in November 2010 and immediately named it the Graff Pink. Its origins, its history and its current location or ownership are unknown – having briefly emerged into the light it has again disappeared into mystery and speculation. It is the tension between high value and extreme vulnerability to theft that lends these large diamonds their allure; it is as though naming them might secure them. John Ruskin purchased for £1,000 a very large diamond (133.1450 carats) which he presented to the British Museum (subsequently the Natural History Museum) in 1887; he named it the Colenso diamond 'in Honour of his Friend, the loyal and patiently adamantine First Bishop of Natal'.[78] This did not prevent it from being stolen on the night of 28–9 April 1965 by someone who had climbed a drainpipe to the first-floor Mineral Gallery and cut through two iron bars.[79] It was never recovered.

Although prior to the seventeenth century a diamond might have been broken by a massive blow with a hard instrument on a cleavage, the idea of rapidly disguising a large diamond by cutting it would have been impossible. Thus it was that the Koh-i-noor survived intact until Queen Victoria acquired it. The early and confused history of this stone, originally from the Golconda Mine and named descriptively (Koh-i-noor means 'mountain of light'), is bound up with the name of the ruler Babur, the 'Lion of the North', though the stone must have been around a great deal longer. Born in 1483 and the first of the Mughal rulers of India, Babur claimed descent from Tamerlane and Genghis Khan. He was not only a warrior but a cultured man and a poet, according to an account in his memoir, *The Baburnama*. At the Fort of Agra in 1526 his son was given a quantity of jewels and precious stones by the defeated ruler Vikramaditya, including one famous diamond which had been acquired by Sultan Alauddin. This diamond was so valuable that a judge of diamonds assessed it to be 'worth half the daily expenditure of the whole world', clear evidence, were it needed, that hyperbole concerning diamonds is nothing new.[80] Babur's son, Humayun, was allowed to keep this big diamond but, having succeeded his father, his reign was unsettled; he was driven out of India by Afghans and was compelled into fifteen years of exile in Persia, during which time he kept the stone, known as 'Babur's Diamond', with him.[81] It was in Persia that he finally parted with it, presenting it to Shah Tahmasp, who subsequently returned it to India as a gift for Burhan Nizam, Shah of Ahmednagar.

From 1547 to the Sack of Delhi in 1739 the history of Babur's diamond is obscure. However, Ian Balfour suggests that Shah Jahan (great grandson of Humayun), who was reigning Mughal emperor in the 1650s, may have struck a deal with Mir Jumla, disgraced First Minister of the king of Golconda. Mir Jumla was a diamond dealer, famous in Persia, and the deal was that in return for the gift of a celebrated diamond, Shah Jahan's son Aurangzeb would wage war on the king of Golconda.[82] Having acquired Golconda, Aurangzeb rid himself of his father and brother, the former having relinquished his precious stones to his son. While in Aurangzeb's possession, the diamond was badly cut by a Venetian lapidary, thus diminishing its weight. At this point Jean-Baptiste Tavernier, whose *Six voyages* was published in 1676, both clarifies and further confuses the story of the Koh-i-noor. Among the stones given to Shah Jahan were two extremely large diamonds, one uncut and today thought to be 'the Great Mughal' which Aurangzeb showed Tavernier in 1665.

When the Koh-i-noor arrived in England in 1850, there was speculation that the Great Mughal and Babur's diamond were one and the same. Distinguished mineralogists and gemmologists fought over this in print.[83] Further arguments about the stone's identity were put forward by Valentine Ball in appendices to his new translation of Tavernier's travelogue.[84] Ball was the officiating superintendent of the geological survey of India and author of several important books, including *The Economic Geology of India* (1881), of which the first chapter deals with 'the diamond'. In the 1960s it was possible to examine a great diamond in the Iranian treasury, the Darya-i-noor (Sea of Light), which like the Koh-i-noor came from the Mughal treasury, as well as the Orlov diamond, set in the Russian imperial sceptre since 1784 and now in the Kremlin State Diamond Fund (illus. 24). Taking into account all the physical characteristics, including weight and colour, of these diamonds, and the (however inconclusive and contradictory) documentary evidence available, Balfour believes that a very strong case exists for identifying the Orlov with the Great Mughal, as does a valid case for regarding the Koh-i-noor as Babur's diamond.[85]

The more recent history of the Koh-i-noor involves a change of hands after the Battle of Karnal in February 1739 when the Persian Nadir Shah defeated the last of the Mughal emperors, Mohammed Shah, and marched into Delhi. In restoring his throne to him, Nadir Shah tricked Mohammed Shah into showing him the hiding place of his great jewel – it was in his turban – and

24 The Orlov diamond, set in the Russian Imperial sceptre in 1784.

it was he who named it Koh-i-noor. After the Battle of Karnal the Persians sacked Delhi and the Koh-i-noor returned to Persia with the victors and was then taken to Afghanistan, where it was the object of envy, negotiation, demand, theft and extortion by warring factions across both territories until finally in 1813 it was seized by Ranjit Singh, known as the 'Lion of the Punjab'. He wore it set in an armlet between two smaller diamonds,[86] an arrangement that added to its exotic interest in 1851 when a replica was shown in an Indian armlet alongside the diamond itself at the Great Exhibition in London. It was from Dhulip (more commonly spelled Duleep) Singh (1838–1883), the last of Ranjit Singh's sons and a minor when he inherited, that the Koh-i-noor was taken, following the annexation of the Punjab by the British on 29 March 1849.

In 1851 the Great Exhibition of the Works of Industry of All Nations opened in Hyde Park in London. It was housed in the Crystal Palace, a proto-modernist building for a modernist event celebrating manufacture. Multiple and disparate meanings were produced around this imperial spectacle of a commodity world. As India was 'pre-eminent' among Britain's colonial possessions,[87] the jewel in the imperial crown, the Indian Court was

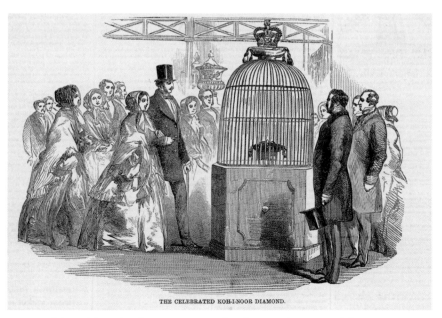

THE CELEBRATED KOH-I-NOOR DIAMOND.

25 'The Celebrated Koh-i-Noor Diamond as shown at the Great Exhibition 1851', illustration from the *Illustrated London News* (7 May 1851).

a key attraction. But the most eye-catching and discussed exhibits originating in India were not in this section; they were the East India Company's display of jewels and the Koh-i-noor diamond that belonged to Queen Victoria and which was exhibited on its own in a gilded cage (illus. 25). The objects in the East India Company's display represented – or stood in for – the Indian rulers whose wealth had been despoiled, whether as booty or as tribute:

> not a few were tributes offered on the occasion by native princes and other *magnates* of the East . . . comprising natural products, native manufactures for domestic use, Models, and a wondrous display of the richest articles of jewellery and luxury.[88]

Unlike later world fairs such as the Colonial and Indian Exhibition discussed earlier, the Great Exhibition did not showcase living villages. Workers were effaced. But there was an exception; in the Indian Court a collection of 'ethnographic models' was shown – over 150 miniature figures representing Indian trades. These figures were viewed as repulsive: one writer found himself sickened by the 'distorted bodies of the models', and another described the Indian labourers as 'a lean starved-out regiment of squalid beggars, half naked, or with scanty folds of coarsest cotton flung around their wasted limbs'.[89]

In 1843 Duleep Singh, during whose reign the two Sikh wars were fought, had become the recognized ruler of the Punjab. The Punjab was the only Indian state not under European rule at the time. On 23 March 1849 the British flag was hoisted on the citadel of Lahore and the Punjab was proclaimed to be part of the British Empire of India. One of the terms of the Treaty of Lahore was that 'the gem called the Koh-i-noor which was taken from Shah Shuja-ul-Mulk by Maharajah Ranjit Singh shall be surrendered by the Maharajah of Lahore to the Queen of England.' The treaty also required that Duleep Singh resign for himself, his soldiers and his successors all rights to the sovereignty of the Punjab; that all property of state be confiscated to the East India Company in part payment of 'the debt due by the State of Lahore to the British Government and of the expenses of the war'; that Duleep Singh should receive from the Company a pension to support himself, his relations and the servants of the state; and that he should be treated with respect and

26 Franz Xaver
Winterhalter,
*The Maharajah
Duleep Singh*, 1854,
oil on canvas.

honour, retaining his title and receiving his pension, provided he 'reside at such place as the Governor-General of India may select'.[90]

Accordingly the Koh-i-noor was ceded to the Governor General, Lord Dalhousie, who, not without intense secrecy, brought it back to England aboard a ship of the Queen's Navy named HMS *Medea*. 'Why', as one Indian writer has asked, 'was this historical diamond snatched away from the young

Maharaja? There was absolutely no justification for this [grabbing].'[91] Given that the Koh-i-noor diamond already had the reputation of bringing bad luck to any man who owned it – a story that inspired Wilkie Collins in his novel *Moonstone* (1868) – one might have thought that they could have found a ship with a more auspicious name. The person responsible for actually taking the diamond out of the Lahore jewel house, Dr Login, was also entrusted with guardianship of the eleven-year-old maharajah. The jewel house had been in the sights of British government representatives even before the signing of the treaty and Lord Dalhousie had ordered an inspection and issued strict orders that nothing should be removed. The Koh-i-noor was merely the most notable item in the collection, all of which became British property. The East India Company was annoyed because they wished themselves to present the diamond to the queen as a gift, but Dalhousie insisted that it was more in honour of the queen 'that the Koh-i-noor should be surrendered directly from the hand of the conquered prince into the hands of the sovereign who was his conqueror, than that it should be presented to her as a gift – which is always a favour – by any joint stock company among her subjects'.[92]

The young Duleep Singh was tutored by devout Christians and then sent to Britain in 1854, where he was first housed at Claridge's Hotel before the East India Company found a house for him in Roehampton. When he expressed a desire to return to India, he was sent on a tour of Europe. Queen Victoria found him exotically charming and had him portrayed by Franz Winterhalter, who was 'in ecstasies at the beauty and nobility of bearing of the young Maharajah [illus. 26]. He was very amiable and patient.'[93] He is shown wearing a miniature of the queen set in diamonds. Thereby the deposed and dispossessed young Indian presents himself for perpetuity in the artistic idiom of the conquering nation. This is not only a portrait but an image of imperial power. Within it is the second image, that of Queen Victoria encircled by diamonds; it references India in the material sense while simultaneously suggesting subjugation. A portrait of the queen executed in 1856 shows her *wearing* the Koh-i-noor diamond (illus. 27). Originally a flat Indian lasque cut, as seen in the illustrations of the Great Exhibition, it had by then been recut and thereby rendered more brilliant but also much reduced in size (it lost 43 per cent of its weight). While the Maharajah wears *her* portrait, the queen, who would be declared Empress of India in 1877, is depicted wearing one of the largest and most valuable Indian diamonds ever known, a jewel that, as everyone knew, had belonged to the young man. As with the brightest jewel in Queen Victoria's crown, 'an emblem of prosperity and dominion', there could be little doubt, it was remarked in 1851, of the Koh-i-noor remaining 'what it has ever been, a brilliant token of power and ascendancy'.[94]

How is it then, that when it was exhibited at the Great Exhibition, after a fanfare of publicity about its journey from India, the Koh-i-noor diamond disappointed the viewers who queued up to see it in its specially constructed cage, surrounded by an iron railing with a policeman in attendance? For many, it epitomized that 'other', the Orient with its useless, pre-industrial, pre-technological ornamentation – the antithesis of Britain's arts of manufacture:

> After all, there is but poor satisfaction to the mind, that is gifted with a ray of intelligence, in the contemplation of these glittering toys, and more especially so, when they are too bulky or precious for use. Witness the great Koh-i-Noor, imprisoned like a robber in his own iron cage; the tribute of admiration bestowed upon which was not equal to that elicited by the most trivial piece of machinery that was applicable to the use or service of man.[95]

Others blamed the fact that the diamond did not seem to glitter on the failure of its cutting in India; preserving as much of the stone as possible was an Indian priority but the Venetian who had cut the Koh-i-noor had been criticized for the result. Judging by the crystal replica made before it was recut in London, the diamond was a classic flat cut, a so-called lasque. Blaming India for the failure of the Koh-i-noor locks into the colonial discourse of the incompetent native, justifying the 'rescue' of so valuable an object for safe keeping in the West:

> Notwithstanding the enormous value at which it has been estimated . . . [the Koh-i-noor] has disappointed public expectation in no ordinary degree: the ungraceful peculiarity of its shape, and the ineffective manner in which it has been cut, although more than half its weight

27 Franz Xaver Winterhalter, *Queen Victoria Wearing the Koh-i-noor as a Brooch*, 1856, oil on canvas.

has been wasted in the operation, having deprived it of much of the brilliancy and beauty of which no doubt the original stone would, in skilful hands, have proved susceptible, and in spite of the various costly expedients that have been resorted to for the purpose of exhibiting it to the best advantage, it is still very far from realizing the anticipations that had been formed of its attractions.[96]

In its cage the Koh-i-noor seemed much less luminous and light-projecting than the glass fountain that had been erected as the centrepiece of the main transept of the Crystal Palace, itself a miracle of glass. *The Times* asserted: 'after all, the diamond does not satisfy. Either from the imperfect cutting or the difficulty of placing the lights advantageously, or the immovability of the stone itself, which should be made to revolve on its axis, few catch any of the brilliant rays that it reflects when viewed at a particular angle.'[97] James Tennant, the distinguished mineralogist, valued the Exhibition as an opportunity for the study and comparison of precious stones from many private lenders and jewellers, but he remarked on the fact that its imperfect cutting and fractures produced by rough usage 'disappointed many a high-raised expectation'. It yielded its brilliancy when the sun's rays fell upon it from two to three o'clock but at other times of the day 'it was so devoid of lustre as to excite the suspicion in many minds that it was no diamond at all – in fact nothing but a piece of glass.'[98] According to some accounts, the 6-ft-high cage in which the Koh-i-noor was displayed, and which enabled it to be lowered into a safe each evening, featured a system of gaslights intended to illuminate it from below.[99]

It is not possible now to assess the accuracy of Tennant's criticism. However, there were glass replicas: one manufactured by Apsley Pellatt was on show at the Exhibition on the floor above the actual diamond and replicas were for sale on The Strand.[100] Accounts of the Koh-i-noor, both in the official guide to the Exhibition and in the newspapers, unofficial guides and the *Illustrated London News*, offer a narrative of the stone's confused history steeped in violent warfare, murderous tribal dissent and cupidity.[101] Alongside this is a discourse of illumination both literal and metaphorical. Thus on 17 May 1851 the *Illustrated London News* published a long article on 'Light and Its Applications' ranging from electricity to daguerreotypes and then to 'the mountain of light' and other diamonds in the Exhibition, like the Hope diamond (see illus. 11), admired for the way they 'almost emit light'.[102] The Koh-i-noor diamond in these accounts is conflated with India: its shortcomings mirror those of the unruly subcontinent; its murky failure to send forth rays of light is symptomatic of the impossibility of illuminating India, which will always be rough, like an uncut diamond. The suspicion that a celebrated diamond shown in a palace constructed of glass might have no more value than a piece of glass (or, as *The Times* averred, 'a large piece of carbon') not only constructs glass as a kind of ghostly equivalent to diamonds, as Armstrong has argued, but images the anxieties inherent in the colonial enterprise.[103] Might it be that the empire was not worth the material it produced? Might it be that the imperial power was, at the end of the day, a delusion? While it lured spectators, the diamond did not fit in with the Crystal Palace's progressive and utilitarian economic agenda.[104]

Described as an object 'where the difficulty of the issue of "return" is amply illustrated',[105] the Koh-i-noor's post-Punjab history exemplifies a form of imperialism that hinges on cultural capital rather than mineral exploitation. Its status is therefore worth more than its financial value. In 1947 and 1953 the government of India asked for the Koh-i-noor's return. In 1976 the prime minister of Pakistan requested its return to Lahore, a request that was refused at the same time as an assurance was given that it would not be handed over to any other country (such as India). Subsequently Iran claimed it, asserting that it was a Persian possession. This much travelled jewel has been in Mughal possession in India for 213 years, in Afghan possession in Kandahar and Kabul for 66 years, in Sikh possession in Lahore for 36 years and in British possession for 163 years. 'It is true', it has been stated,

> that when acquired by the British, it was in Lahore, now in Pakistan, but it is clear that there are other prior claimants in the field. The Moguls of Delhi were of Turkish origin, and the rulers of Lahore, when the stone came into British hands, were Sikhs, in which case it has been stated the word 'return' to India would hardly be applicable.[106]

Nonetheless, in 2013, on the final day of an official visit to India, the British prime minister was asked about the Koh-i-noor and ruled out the possibility of its return.[107] The stone is undoubtedly of Indian mineralogical origin but its status as cultural property has been hugely complicated by centuries of ethnic war, religious dispute, conquest and changing national borders, not least the division of the Punjab by the British in 1947. The British government has always repudiated claims on the basis that the diamond was not seized but presented. This is not a view that finds favour among Indian authors, who naturally point out the unequal forces of the British government and the East

India Company on one side and a boy maharajah on the other. But as with other claims for restitution of cultural property, it seems unlikely that a jewel that encapsulates the relationship of diamonds to empire will be travelling anywhere beyond the Tower of London in the foreseeable future.

TWO

DIAMOND BUSINESS

Cutting and Polishing

To UNDERSTAND WHAT HAPPENS WHEN DIAMONDS have left the mine, it is important to recognize the day-to-day practicalities of diamond processing (now and in the past). Diamond dealing as a profession is founded on extreme reticence and therefore evidence is necessarily somewhat haphazard. For this reason, rather than a sustained economic history the aim here is to offer some insights into how dealing in diamonds happens, both legally and illegally, by examining some of the records of independent diamond merchants. First, who are the people who work on diamonds and what do they do?

In a long, narrow, windowless room, accessed only after passing through security and yielding up one's passport, sit around fifteen men and women at the long work benches that run the length of the walls illuminated by ultra-bright artificial light (illus. 28). They wear red T-shirts branded with the name of Meylemans & Somers. This is a workshop of *diamantslijpers* (diamond polishers). From the mine, it is to workshops like this one in Antwerp's diminished but still active diamond district, close to the city's grandiose marble-ornamented nineteenth-century railway station, that the raw stones are brought. Despite the loss of much business to India, the whole process of turning raw stones into desirable gems is still accomplished here. At either end of this long room are glass-partitioned sections. At the front is the diagnostic equipment. Here a rough diamond can be scanned with software that will deliver information accurate to a degree far beyond the capacity of a human eye – data about the external and the internal characteristics of a stone (illus. 29). The stone seen

28 Meylemans & Somers workshop, Antwerp, 2014.

on the monitor here is 41.840 carats, a very large stone, and the inclusions are shown in turquoise. Inclusions occur in diamonds as a result of flaws in the structure of the diamond or foreign material incorporated into the stone. On the surface, which is never smooth, just as the shape of a stone is rarely a pure octahedron or dodecahedron, there may be blemishes. The scan will not only give information on the diamond's weight and mineralogical characteristics, but will create a diagram of the possibilities for cutting the stone while avoiding inclusions and any weaknesses that may cause it to split. A large stone may be cut into several smaller stones but the objective is to avoid wastage. The dealer who has brought in the stone will then decide which of several options to pursue.

At the far end of the room is an area that contains a laser diamond-cutting machine (illus. 30). Until relatively recently, the cutting of a diamond was an occasion that generated extreme tension. A skilled diamond cutter would spend months and even, in the case of an especially large diamond, years studying the stone to work out the cleavages, as crystals tend to split along certain lines. Then when he (and it was invariably he) was ready the cutter would cleave the diamond by fixing it firmly in place and then placing a purpose-made cleaver on it, taking a hammer and hitting it with a single blow. Although this method is still sometimes used, laser cutting is preferred, though this is not without dangers. The process is semi-automatic. The stone is placed in the machine and the cutter can adjust it as she or he monitors progress of the cutting on a screen where two overlapping images of the stone can be seen, with pink showing what is being removed and blue showing the shape in which the stone will finally emerge. On the left side of the monitor the actual cutter can be seen; the diamond is clamped into the central section. The machine and monitor fit comfortably onto a desk. The unseen diamond, minuscule compared to the machine, is cooled by running water; a build-up of heat can cause a diamond to explode or, in the terminology of the workshop, 'bomb'. Each stone is accompanied on its progress by a small, seemingly insignificant slip of paper in which it is wrapped (illus. 31). On this are recorded all the characteristics revealed in the scan, as well as a diagram showing how it is to be cut, and then a note of each intervention as it is made. Where there is a risk a warning is printed in red – 'Voorzichtig'. Here the word 'Bom' has been added to alert the workers. The word 'cushion' refers to the type of cut: one with rounded corners and curved sides. The dust coming from the diamond mingles with the water to create a dirty grey mud. This is dried and, once mixed with oil, is reused by polishers as the essential abrasive on their wheels.

29 Diamond-scanning equipment, Meylemans & Somers, Antwerp, 2014.

This combination of high-tech and time-honoured artisanal skill is a typical characteristic of the diamond processing business. Once cut, the stone goes to the polishers on their benches where it is faceted (see illus. 28).

Competition between Antwerp and Amsterdam has always been intense. In the seventeenth century, the powerful 'Natie' (guild) of ruby and diamond cutters, founded in 1582, established a monopoly, exerting control over who was permitted to work with precious stones.[1] In 1732 the Antwerp Natie, feeling the pressure of competition, put out a statement claiming that

> Since time immemorial this city has flourished and radiated the shine of diamond cutting and polishing and that to the exclusion of all other cities who have sent their diamonds here to get them cut in all perfection and to keep this lustrous and noble art here and to stabilize and maintain it the laws and legislators of this city made good decisions in 1582.[2]

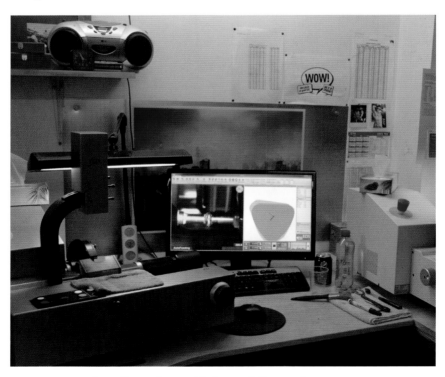

30 Laser diamond cutter, Meylemans & Somers, Antwerp, 2013.

31 Note accompanying a diamond through the cutting and polishing process, Meylemans & Somers, Antwerp.

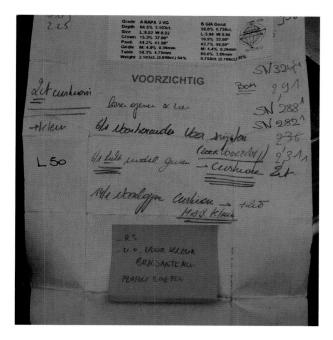

Today it is claimed that 80 per cent of rough diamonds are traded through Antwerp and that all diamonds entering Belgium are certified by the Antwerp Diamond Office, founded in 1944, the year Antwerp was liberated, and part of a scheme to get the Jewish diamond families to return to the city to kickstart the economy. Jews who did not flee the city as the German army invaded Belgium were sent to the concentration camps where few survived. Those diamond workers who had fled to London, Tel Aviv and New York established businesses and were often fearful of returning as they were hearing accounts of continuing anti-Semitism and of the extermination of their Jewish co-workers.[3]

The only way to import or export diamonds *officially* is to register them with the Belgian government. Once graded and valued, diamonds are dispatched to cutting centres across the globe with (it is alleged) the most valuable being kept and processed in Antwerp.[4] The first diamond bourse was established in Antwerp in 1893. There are now four, all of which have glitzy websites, though entry to all but the welcome pages of these sites are for members only. The Beurse voor Diamanthandel, founded in 1904 during the period when diamonds from the Belgian Congo were flooding into the country, is typical

32, 33 Anonymous Anglo-Netherlandish artist, *Henry VIII*, c. 1520, oil on panel, and detail.

(see illus. 19).[5] In a huge refectory-like hall flooded with daylight from a wall of windows down one side are long tables and benches where diamond dealers buy and sell. The bourse was established when dealers were more itinerant and communication technology less sophisticated; now much business takes

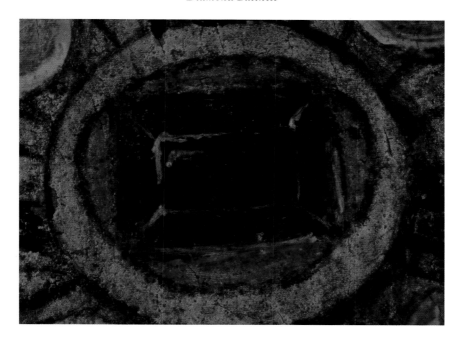

place in offices and the bourse is more of a social club. To become a member a dealer must be approved by all of the four bourses. If a member reneges on a deal then they will be blacklisted not only in Antwerp but in every bourse around the world. Diamond dealing in the high-tech world we have been exploring is still conducted without written documents and on the basis of trust, and the bourses not only fulfil the function of regulation but provide reconciliation and arbitration in disputes.[6] A noticeboard of blue stickers, I was told when I visited, announced members who had been blacklisted; this effectively meant that they would never be able to trade again. White stickers were for those applying for membership and another board was devoted to 'Lost and Found'; diamonds are very small and dealers carry them in their pockets wrapped in paper, as they have always done. Historically diamond dealers have been Jewish and members of close-knit families but now the profession is much more global. I will have more to say on this but for the moment let us return to the *diamantslijpers*.

During classical antiquity and the Middle Ages gemstones were valued for their colour, their medicinal and magical properties and for the markings on them, which were read as signs. These markings were either natural or, in the case of intaglios, carved. It is easy to see how in the Middle Ages an agate with the shape of a head or an onyx from Roman times carved with an emblem could be understood as a divinely devised image. Polishing enhanced the colour of stones and a skilful craftsman could bring them to a round or oval shape (a cabochon). But certain stones like diamonds and spinels, on account of their crystalline structure, could not be worked on in this way because they would fracture along flat surfaces. Gradually it was discovered that by improving the symmetry of these stones they could be made to exhibit brightness or 'fire'. First, the four octahedral upper faces of the diamond were polished and then, probably around 1380, jewellers began adding new diagonal facets. Pointed diamonds (the natural octahedral shape) and diamonds which had been polished to make a flat upper surface (table-cut) can be seen in early portraits of royal subjects, in which black rectangular stones set in gold jewellery are worn as ornaments (illus. 32, 33).

By 1439 a lapidary wheel was in use in the Low Countries.[7] The real breakthrough occurred some time between 1530 and 1538. A cut consisting of an octagonal section with sixteen lower facets and a flat top (the *tavola*) was practised in Augsburg in 1538 and at roughly the same time in Antwerp the rose was developed with its hexagonal shape, six nearly flat-top facets and twelve more inclined facets next to the table.[8] The rose has a flat bottom which is usually its cleavage plane; as many diamonds imported from India were already cut into flat lasques, it was possible to modify these to turn them into the roses that were regarded as desirable in Europe.[9] These modifications that changed the octahedral surfaces of the raw diamond and produced the cuts that dominated European elite fashion for several centuries (illus. 34) were achieved by the use of abrasive powder made from grease and diamond dust – as we have seen, this remains the standard method used today. It was known in Venice in 1530 but may have originated in India.[10] A late seventeenth-century Dutch engraving (illus. 35), formerly in the possession of the great collector Sir Hans Sloane, shows such a wheel being driven by a woman. The accompanying verse translates as: 'The rough diamond, how obscure, receives all his splendour in polishing. That which turns out pure of water, and large of body, is called a gem.' What had been recognized since Pliny the Elder's *Natural History* as the hardest stone could only be cut or polished by using the same mineral; from this comes the widely employed metaphor of 'diamond-cut diamond'. By the time of the publication of Diderot and d'Alembert's *Encyclopédie* (1751–77) it was possible to illustrate a remarkable variety of facets belonging to the brilliant cut (illus. 36); this glittering diamond cut, devised at the end of the seventeenth century, virtually eclipsed the table cut and the naturally pointed octahedron (the bottom half of which might be invisible in the setting of a ring or which might be cut into two; illus. 37) as well as the rose or 'à la mode' cut. Roses were recut as brilliants, just as early pointed diamonds had been later refashioned into tables.[11]

Fashion is fickle and by 1678 table diamonds, like that depicted in illus. 33, had become difficult to sell. In January of that year, the English merchant John Cholmley wrote to his brother Nathaniel in India to tell him that he

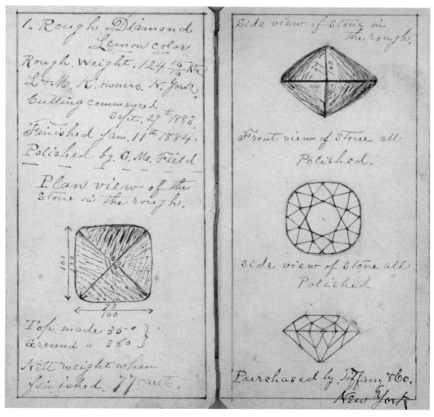

34 Charles M. Field's drawing of facets of a yellow diamond (subsequently sold to Charles Lewis Tiffany), from the personal scrapbook of Charles M. Field (1860–1940).

35 'Diamond Polisher', Dutch engraving, from Joannes Antonides van der Goes, *Menschelyke beezigheeden* (Human Occupations; Amsterdam, 1695), Anthonie de Winter (after Caspar Luyken and Jan Luyken).

and his partners had made between 50 and 80 per cent profit on diamonds Nathaniel had sent and he was relieved to have sold 'a greater table' for £7,000. He continues:

> We are glad 'tis disposed off, for stones of that magnitude and value are esteemed in India 50 per cent more than other goods. And wee have noe market to dispose of such but France, which theire jewellers and the Jewes know and accordingly make their advantage, besides table stones are almost out of fashion in Europe and their price in Germany much fallen in few yeares. This stone was bought for France to make an a'lmode, is now offered to be sold there for £8,000.[12]

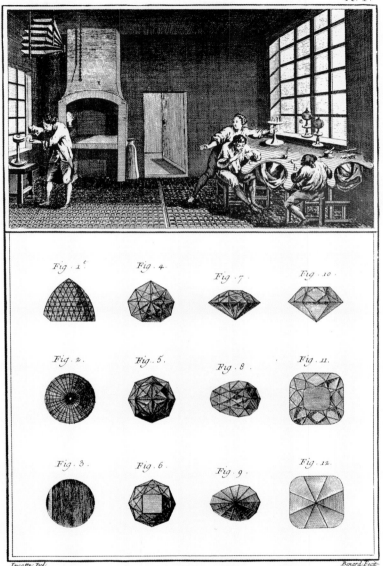

Orfèvre Jouaillier, Metteur en Œuvre,
Brillans Rares.

36 Diamond cuts including (10–12) elevation and two planes of a rose-cut diamond, an illustration to accompany Diderot and d'Alembert's *Encyclopédie* (1751–77).

The standard method of modifying a diamond to produce the facets that will enhance refraction and the polish that will generate reflection is, as we have seen, to use a fast-turning wheel (scaife) on the surface of which has been spread the aforementioned diamond dust mixture. The diamond is fixed into a dop or small cup attached to a tang, a kind of arm, which is then lowered over the revolving table or mill. Until the invention in 1933 of a mechanical dop that clasps the diamond and which can be adjusted to virtually any angle that the polisher needs, the diamond was fixed into the dop by means of a solder made of a heated mixture of lead and tin, and had to be taken off each time a new facet was started.[13] In some Antwerp workshops today the old dop with solder to hold the diamond in place is still used for the first basic facets; both old and new methods are shown being used concurrently here (illus. 38). In the photograph the packets bound with wire are lead weights. Prior to the advent of a mechanical dop, for the 57 facets of a brilliant-cut

37 Sixteenth-century gold fede ring with point-cut diamonds.

38 Antwerp diamond polisher using a scaife and old and new dops, lead weights etc., 2014.

diamond, the stone had to be moved 57 times. The work of making the dops was often done by women and was extremely unhealthy owing to the heavy metals involved. Until mechanization women were not accepted as cutters and polishers but were employed in hard labour (see illus. 35). Today, the polisher may have several diamonds on the go at once, taking them off the wheel every few seconds to check progress with a loupe or magnifying glass.

In her novel *Diamonds*, set in Antwerp and London just before and during the First World War and first published in Yiddish in 1944, Esther Kreitman describes what Dovid, son of a wealthy diamond merchant, experiences when he breaks class taboos and enters an Antwerp workshop in 1913, emphasizing the contrast between the dirty blackened surroundings and the glittering diamond:

> The workers, in their dirty, often torn overalls followed the revolv-ing wheels with their experienced eyes. They spun round faster than the layman's eye could see, and all Dovid saw was a circular blur of gleaming metal. On the wheels, diamonds of all sizes and colours were being polished: single cuts, small stones with only eight facets, as well as large valuable full cuts with fifty-seven facets . . .

39 The Nijlen diamond workshop, province of Antwerp, before its restoration as a museum, 2014.

As soon as one facet was finished, the stone was taken off the disc, which then began flying round again at dizzying speed, like magic. A worker took the diamond off the dop, melted the lead on the little blue gas flame which, like the flames of hell, never went out, put the stone back on the dop and another facet was polished. The workers clustered round the scaife even though they didn't have a great deal to do. Looking was the most important activity. They all looked grubby, as if they worked in a coal mine instead of polishing diamonds to glitter on the necks, arms and breasts of leisured ladies and gentlemen. Even Dovid's hands were grimy, and, under his beautifully manicured fingernails, a layer of dirt built up; this was the black diamond powder mixed with oil, which clung to the skin as soon as one went near it.[14]

40 The Nijlen workshop in an anonymous photograph of *c.* 1920.

In a rural area of Flanders known as De Kempen, a few miles from Antwerp, a workshop survives in the village of Nijlen (illus. 39) which has now been transformed into a museum but which, in its frozen time warp, demonstrated in 2014 something of what life was like for the diamond polishers who, with little training, were recruited to workshops after 1900, when vast quantities of diamonds began to be extracted and exported from the mines of Pretoria. A single engine powered a belt, which in turn powered the individual wheels arranged at regular intervals along the bench (illus. 40). Electricity came to De Kempen around 1928 but prior to that the engine would have been driven by coal-produced gas. The transverse belts were now missing but much else remained in place: the single stove for heating, the lead-covered window sills, the lamps with their green metal shades, the regulations governing the workshop framed on the wall, and tools left lying around, such as an implement that looks like an ice cream scoop but that was used for making dops (illus.

79

41 Dop-making device left in an abandoned workshop at Nijlen, 2014.

41). The owner of the workshop installed the equipment but workers had to rent a place and buy their own tools (illus. 44). These village workshops had all closed by 1980; the area was very poor, with sandy soil and an inadequate transport system, and the badly educated, scarcely trained workers, who were allowed only to make eight facets, were paid by the stone rather than, as in Antwerp, by the day (which is still the case). Consequently the work was of poor quality. With electricity it became possible for the polishers to set up in their own backyards, avoiding taxes. Some villagers became rich and emigrated to Africa, India or China, but many in an ununionized craft were exploited. All diamond work ceased in De Kempen after the government clamped down around 1970, fearful of the damage to Antwerp's reputation from inferior work, and challenged by the uncontrolled nature of this rural industry. Between 1950 and 2003 some of the workers made redundant by this decision, and their children, were employed by the nearby British Army base.[15]

Once faceted and polished, the diamond leaves the cutting and polishing shop where it has lived for the duration, either on the wheel or in its little white paper packet (illus. 42), and is sent on to the jewellers, from where it ends up in high-end stores like Tiffany & Co. in New York, Cartier in Paris

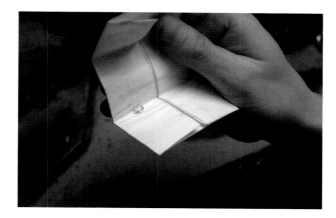

42 Pink diamond in the final stages of faceting, Antwerp workshop, 2014.

43 Touting for business at the Jewelry Exchange, West 47th Street, New York City, 2011.

or De Beers in London. Small stones – mounted to appear much larger than they are – that are set in engagement rings in high-street stores or available online will have come in all likelihood from a cutting and polishing shop in India, Israel or Russia. But what of the diamond dealer who brings the diamond to be cut and polished? A stroll round Antwerp's diamond quarter or New York's West 47th Street leaves little doubt that whereas cutting and polishing is largely gentile and international, the trade is still, as it has been for centuries, dominated by Jewish *diamantaires*. Orthodox Jews in black clothes

44 Diamond polishers at their scaifes in Berlaar near Antwerp, 1920.

and tall hats talk earnestly in front of the shops selling advanced computer software designed for the most up-to-date analysis of precious stones. At the bottom end of the diamond chain, casual labour is employed to attract punters (illus. 43).

Trans-global Diamond Trading in the Seventeenth and Eighteenth Centuries

Despite the secretiveness of the diamond business, a considerable amount of documentation survives owing to its transglobal nature: letter books contain copies of letters sent and received, and bills of lading record the cargo of particular ships. Then there are the records of the East India Company, which registered every official import. However, diamonds are very small and the possibilities of employees defrauding the company were many. Historiography of the diamond trade is diasporic on the one hand and, on the other, a narrative of consecutive and largely futile attempts to prevent smuggling. The first great diamond diaspora was the result of the Inquisition's persecution of Portuguese Jews, which brought wealthy and highly skilled diamond dealers to London, often under assumed names. They assimilated but struggled to attain citizen's rights until the Jewish Naturalization Act of 1753, for which the head of the leading merchant house of Salvador made representations in print.[16] It has been reliably claimed that London achieved its position in the diamond trade in the eighteenth century as the direct result of the immigration of Jewish diamond merchants from the Netherlands and Portugal, and later also from Leghorn and Germany.[17] After an Act of Parliament in 1732 abolished customs duties on uncut stones, London enjoyed a virtual monopoly. Indian stones were imported from Fort St George (illus. 45), subsequently Madras and now Chennai, sent to Amsterdam and Antwerp for cutting and polishing, then reimported and further exported around the world. Silver and coral were the currency with which diamonds from India and Portuguese Goa were purchased. Coral came from Naples, Genoa and other sites around the Mediterranean and was popular in India for jewellery. As the export of silver was restricted, Spanish pieces of eight and other foreign currencies were bought up for shipment to Asia.[18] The East India Company regulated imports with the effect that in the seventeenth century, although conditions fluctuated, private merchants had relatively limited opportunity for trade. However, there was one breach in its monopoly, which was the privileges of ships' officers employed in its service. They were allowed to take a certain quantity of goods on each voyage, depending on the officer's rank. As they themselves had limited resources, they 'sold' their rights to a merchant or a loan was made that was paid back if the voyage was successful. As we shall see, ships' captains might also be asked to transport bulses of diamonds that were small-scale, high-value and relatively easy to conceal on a person.

In the late seventeenth century and through the eighteenth century, the Company grappled with the problem of illegal trade and eventually opted for liberalization. India was the destination for many younger sons in the eighteenth century, and the word 'Nabob' was invented to describe a newly wealthy social nobody; those who had worked for the Company and brought diamonds back with them became the object of opprobrium and anxiety back home. The Nabob's immense wealth, transported as diamonds, enabled him to acquire land and therefore to join the nation's elite. Trading in diamonds became a vehicle for those who made the largest fortunes in India and men like General Robert Clive became almost like gem specialists, able

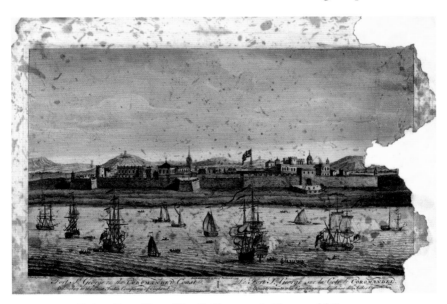

45 Robert Sayer, *View of Fort St George on the Coromandel Coast*, 1754, hand-coloured etching.

46 Drawing showing the elevation of the garden facade of Claremont House, Esher, designed by 'Capability' Brown for 'Clive of India', 1774.

to recognize what the best stones were that they were receiving in exchange for their rupees. But Clive was only the most prominent – and publicly criticized – of the Nabobs. Walpole famously remarked to Horace Mann in 1760: 'General Clive is arrived, all over estates and diamonds. If a beggar asks for charity, he says, "Friend, I have no small brilliants about me."' Clive had just purchased Claremont Estate for £25,000 (illus. 46).[19]

Trade in luxury goods, of which diamonds are the quintessential example, flourishes in peacetime and is disrupted by wars, religious and other forms of persecution, famine and disease. When John Cholmley told his brother that France was the only market for the very large diamond he was trying to sell, he did not need to explain why: for much of the period 1652–74 England was at war with the Netherlands over trade routes and was subsequently, 1701–14, heavily involved in Continental Europe in the wars of the Spanish succession. Taking into account the difficulty of accessing the Golconda mines to acquire diamonds in the first place, and the chief concerns of the Company that were in bulk goods like cloth, it is surprising that such efforts to regulate the import of diamonds were made once it became aware of the sums that were being imported in this form. Further disincentives to merchants were the fluctuation in diamond prices owing to unpredictable factors like the Portuguese Inquisition, the plague and the Great Fire of London, not to mention common factors like shipwrecks and the time lag (which was generally years) between initial investment and final sale. It is extraordinary that so many merchants entered into the business and that more did not founder.

The import and export of diamonds was dependent on systems of credit: on the one hand the availability of cash and credit influenced the demand for luxury goods and on the other, merchants depended on the arrival of the Rio fleet (from Brazil) and the India ships for the realization of their capital. The artist Peter Paul Rubens (1577–1640), who lived in the port city of Antwerp, acted as a financier without charging interest to his fellow citizens.[20] This is not at all surprising given that the economy of Antwerp depended on ready credit and many others must have done likewise and improved their social standing thereby. Merchants did not deal exclusively in precious stones, but the combination of high worth and small weight united with fashion meant that, as independent merchants became more prosperous and brokered ever larger sums, diamonds took precedence. Sir John Chardin (born Jean-Baptiste Chardin, knighted by Charles II in 1681, an associate of Josiah Child, Chair of the Company, and of John Evelyn; illus. 47) and his partner, the Jewish merchant Francisco Salvador, shipped coral beads and pieces of eight (silver) in large quantities to Fort St George, where the Honourable William Gifford and Elihu Yale (subsequently founder of Yale University) took delivery for John's brother Daniel Chardin and Francisco's brother Rodriguez Salvador. John Chardin wrote to his brother on 2 January 1700 complaining that their coral had sold at a loss and declaring: 'After twelve years of business collaboration the experience shows that the best merchandize is on my side gold and silver, on yours diamonds. We should stick to that in future.'[21] By 1700, the demand for brilliant-cut diamonds was evidently driving the business, with John Chardin writing to his brother on 2 January 1707/8 that diamond prices were going up and down according to their weight and the quality suitable for making brilliants of good shape and 'water' (the purity and translucency of the stone, the most perfect of which should be as clear as water).

We tend today to think of the developed world as a globalized society in which we are all networked and the transmission of news is instant and more

47 David Loggan
(?), *Sir John Chardin*,
1643, engraving.

JOHANNES CHARDIN MILES.
Natus $\frac{6}{16}$ novembris, 1643.

or less accurate in contrast to a past that somehow lacked these connections. The Chardins and James Dormer, an Antwerp merchant operating in the first half of the eighteenth century, exemplify what has been described as cross-cultural cooperation, showing how 'in the diamond trade, at the level of international imports and exports, merchants of different religions and Company officials were interconnected at a personal and commercial level, both in London as well as in India. The Salvadors were Jews, the Chardins Protestant Huguenots.'[22] Admittedly news travelled slowly but it is nonetheless instructive to read the correspondence of these merchants and to recognize their command of events, and the human and business associations they forged across national boundaries. Interestingly, of the three merchants examined here, none was regarded as in any significant way inferior to the gentry and aristocracy with whom they socialized as well as did business. Yorkshire-born John Cholmley was established in London by December 1664 (when the surviving correspondence with his brother commences), dealing mostly in diamonds but also in a range of other commodities not regulated by the East India Company, such as rubies, sapphires, opals, musk, ambergris and sandalwood. He never married and when he died suddenly in 1694 his estate passed to his brother Nathaniel's infant sons. Nathaniel arrived in India around 1662 and remained in Masulipatam (Metchlepatam) until 1675, when he moved to Golconda and built a house there, remaining for two years before moving to Fort St George, where he was resident in 1677. His correspondence with his brother reveals that he faced many difficulties in trading in India; at first he was obliged to work under the protection of an East India Office commissioner who charged 12 per cent commission for diamonds purchased in Golconda, but passed only 2 per cent to Nathaniel. At one stage he was imprisoned on a charge of treason for his part in a feud between two agents. Nonetheless, when he sailed home in 1682, he was worth at least £100,000, as this was the sum he was forced to pay for a bond to the captain of the ship that he was not carrying diamonds. The year after his return Nathaniel married a very well-connected woman, his first wife having died in India.

John Cholmley acted as an intermediary (broker) for English customers who wanted to buy diamonds from India, handled the business transactions of those who worked in India, sold jewels for them, arranged credit and banked their money. Clients for whom John engaged to import diamonds included Lady Villiers, the Countess of Pembroke and Lady Berkeley, all of whom wanted the stones for investment and subsequently sold them at a profit, casting an interesting light on the importance of jewels to women's financial independence in the early modern period. Among very large investments totalling thousands of pounds, he sent '5 doubloones to lay [invest] for N[ur] S[e] Frisby in a rough stone'.[23] Nathaniel's task was to get to the mines as quickly as possible after receiving the funds to select the best stones to be dispatched back to England as quickly as possible. He spoke the language and used Indian brokers but he was evidently also a skilled lapidary able to select stones directly from the mines; if good enough stones were not available, he retained the funds until they were. In 1674 John wrote to Nathaniel anxious about the arrival of the ships being so late that 'you'll not have time to make your investments at the mines to your owne and Correspondents satisfaccion.' He reported that: 'Mr Sheldon sold his great laske for between 5 and £600 and twas well sold.' Mr Sheldon evidently recouped his investment but sending these flat Indian cut stones must have been regarded as a bit risky, as John continues: 'Send no lasks except very good round and smooth, they generally proving browne water, which is not readily discerned because lying flat on the top and noe point they have noe play, but your high Labradores show theire water.'[24] The reservations about lasque diamonds do not appear to have been shared by the top rank of French dealers as many of those sold by Tavernier to the French monarch were lasques, including the famous 'French blue (see p. 25), and many were cut into roses by the royal lapidary Jean Pittan. John Cholmley's very precise advice to Nathaniel indicates that what was being valued in these imported diamonds was 'water', which could not be judged adequately on a flat stone because, having no point, or in other words no octahedral angles, there could be no 'play' of light.[25] Gems that arrived in England John showed to jewellers on behalf of his clients, and any that he was unable

48 Collection of uncut diamonds of varying shapes and water,
including some that are octohedral.

to sell because they were too flawed were not cut and polished but 'bought for Rushia', suggesting a secondary market.[26]

Even in 1687, when the Cholmleys were complaining about the decay in the diamond trade caused by the Company having included the diamond among its protected commodities, and of a glut in the market of stones sold at less than prime cost, sums of up to £100,000 were being sent in silver pieces of eight to purchase Indian diamonds. John's letters provide invaluable evidence of just how discerning these merchants had to be. In 1687, by which time Nathaniel was back in England, a letter was sent from John Cholmley & Co. to Daniel Chardin and Rodriguez Salvador along with £4,757 sterling in pieces of eight on board the HMS *Resolution*, to be changed into pagodas (the Indian currency) and used to purchase diamonds (illus. 48):

> In general our desires are for rough diamonds from five mangaleens to twenty, to be of a christaleen water, and as well spread and cleare of foules as you can procure them. If it happen you meet with a large stone or stones that have foules in them (of a bright water), that lye soeas to bee taken out in splitting, sawing or making to bee brought reasonable provide us such. Send noe cut stones or laskes except very good, round, smooth edges, and flatt in the collett . . .[27]

In between instructing him on the minutiae of gem valuation and the challenges of profit margins, John Cholmley also kept his brother au fait with the broader picture of international diamond business. Writing in 1669, John told Nathaniel:

> diamonds are att present so greate a drug there's now encourage-ment to send adventure for them. I conceive 'tis chiefly in regard of their raiseing their value att Flanders etc. and building in London there's few buyers and they are fallen in value 20 per cent. The Jewes have greate quantities & cannot sell either here or abroad. The King of France bought all that [Jean-Baptiste] Tavernier bought last year rough for 300000 Crownes & had them cut. I know not any this yeare sold for 40 per cent profit except Mr Hernes.[28]

The following year, John Cholmley sent his brother further news of French activity in the field, enclosing a letter from M. Raisin who, with M. Chardin, had sold rough diamonds there worth 350,000 livres. This was Antoine Raisin, a famous French Catholic dealer and jeweller who in 1670 signed the first of two contracts of association with John Chardin. He died single and childless in 1681 at Bandar Abbas, a port on the Persian Gulf in present-day Iran, leaving considerable assets around which years of litigation ensued.[29] Cholmley reports on the Frenchmen's plan to go to India and how they were preparing commodities to the value of £100,000 sterling. There was a considerable profit margin to be had in exporting to Persia high-quality European silverware, jewellery, watches and arms; the proceeds were reinvested in diamonds to be imported from India. John Chardin went on to write a popular travel book about his experiences.[30] Cholmley's gossipy letter gives a remarkable picture of those luxury European manufactures that were attractive to the Indian market and that could be exchanged for diamonds; it also provides the latest gossip about how Tavernier has invested the wealth he has accrued from his sale of diamonds to the French crown. The commodities purchased would be taken

> to sell in Turkey, Persia etc. as pendelock pearles, made up in great broaches, with rubies, dyamonds, emeralds, topasses and all other coloured stones of value (except saphires) curiously wrought in severall fashions for pendants and brest jewells of several sizes. Also looking-glasses of christall garnished richly with gold, christall cups, amber and coral beads, watches and many such kinds of merchandize of which I am told they make 3 for one. About 6 moneths hence goes for India Sen. Alvares & 4 more of Paris for the like trad[e]. Young Tavernier is now in those parts, his father hath purchased a great estate in Switzerland where he now lives.[31]

The length of time it could take for a ship that left an English port to arrive at Fort St George (approximately six months) effectively meant that merchants had to factor into their calculations not only the chance of a sudden drop in the price of diamonds or a glut in the supply of commodities sent as exchange, but the decease of creditors or partners and, above all, the possible loss of a whole ship. In 1672 John Cholmley was obliged to approach the executors of Alderman Knight, as both Knight and his son had died before payment had been made for diamonds that Knight had ordered.[32] For their part, in an era before organized insurance, the Chardins took precautions against unseen accidents. An undated draft from John Chardin to his brother and Salvador to accompany a chest of silver states: 'if it should come to pass one of you die before returning of 6000 wch God forbid we desire you to come in w^t ye survivor for ye investing of ye goods & ye sending home of it in diamonds upon ye next ship.'[33] Despite these precautions they had to litigate after the death of Chardin's partner Raisin for money owed to them.[34] The great fear of those waiting for the ships to arrive was the loss of a cargo either through piracy and enemy action or – all too commonly – through shipwreck. One such shipwreck occurred in 1741 when the *Luccia*, on the way from Bengal, struck rocks off North Ronalshaw, west of Orkney, and went down with the loss of a full cargo and many men. Hugh Campbell, a Scottish merchant, wrote immediately from Gothenburg to a colleague in Antwerp to express 'the greatest concern I have had for the late misfortune of our ship Luccia nay for the loss of so many honest gentlemen that perish'd with her'.[35] The recipient of this sad news was James Dormer, another merchant, and one about whom we know a remarkable amount.

In Antwerp's city archives, now housed appropriately in an airy and light-filled converted warehouse on the harbour front, Dormer's business correspondence is preserved in dozens of boxes.[36] He was born near Southampton in 1708 into a Roman Catholic landed family. After his father's death had left the family in pecuniary difficulties, his mother could not afford to apprentice him in London so instead sent him to Bruges where, at the firm of Prosser & Porter, she had only to pay £40 per annum and was assured that after five years he would be qualified. James's elder brother Walter had made money in Bengal and wanted James to join him. But having made the acquaintance of the established Antwerp merchants De Pret & Proli, he was commissioned in 1731 to go and sort out the business interests of their Ostend Company in Canton. The De Pret family had been importing diamonds for two generations. After a successful mission he returned to Antwerp to acclaim for his business acumen. Thus began his rapid ascent in Antwerp society and his accumulation of wealth and a degree of power. The young James had evidently understood contemporary taste and had brought back from the Far East a bag of luxury commodities. Arriving back in Antwerp, he received a letter from the Comte de Calenburg in Brussels:

> Having learned that you have brought back from your journey to China some well-chosen and tasteful curiosities, I wanted to write this to you, Sir, to request, to know if you would extend to me the friendship of sending me a little list of what you have brought back either pretty or curious, and if you would care to add to it the price you would oblige me and I will keep it for myself alone, I congratulate you, finally, on your happy return and on the part you have played in the good and prompt expedition of the affairs of the Company . . .[37]

Through his first marriage, probably in 1735, to Maria Magdalena Emtinck, Dormer became related to the old patrician merchant families of Antwerp like the Van Colens, and also to the bishop of Bruges. When his wife died in 1737, the couple were residing in a fine house in Venusstraat, not far from the docks and the Custom House. His second marriage, a year and a half later, was to Joanna Theresia Goubau, who was well educated and a capable collaborator.[38] When Dormer died suddenly of a stroke in 1758 while selling Austrian lottery tickets illegally in England,[39] he had moved from importing all manner of goods (including precious stones) to specializing in gems and banking. He owned a modest country estate, acquired a collection of paintings (he appears to have favoured Frans Snyders) and had become a major figure in the civic life of Antwerp.[40] He effectively founded a trading house, a bank and an insurance company, and he obtained credit for Empress Maria Theresa and arranged for the payment of British troops. After his death, his widow and his son by his first wife formed a company, but Jacob-Albert Dormer lacked his father's skills and the bank failed. Diamonds – and James Dormer's knowledge of them – were undoubtedly the foundation of his success. And he dealt on a large scale: his memorandum book contains the following note for 1747: 'Mem^d The great Diamond Carat 88 ¾ is in the hands of Messrs. Rensuards of Amst[erdam] the price £10,000'.[41] The Dormer archive contains evidence of his dealing on behalf of Jews and gentiles alike: among his clients were the Jewish-British banker Sampson Gideon and the London jeweller Charles Belliard, of whom I shall have more to say in Chapter Four.[42] His partners included Francis Salvador (a Portuguese Jew) in London as well as aristocrats like Lord Gray, Lord Stafford, Lord Albemarle, Lord Rivers and Viscount Fairfax.[43] He also appears to have sold direct to jewellers.[44]

In a recent study of mercantile networks, James Dormer's business transactions have been drawn on to demonstrate how a cross-cultural trade network functioned during the eighteenth century. It included Sephardic Jews, Flemings, Huguenot French and English Catholics and Protestants. They worked as individuals and companies in Antwerp, London, Amsterdam, Rotterdam and Lisbon. They supplied diamonds, travelled as agents, arranged the cleaving and cutting of diamonds, financed ventures and, as intermediaries, brokered deals.[45] Many parcels of diamonds were sent backwards and forwards between London, Lisbon, Antwerp and Amsterdam in search of the best possible price. As with the Cholmleys, Dormer and his associates were very particular about what they wanted and showed a keen eye for market fluctuations. George Clifford & Sons in London asked Dormer to obtain the diamonds most in demand in Amsterdam: 'rozes that are well spread x pretty clear, but not of quite the first water'.[46] Similarly, Dormer's correspondents in Lisbon also kept an eye open for what was fashionable. On one occasion, Dormer had sent Berthon & Garnault, sales agents in Lisbon, yellow diamonds whereas the Portuguese wanted white stones: 'White as much in roses as in brilliants are desired and furthermore with these last [brilliants] perfect, well cut and above all well spread.'[47] As the historian Tijl Vanneste concludes, had Dormer not operated within a network, he would have had to choose between the commerce in polished or in uncut stones; commodity circulation would have been more difficult and the network made possible an ease of transaction between the four markets in which Dormer was active.[48]

Dirty-looking Stones

While diamonds are germane to accounts of mercantilism in the early modern period and, as we have seen, were imported and re-exported by reputable merchants who kept good records of their transactions, diamonds have also always played an important role in the murky underworlds of international crime, bribery, extortion and what we now know as money laundering. Today, the global reach of the corporate diamond business is far more extensive, the sums involved are stupendous, reputational damage is endemic and news travels instantly around the world. To conclude this chapter, I return to the present day to consider how, in one instance, the underbelly of the contemporary diamond business was exposed to general view. In August 2010 the supermodel Naomi Campbell was summoned to appear at the war crimes tribunal in The Hague at the trial of Charles Taylor, former president of Liberia. Campbell allegedly claimed that when, on 25 September 1997, she had sat next to Taylor at a dinner in South Africa organized by Nelson Mandela, she had never heard of Liberia and had no idea who Charles Taylor was. With great reluctance, she testified that during the night following the dinner some men came to her hotel room with a pouch containing what she is reported to have described as 'dirty looking stones'. At the same time she claimed that she was ignorant of the source of this gift of what were, of course, rough diamonds.[49] The episode was of considerable interest to the tribunal as Taylor, who was facing crimes against humanity including terrorism, murder, rape, sexual slavery, use of child soldiers, forced amputation, enslavement and pillage (to all of which he pleaded not guilty), was alleged to have financed the Revolutionary United Front's (RUF) invasion of Sierra Leone by trading weapons for looted diamonds. Arms were smuggled to Sierra Leone, it was said, in sacks of rice, and diamonds sent back in a mayonnaise jar. Had Campbell taken diamonds out of South Africa, it would have been an indictable offence. The Taylor trial, which concluded in 2013 with his conviction and sentence to fifty years in prison, was the first completed criminal appeals process judging a former head of state in modern criminal law, and has been subject to a great deal of interrogation by lawyers.[50] For much of the general public, however, the Taylor trial, with Campbell's high-profile appearance (not to mention the seemingly contradictory testimony of Mia Farrow who, along with Imran Kahn and his then wife Jemima Goldsmith, was also at the dinner), was the first time they had been made aware of just what trading in 'dirty stones' across Africa's war-torn borders actually meant. To be sure, *Blood Diamond* (2006), starring

Leonardo DiCaprio, familiarized audiences with the phrase 'blood diamonds', but the film, directed by Edward Zwick, is a sensational thriller with a storyline that fails to engage with the gravity of political reality in the region.

It is certain that the discovery of diamonds in many areas of southern Africa, combined with new mining technologies, has resulted over the past 120 years in the kinds of production levels that our merchants of the seventeenth and eighteenth centuries could scarcely have imagined. While this has brought wealth to some, it has been largely the colonial powers that have benefited, along with corrupt rulers of recently independent states. More needs to be said about this, but first let us focus for a moment on the notorious pouch of dirty stones that Naomi Campbell allegedly accepted from Taylor. Campbell claimed to have given them immediately to someone running a charity but the question remains of what Taylor might have hoped to obtain; diamonds changing hands undercover immediately arouses suspicion of a bribe. Diamonds have long been regularly given as diplomatic gifts, in recognition of services rendered and expectation of some kind of loyalty, reciprocation or lasting association. In 1630, in recognition of his efforts to further an entente between the Spanish Habsburg rulers and the English, Peter Paul Rubens, who was both an artist and a diplomat, was knighted by Charles I and presented with a diamond hat ornament and a diamond ring. Probably one of the largest diamonds seen by Tavernier in the collection of the Great Mughal and now one of the treasures of the Kremlin State Diamond Fund, the Orlov diamond (see illus. 24) was acquired by Count Orlov (1741–1783), the lover of Empress Catherine of Russia. Eventually rejected by Catherine, he sought unsuccessfully to regain her favour by presenting to her this huge stone. Diamonds as gifts seem to be especially open to suspicion of corruption, the purchasing of favours and improper attempts to influence those in power. It is no accident that the events leading to the fall of the Ancien Régime in France were triggered by the *affaire du collier*, the mysterious theft of the biggest piece of diamond jewellery ever made, in which Marie Antoinette was falsely and damagingly implicated and about which I write in Chapter Five.[51] Aside from Naomi Campbell's protestations that it was inconvenient to her to have to attend the trial in The Hague and that she feared for her family's safety, she must also have been well aware of the reputational damage she risked through her association with a surreptitious nocturnal gift of diamonds. That she is a black woman merely served to intensify the risk that she might become not only a figure of women's insatiable appetite for the consumption of luxury goods but a symbol of the exploitation by a minority of powerful black people of the impoverished majority, and of the inhumane treatment of civilians.

Since the 1990s, as Franziska Bieri aptly puts it, to the four Cs by which diamonds have been judged since the Renaissance – carat, colour, clarity and cut – has been added a fifth C, standing for conflict.[52] Writing in 2010, Bieri assessed that four million had died in the 1990s and that between 3.7 and 20 per cent of the total numbers of diamonds traded during that decade were so-called 'conflict diamonds' or 'blood diamonds'. The seemingly emotive terminology relates to diamonds that are mined in war zones and used to finance insurgency or the activities of warlords. Diamonds have fuelled wars and refugee crises not only in Sierra Leone but in Angola, the Democratic Republic of Congo and Côte d'Ivoire. In 1998–9 a number of non-governmental organizations and the United Nations summoned a forum involving the diamond-producing states. A great deal of pressure came, and continues to come, from Global Witness, whose vigilance, expertise and postings tackle the problem at every level. Typically, for example, on 8 February 2010 they posted a notice for Valentine's Day, exhorting those inclined to sell or purchase diamond rings on that occasion to ask the following questions: do you know where the diamonds you sell came from? Can I see a copy of your company's policy on conflict diamonds? Can you show me a written guarantee from your suppliers that your diamonds are conflict free? How is the supply chain audited?[53]

49 A rough, uncut, brown diamond.

THREE

DIAMOND: SHAPE, PATTERN, SYMBOL

Twinkle twinkle little star
How I wonder what you are
Up above the world so high
Like a diamond in the sky...
NINETEENTH-CENTURY LULLABY[1]

'Diamond' by Design

ADIAMOND IN ITS NATURAL STATE is an octahedron (illus. 49), though generally not a regular one. Viewed when lying on a flat surface, a symmetrical uncut diamond crystal will appear roughly four-sided or pyramidal. In Euclidean geometry this form is a rhombus – that is, a quadrilateral whose four sides have the same length. The word diamond is used to describe this shape; so too is the word 'lozenge'. These terms are widely employed interchangeably, though 'diamond' sometimes refers specifically to a rhombus with a 60-degree angle and 'lozenge' to one with a 45-degree angle. Diamond and lozenge shapes are parallelograms; they differ from the square in not having right angles. A close relation is the square tipped onto a point – the poised square. This chapter explores two interconnected aspects of the diamond shape as a significant presence in history and culture. On the one hand, I will consider how the natural form of the crystal has contributed to the history of design in the widest sense of the word. By 'design' I intend the Italian Renaissance *disegno* as that which is fundamental to the transfer

50 American feathered diamond quilt, *c.* 1988, cotton.

of an idea distinct from colour and other aspects of artistic practice. On the other hand, I shall be exploring how the rhombus, or diamond form, as well as the diamond itself, functions as a universal symbol standing for adamantine beauty across generations and cultures worldwide.

One question underlying this chapter is, why should a poised square have apparently so much more potential in terms of pattern, meaning and affect than a simple square (illus. 50)? How much less pleasing to the eye this woven cotton quilt in two colours would be without the poise and balance conveyed by the diamond shape. Another question relates to the power of the diamond as an image. How is it that, centuries after it was demonstrated incontrovertibly that the 'incorruptible' body of the diamond could disappear under intense heat, the idea of a diamond, represented by the basic rhombus, remains synonymous with endurance and fortitude? In 1771 Horace Walpole lamented to Lady Mary Coke in a letter from Paris: 'Yes, Madam, diamonds are a bubble, and adamant itself has lost its obduracy.' Describing Antoine Lavoisier's experiment during which an emerald and a ruby put in a furnace survived while the diamond was destroyed, he predicted that 'no woman of quality will deign to wear any more diamonds' and claimed that if he were to compliment his correspondent on her eyes he would now have to compare them to rubies.[2] He was, however, wrong.

The abiding notion that a diamond stands for what is indestructible is a triumph of imagination over reason. The very fact of a diamond's superlative hardness, its resistance to wear, is enough to ensure its continuing

51 Trade catalogue cover, London Aluminium Co. Ltd, 1934, Head Office, Witton, Birmingham.

52, 53 Diamond Sutra, Dunhuang, 868 CE, ink on paper, and detail.

metaphorical value, not least in marketing everything from car tyres to kitchenware: typically, for example, in 1913 *The Sun* (New York) advertised 'Diamond vitalized rubber tyres' and in 1934, the English manufacturers of Diamond aluminium saucepans (illus. 51) were in no doubt of the value of the idea of permanence that the word diamond – and a trademark based on a lozenge – would bring to their product. The combination of resistance to damage (except by extreme heat) and the generation of light appears to have been particularly alluring to those responsible for selling products from time-shares to streetwear.[3] Songwriters have employed the diamond as a simile for a star whose light radiates into outer space, and when the UK's synchrotron opened at Harwell Science and Innovation Campus near Oxford in 2007 it was named 'Diamond Light Source', even though no diamonds were used in its construction and none are used in its procedures. 'Diamond', the abbreviation by which it is generally known, speeds up electrons to near light speed so that they give off a light ten billion times brighter than the sun. These bright beams are then directed off into laboratories known as 'beamlines'. Here, scientists use the light to study a vast range of subject-matter, from new medicines and treatments for disease to innovative engineering and technology.[4] For conceptual and abstract artists of the late twentieth and twenty-first centuries, diamonds have similarly provided, as we shall see in the final part of this chapter, a remarkably rich source of imagery.

Religions and philosophies have drawn upon diamond imagery from time immemorial as a way of expressing what is incorruptible and beyond price. The fact that a diamond could only be cut by using another diamond lent force to this image of some element independent of human meddling and true only to itself. The Buddhist faith, which was founded in India, does not believe in a deity and does not look for a relationship between God and man. Rather it centres on the search for enlightenment through the practice and development of morality, meditation and wisdom. Central is the idea of finding a middle way through life's challenges. According to tradition the founder of Buddhism, Siddhartha Gautama, was born in 566 BCE, the son of an Indian prince, and led a sheltered and luxurious life. But one day, when he was 29, he disguised himself and went off to explore. He went in four directions and saw four things that filled him with sorrow: a decrepit old man, a diseased man, a dead man and a monk. The sight of this misery inspired him to adopt a life of self-denial. Eventually he adapted the total deprivation to which he had committed himself and found the middle way. He thus became the Buddha, or 'Awakened One'. The Buddha's teachings, called sutras, were committed to memory by disciples and eventually written down. The world's earliest surviving complete and dated printed book is called the Diamond Sutra (868 CE; illus. 52).[5] The text (in Chinese) explains how an elderly disciple asks the Buddha how the sutra should be known. The answer is that it should be called 'The Diamond of Transcendent Wisdom' because its teaching will cut like a diamond through worldly illusion to illuminate what is real and everlasting. Jewel imagery is important in Buddhism: at the centre of the faith are the three jewels, or triple jewel: the Buddha, his teaching (the Dharma) and the spiritual community (the Sangha). A popular Buddhist parable recounts how a poor man travels through life unaware of the precious jewel that has been sewn into the hem of his coat by a well-meaning friend. An illustration to the Diamond Sutra shows the Buddha expounding the faith to his disciple with, on a table in front of him (illus. 53), three caskets containing the three jewels of his teaching.

The Judeo-Christian tradition also employs the imagery of precious stones. Caution is needed, however, because of the difficulty of translation: references to hard stones in the Old Testament are sometimes translated as diamonds and sometimes as flints or emery, as with Ezekiel 3:9 where the line 'Like adamant harder than flint I have made your forehead' has been variously translated.[6] Diamonds are included in lists of precious stones when God instructs Ezekiel to go to the king of Tyrus, who has defiled God's sanctuaries by his iniquities. He had been given by God gifts of beauty and wisdom but has 'set his heart as the heart of God':

> Thou hast been in Eden the garden of God; every precious stone was thy covering, the sardius, topaz, and the diamond, the beryl, the onyx, and the jasper, the sapphire, the emerald, and the carbuncle, and gold.[7]

In Exodus appears the description of the breastplate of righteousness that God commands should be made for Aaron (and for his sons) so that he may minister as a priest of the Lord. The instructions are very precise and include a whole series of precious stones that are to be engraved with the names of the children of Israel. The breastplate itself is to be four square and set with four rows of stones: in the first row a sardius, a topaz and a carbuncle (ruby); in the second an emerald, a sapphire and a diamond; in the third a ligure, an agate and an amethyst; in the fourth a beryl, an onyx and a jasper.[8] Each stone stood for one of the twelve tribes of Israel but beyond this any particular symbolism relating to the individual stones is obscure. Presumably these were regarded as the most precious stones known at the time.

A quadripartite structure underpinned early Christian and medieval ideas about the world.[9] The four gospels dominated Christian iconography: the four living creatures, symbolic of the evangelists, were frequently represented around the divine throne amid cosmic portents underscoring the four-square nature of the earth, with angels standing at the four corners, holding back the four winds.[10] Commentators on the Book of Revelation probed the mysteries of space, time and matter as part of a fourfold ordering of the world: four winds or cardinal directions (oriens, occidens, aquilo, meridies); four seasons of the year, four elements (earth, fire, air, water) and their properties; four humours of the human microcosm (sanguine, choleric, melancholic, phleg-matic). The underlying unity of this quadripartite world was seen to flow from the divine creator made known in Christ and revealed through the four gospels. Diagrams habitually employ a poised-square format to indicate the four elements and their properties in different colours, but these are simple compared to the diamond structures devised by medieval commentators and theologians who produced elaborate figured diagrams that served a decorative as well as a religious function. In the frontispiece to the gospels in the Vivien Bible made in Tours 845–51 (illus. 54), a strong quadripartite structure centres on a central lozenge or rhombus with Christ as described in the Apocalypse enthroned at the centre and evangelists and their symbols disposed in circular medallions at four cardinal points of the lozenge and in the spandrels or four corners of the rectangular outer frame (head and shoulders in the medallions and full figures at the corners).

In England around 1011, Byrhtferth, a priest and monk at the Abbey of Ramsey, made a complicated diagram (illus. 55), which has been described

54 *Christ in Majesty Surrounded by Four Evangelists and Four Great Prophets,*
from the Vivien Bible, AD 845–51.

as part of a natural science endeavour, incorporating Christian cosmological
doctrine into classical theories on the structure of the heavens and earth, unit-
ing geography, physics and computation of time to demonstrate the harmony
of creation.[11] Byrhtferth's diagram, of which several later copies exist, sets out
the harmony of the macrocosm and the microcosm through correlating the

55 Byrhtferth's diagram, in
a manuscript from St John's
College, Oxford.

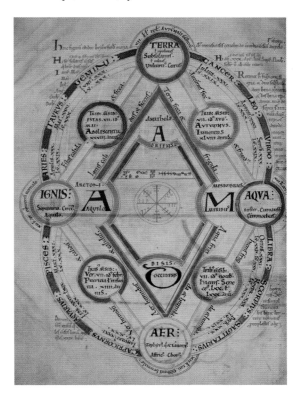

quaternities of time, space and matter. We see the four seasons together with
the signs of the zodiac and related months, four cardinal directions and winds,
four elements and properties, four humours and ages of man. The inner of
two rhomboids is inscribed with the name of A-D-A-M (four letters, as in the
name of Christ – Deus). Critical to this disposition and to the melding of
word and image is the diamond structure of the central frames.

In a sinister postscript, it is worth remarking that the self-styled Night
Wolves, the pro-Kremlin religious patriot biker gangs alongside whom
President Vladimir Putin likes to be photographed and who were reported to
have been seen erecting road blocks in the 2014 invasion by Russia of Ukraine,
use as their insignia the head of a wolf inscribed within a diamond surrounded
by runic script. Accordingly the flaming wolf head set against a full moon is
configured as a horizontal rhombus in the bikers' badge (illus. 56), which is
inscribed with the words 'The Night Wolves. Moscow.' Writer and journalist
Peter Pomerantsev has described 'a great stone at the entrance to their kingdom

on which is engraved one of the Hell's Angels' symbols, a one per cent sign inside a diamond'. In Hells Angels lore, he states, it stands for the 1 per cent who are outlaws, but the Night Wolves have engraved a new text in gothic Cyrillic around the diamond, signifying that 'in heaven there is more joy at the one per cent of sinners who confess than the ninety nine per cent who have no need of salvation.'[12] In a reinvention of the mythology of Holy Russia the diamond serves to convey timelessness and endurance as well, perhaps, as the traditional quaternities discussed above.

In Christian teaching the diamond is regularly invoked on account of its clarity and resistance to damage. In the writings of the mystic St Teresa of Avila (1515–1582) it is clear that the author is aware not only of the mineralogical characteristics of diamonds but of how they are worked on in her own time. For example, she likens her inner visions to 'The brilliance . . . of

56 Member of the Russian biker group Night Wolves.

an infused light coming from a sun covered by something as transparent as a properly-cut diamond'.[13] For St Teresa, diamonds are paradoxically both the measure of how inferior the best things of this world are to the treasures of divine revelation and, simultaneously, a means of conveying the intensity of the relationship with God of which the soul is capable. Thus in the book she wrote about her life, St Teresa describes a visionary conversation with Christ, who took from her the cross she was holding attached to a rosary. When he gave it back it had been transformed into four large stones (symbolic of the quaternities discussed earlier); the stones were 'incomparably more precious than diamonds', she tells her readers, 'there is no appropriate comparison for supernatural things. A diamond seems to be something counterfeit and imperfect when compared with the precious stones that are seen there.'[14] While diamonds are paltry imitations of the true jewel – that is, Christ – Teresa also grounds her account in the imagery of jewellery that would have been familiar to an elite readership: 'the representation of the five wounds was very delicate workmanship. From then on [Christ] told me I would see the cross in that way.'[15] In another work, Teresa compares the body to the setting or frame of a jewel, lamenting that we ignore the jewel that is the soul while fussing over the body in which it is set: 'little effort is made to preserve [the soul's] beauty. All our attention is taken up with the plainness of the diamond's setting or the outer wall of the castle; that is with these bodies of ours.'[16] Elsewhere, the divinity itself is compared to a diamond: in a passage that appears to demonstrate the author's knowledge of the fact that diamonds regularly contain inclusions (flaws), Teresa states:

> And we could say that everything we do is visible in this diamond since it is of such a kind that it contains all things within itself; there is nothing that escapes its magnitude. It was a frightening experience for me to see in so short a time so many things joined together in this diamond, and it is most saddening, each time I recall, to see appearing in that pure brilliance things as ugly as were my sins.[17]

The passage looks forward to Gerard Manley Hopkins's lines on the comfort of the Resurrection:

57 Gabriel
Rollenhagen,
*Selectorum
emblematum
centuria secunda*
(1613).

In a flash, at a trumpet crash,
I am all at once what Christ is, | since he was what I am, and
This Jack, joke, poor potsherd, | patch, matchwood, immortal
    diamond,
Is immortal diamond.[18]

The emblem books that were so popular in sixteenth- and seventeenth-
century Europe offered wisdom in a concentrated form; a pictorial image often
representing an abstract concept is accompanied by an elucidatory motto
(epigraph) while underneath or alongside is printed a short text providing an
example. Gabriel Rollenhagen and Crispin van der Passe's 1613 book, extended
and widely disseminated by George Wither in *A Collection of Emblemes* (1635),
shows a diamond fixed with lead on an anvil with a hammer poised above it
and the motto '*True* Vertue, *firme, will always bide, / By whatsoever* suffrings

464   DE SYMBOLIS HEROICIS

Cæfar Laurentius ex noftrâ Societate, alteri eum honorem declinanti pariter, dedit pro teſſerâ pyxidem, quibuſdam intus gemmis inſtructam, quæ lucem in Sole hauriunt, & ſeruant, egeruntque; ſi pyxis eadem, vbi clauſa fuerit, recludatur in tenebris. Erat verò Epigraphe; A M A T O B S C V R V M.

Nimirum etiam ipſe lucem animi faciliùs erat explicaturus in priuato, & minùs celebri conſeſſu.

tride' (illus. 57).[19] In a 1682 collection, we see a treasure chest set in a niche surrounded by a cartouche. The embrasure is dark but the lid of the chest has been opened and dazzling rays of light emanate from the heap of diamonds inside (illus. 58). The epigraph reads: 'Amat Obscurum' and derives from a verse by the Latin poet Horace: 'one [poem] courts the shade; another, not afraid of the critic's keen eye, chooses to be seen in a strong light; the one pleases but once, the other will still please if ten times repeated.'[20] The exemplum (referring to diamond's phosphorescence) tells of a contemporary Jesuit: 'Caesar Laurentius [perhaps Cesare Lorenzo] of our Order [Jesuit] gave for his token [emblem] a box filled with gems, which take up [literally drink] their light from the sun and preserve it, and need to do this if the same box, when closed, is shut away in a dark place.'[21]

Diamond or lozenge shapes are endemic in pattern and design across many cultures. In Islamic art and architecture rectangles and lozenges are

59 Interior brickwork in the Mausoleum of Ismail Samani, Bukhara, Uzbekistan, 10th century.

a fundamental part of the decorative vocabulary of surface coverings of buildings and artefacts, both in secular (court) art and in religious buildings. At Bukhara in Uzbekistan, where the Mausoleum of Ismail Samani (begun 892 CE; illus. 59) has been described as a 'major masterpiece of ornament',[22] the upper part of the brickwork interior is covered with a rich surface in which squares and lozenges alternate. The anthropologist Alfred Gell asked how it is that sequences of repeated geometric forms 'induce animacy'. Why, in other words, do we read them as dynamic rather than static? He suggests that the process of seeing a pattern involves progression and mental transference of the motif in order to register congruence – that is, to recognize like with like – and that this leads to a sense of agency and motion that appears to adhere to the motifs themselves.[23] Geometric patterns are neither an Islamic invention nor an exclusively Islamic device. But it is the case that some of the most spectacular geometric ornamentation involving diamond shapes is found on artefacts and buildings produced in Islamic cultures where, as Oleg Grabar succinctly puts it, ornament is both 'slave and master of the space on which it occurs'.[24] In Western Europe, heraldry gave prominence to certain shapes and their influence permeated many fields of representation. For example, in 1589 the English writer George Puttenham united heraldry and information he states as coming from 'Orientall parts of the world' when he describes lines of poetry put into the form of a fuzie (an elongated lozenge; illus. 60). The lozenge is, he asserts, 'the most beautiful figure & especially fit for this purpose [of writing poems], being in his kind a quadrangle reverst, with his point upward like to a quarrel of glasse the Greekes and Latines both call it *Rombus*'. He also likens it to the turbot and states the fuzie as 'of the same nature but that he is sharper and slenderer', and goes on to tell a story about a lady presenting an emperor of Tartary 'with this Lozange made in letters of rubies & diamants entermingled thus'. There follow Puttenham's shaped verses.[25]

Diamond shapes work in two different ways on patterned surfaces. In the first place they form a closed design, which is confined in its own border and which may frame other forms, such as representational or semi-representational organic motifs like flowers or leaves. In the second place, through repetition they are used to create a background or a surface design (such as we see at Bukhara or in English medieval ecclesiastic buildings like the cathedrals of Durham and Norwich (illus. 61)). Squares and lozenges, it

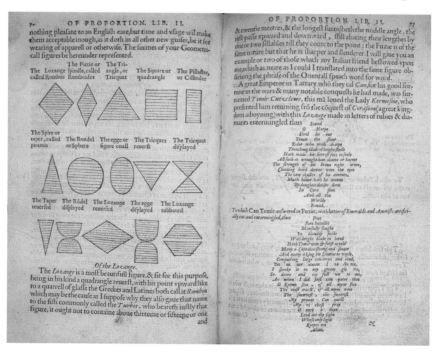

60 George Puttenham, *The Arte of English Poesie* (London, 1589, facsimile 1966).

61 Norwich Cathedral, 12th century, north aisle: this tympanum is filled with geometrical blocks laid at 45 degrees with their faces bevelled into squares to give a latticework effect, and the archivolt has regular voussoirs each incised with a simple poised square.

has been remarked, lend themselves relatively easily to perforation and have been used frequently for wooden screens and window grilles.[26] The lozenge as a frame for embroidered flowers and pearls is common in the dress represented in portraits of Elizabethan elite women, and also appears on its own as a shape embroidered onto sleeves, as in Hans Eworth's *Margaret Dudley, Duchess of Norfolk* (1562),[27] whose sleeves are embroidered with lozenge shapes and who wears a diamond cross round her neck, and *Katheryn of Berain* by an unknown Netherlandish artist (1568; illus. 62), who has diamond motifs richly embroidered on her sleeves. She also wears four diamond rings, one set with a very prominent pointed or pyramidal stone.[28]

The diamond shape was also attractive as a way of introducing a sense of order – and thereby of harmony – into the profusion of natural motifs in Elizabethan embroidered gowns; it is as though a lattice structure is introduced to bring order to nature. Diamond jewels are represented widely in Tudor and Stuart portraits, always dark or black. Unlike today's diamonds, they were unfaceted and set directly into their mounts without being lifted on claws to permit the light to penetrate from below. Sometimes foil was used to increase the reflection but they remained extremely dark, as may be seen by looking at a rare sixteenth-century ring in the Ashmolean Museum (see illus. 37), where the central and four surrounding diamonds, almost certainly uncut though given a polish, have been set into a deep bezel, meaning that the gold surround and the diamond itself project. Such rings must have been heavy to wear and difficult to maintain in a stable position on the finger. An example of a seventeenth-century ring in the same collection demonstrates how one large and six smaller table-cut diamonds could be set in a way that emphasizes their lozenge shapes.[29] As we have seen, artists portraying subjects wearing these jewels were remarkably diligent in representing the precise cut (see illus. 32, 33).

In Tudor and Stuart portraiture the diamond or lozenge motif appears to be confined to female dress and may therefore relate to rules governing heraldry in which the mascle (a voided lozenge-shaped opening through which the ground appears) is a peculiarly female sign. It has been argued, however, that the lozenge motif dates back to Neolithic and Palaeolithic times and that, indicating the pattern of sewn fields, it is a sign of female fertility.[30] Sigmund Freud adopted the theory of the diamond as vulva in analysing what he calls the 'sleep-ceremonial' of a nineteen-year-old girl. This involved various nightly adaptations to her bedroom to allay intense fears that prevented her sleeping. The most significant reorganization involved her pillows and bedclothes: the small top pillow must lie on a large pillow 'in one specific way only – namely, so as to form a diamond shape. Her head then had to lie exactly along the long diameter of the diamond.' After a detailed reading of the symbolic content of all the various objects that had to be rearranged before the girl could sleep, Freud asks why this pillow had to be aligned and her head placed precisely in these ways. His conclusion: 'it was easy to recall to her that this diamond shape is the inscription scribbled on every wall to represent the open female genitals.'[31] It is this image that created a storm of controversy in 2014 when graffiti artist Carolina Falkholt's mural was installed in a Swedish middle school (illus. 63). It is relevant here to speculate on the 'reticulate designs' of diagonal rhombuses that archaeologist John Mitchell identifies in screens closing off the sanctuary in early Christian churches, whether painted or as grilles; he describes them as 'palpable and excluding' on the one hand and 'permeable and offering passing or passage' on the other, conveying the sense

62 *Katheryn of Berain*, 1568, oil on panel.

63 Carolina Falkholt, graffito of female genitalia, *Övermålning/Overpainting* at Alphaskolan in Nyköping, Sweden.

of a 'vibrating oscillating screen'.[32] Is there, one must ask, something here akin to the female hymen? Beyond the diamond shapes is an opening up as well as a closing off, just as, discussing Mallarmé, Jacques Derrida named as hymen that which indicates both proximity and separation.[33]

Architecture and Ornament in the West

In the West the classical tradition was kept alive not only through Greek and Roman architecture but above all through treatises such as that of Vitruvius (d. 15 CE) and subsequently Leon Battista Alberti (1404–1472), Sebastiano Serlio (1475–1554), whose work was translated into English in 1611, and Andrea Palladio (1508–1580). According to these texts, rules of architecture and design should depend above all on the stability of visible verticality. Geometrical forms that deviated met with disapproval. Nonetheless, lozenges creep into architectural design and the diamond has given its name to a particular form of vaulting. Like diamonds themselves, diamond vaults, it has been proposed, 'offered an effective way to give a touch of eye-catching modernity to any structure, and for that reason they appealed to the nouveaux riche and new religious

64 Tower staircase at Albrechtsburg.

orders alike'.[34] Begun in 1471 with work continuing over the next thirty years, Albrechtsburg, a castle that dominates the German city of Meissen (illus. 64), is distinctive for its prismatic vaults, which cover most of the stairs, public rooms and window alcoves. The chief architect, Arnold von Westfalen, produced a spectacular effect in which the segments of the vault delineated are not the spherical webs customary in Gothic architecture 'but rather three-dimensional triangular or rhomboidal cells which give the entire surface an origami-like appearance of multiple facets or folds'.[35] The overall effect is of cut crystal and the style spread across middle Europe until 1550, when this distinctive vaulting disappeared. Around the same time, in Spain, Juan Arfe y Villafañe, the silversmith and author of a 1572 handbook on gems and how to value them, went on to write an architectural treatise (1585) in which he analysed geometrical forms in visual language similar to the crystalline structures he would have encountered in his work as a gem cutter and jeweller (illus. 65).[36]

The use of *bugnati* – or projecting blocks of carved stone – on the external surfaces of buildings both secular and religious evolved in the fifteenth century in Italy into a monumentally decorative form creating variegated

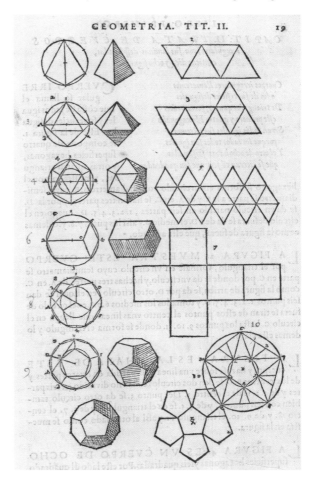

65 Diagram showing regular geometrical forms, Juan Arfe y Villafañe, *De varia Commensuracion para la Esculptura y Architectura* (1585).

and light-reflecting surfaces on the lower parts of buildings. Among the most spectacular examples are the Church of the Gesù Nuovo in Naples (1470) and the Palazzo dei Diamanti in Ferrara built for Sigismondo d'Este by Biagio Rossetti between 1493 and 1503 (illus. 66). Here the entire surface of the building comprises 8,500 marble blocks carved to simulate mounted diamonds, their position varying in order to maximize the light reflecting off the building. In the late sixteenth century, architects introduced the characteristic pointed form of the diamond in three dimensions into their decoration of buildings in England. Among many instances, Audley End in Essex, built between 1605 and 1614 for Thomas Howard, first Earl of Suffolk, with Bernard Janssen as surveyor, has a highly ornamental entrance portico that features lozenges and projecting diamond-like points (illus. 67).[37] The focal point is a pointed diamond projecting from a cartouche from which three tassels are suspended.[38] When Karel van Mander, the Flemish writer and painter, translated a passage from Giorgio Vasari's *Lives of the Artists* describing how Michelangelo had invented all sorts of new orders of architecture and licensed them to break free of the antique and give rein to their imagination, he intensified the passage, expressing disapproval of his countrymen who had misused Michelangelo's imaginative innovations, including specific reference to the diamond points that we see in Elizabethan architecture, much of which was executed by craftsmen from the Low Countries:

> In architecture beside the old common manner of the ancients and Vitruvius [Michelangelo] has brought forth new orders of cornices, capitals, bases, tabernacles, sepulchres and other ornaments, wherefore all architects that follow after him owe him thanks for his having freed them from the old bonds and knots, and given them free rein, and licence to invent something beside the Antique. Yet to tell the truth this rein is so free, and this licence so misused by our Netherlanders, that in the course of time in Building a Great Heresy has arisen among them, with a heap of craziness of decorations and breaking of pilasters in the middle, and adding, on pedestals, their usual coarse points of diamonds and such lameness, very disgusting to see.[39]

66 Palazzo dei Diamanti, Ferrara, 1493–1503.

Living and working in the Low Countries, van Mander (1548–1606) would have been very familiar with the appearance of rough diamonds and those which had been cut to a point – the two cuts at this period prior to the rose cut were 'diamant taefel' and 'diamant punt' or 'diamant punct', table and point cut (as we have seen in Tudor portraits and a few rare surviving rings). Paul Taylor points out that the word 'diamant' in Dutch is used exclusively to refer to gemstones and that when van Mander is talking about diamond shapes, the word 'ruit' or rhombus is used. He has suggested that van Mander was thinking in this passage of Vredeman de Vries's *Architectura* (Antwerp, 1577), in which are fantastical designs for engineering works and architectural ornament, including one plate showing five variations on the Doric order (illus.

67 Entrance portico, Audley End, Saffron Walden, Essex, 1608–9(?).

68).[40] The first two exemplars sport giant 'diamants punct' on their bases as well as the bizarre inclusion of diamond points studded upon the entire height of the first pilaster and on the second, which is a column, in double rows.[41]

Sebastiano Serlio's essays on architecture, published from 1537 and widely translated from their original Italian, included in Book IV a series of diagrammatic illustrations demonstrating how the 'coarse points of diamonds' to which van Mander took exception might be understood to have evolved (illus. 69): 'So from one age to another such work has varied, so sometimes in imitation of a table cut diamond, and sometimes in greater relief.'[42] The text for this page, translated into English and published in 1611, has an interesting variant that suggests diamond had become absorbed into the technical vocabulary:

> After, they devided the stones in more proportion and then with flat lists, and for more beautie, and for ornaments sake made these crosses in them. Other workmen brought in wrought Diamonds and made them decently in this manner and in processe of time, things altered: workmen, for flat diamonds, set flat tables and raysed them somewhat higher, as in this figure is to be seen.[43]

68 Illustration from Vredeman de Vries, *Architectura . . .* (1582).

What is significant for the purposes of my argument is not whether writers were actually thinking of diamonds themselves but how, when invoking a pointed three-dimensional projecting ornament, the word 'diamond' is seized upon. It is hard to overestimate the influence of the characteristic diamond rhombus in northern design, and especially in ornament. It is as though a wave of diamonds flooded the pages of Flemish pattern books at the very time

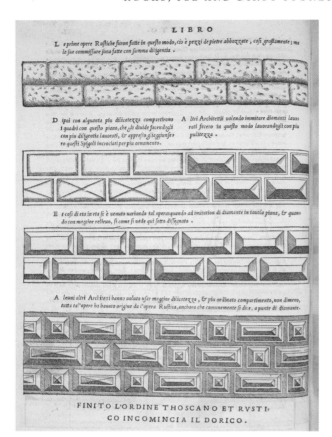

69 Sebastiano Serlio,
*Regole generali
d'architetura* (1537),
f. XVIII verso.

when actual diamond imports from the East Indies were making merchants and dealers wealthy from Venice to Antwerp and Lisbon and from Frankfurt to London and Amsterdam, and when wars and religious persecution meant that diamond workers sought refuge across national boundaries.[44] Attempts have been made to date the development of certain diamond cuts according to the representation of stones in so-called 'black ornament' prints published predominantly in France, Germany and the Low Countries, arguing that they served as models for jewellers and their clients.[45] Certainly there are many collections of prints towards the end of the seventeenth century that feature jewellery designs that might have been intended as patterns for enamellers and goldsmiths, such as those made by Peter Symony and Isaac Brun in 1621 (illus. 70) and by the French jeweller Gilles Legaré in 1663. However, the wild fantasy vegetable and floral forms, landscape panoramas and grotesque figures

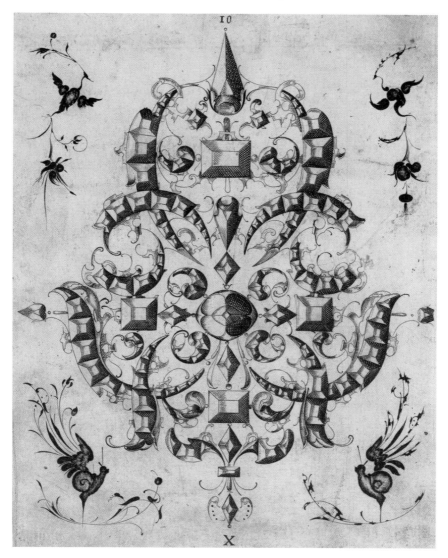

70 Peter Symony and Isaac Brun, *Tabulae gemmiferae*, xxiv, 1621, engraving.

that dominate many earlier suites of prints with their so-called *cosse de pois* (pea pod) curlicues and their table-cut, pointed and rose-cut diamonds belong rather to the world of diamond extravaganza than to any workshop manual. The non-diamond components of these designs cannot simply be set aside when explaining how these prints were understood. Diamonds here signify what is precious in God's gifts and what can be improved through skilful artisanship by man, who is made in God's image. But, represented alongside fantastic figures animal and vegetable, they are also part of the encyclopedic understanding of nature's riches in a world where what we would now call the natural sciences were making spectacular progress.[46]

Diamonds and Artists

If we turn to the *representation* of architecture we see how the diamond shape as a component alongside the regularity of vertical units in the production of a dynamic whole was most intensely exploited. The subject of church interiors in the light-filled art of Pieter Jansz. Saenredam (1597–1665; illus. 71) brought with it unique dilemmas of design. Saenredam made sketches and construction drawings of the Netherlandish church interiors he painted, and 'only with a wide-angle or "fish-eye" lens could the subjects found in most of his work be recorded.' Of course, he did not possess these optical devices but he permitted distortions comparable to the contemporary Mercator projection, a system used in map-making.[47] The churches Saenredam chose to paint had been stripped bare of their furnishings following the Protestant Reformation but even so, compared to the work of contemporaries like Gerrit Berckheyde (1638–1698; illus. 72), Saenredam's interiors are singularly rinsed clean of fittings and by and large also of people. Regular solids such as columns spaced at constant intervals create an extraordinary sense of abstraction. Berckheyde's *Interior of the Grote Kerk, Haarlem* of 1673 and Saenredam's view of the same subject of 1636–7, even allowing for the passage of time, hardly appear to be the same building.

A further distinction between the work of these two artists lies in the way that Saenredam has exploited the large diamond-shaped hatchments that hang on the walls of the churches he depicts. Hatchments are large heraldic paintings that, originally displayed over the front door of a deceased person, were subsequently hung on the wall, often in the nave aisle, of the church where the deceased was buried, to be later removed once a permanent monument was erected.[48] They differ from a coat of arms in comprising not a square but a poised square or lozenge. Why such announcements of death were this shape is not explained but it is tempting to suggest that, once hung in the nave or an aisle of a church, the four points of the diamond signalled the earth beneath, the heavens above and west and east (death and resurrection). At all events, while Berckheyde's cluttered interior is dotted with hatchments, many of which are clearly legible, Saenredam uses this feature as a key element in his otherwise vertical and horizontal design structure. Dark, almost black, and illegible as a coat of arms, these diamond hatchments produce an extraordinary effect in the white and cream matt-surfaced interior.

As a way of trying to explain the remarkable impact of these sombre diamond-shaped objects in Saenredam's light-filled interiors we might turn to American artist Richard Serra (b. 1939). Serra is an abstract artist and the works I am thinking about here are drawings executed in a technique Serra invented using layer upon layer of black paintstick on Belgian linen.[49] The result of the layering is a matt surface that is yielding and tactile (illus. 73) – quite unlike a hard diamond one might say. The shapes that Serra made in the 1970s in a major sequence of large drawings, which were often painted directly onto walls – thereby inviting comparison with installation art – are crystalline: they consist of large-scale triangular and diamond shapes that challenge the architecture on or within which they are mounted.[50] What has been described as the 'anonymous' surface, eliminating areas of reflectivity, has remarkable affinity with the rough diamond (see illus. 49), though here the artist suppresses any inclination of the material to shine.[51] While the tendency has been to compare Serra's drawings with Russian Constructivism, and especially with Malevich, if we listen to what he himself has said, it is evident that the diamond shapes and fractured 'crystal' forms that Serra creates work as architectonic components in the same way as Saenredam's hatchments, enforcing the principle of '*disegno*' in their monochrome effect:

> The black shapes, in functioning as weights in relation to a given architectural volume, create spaces within this volume and also create a disjunctive experience of architecture.
>
> For example, two black shapes installed on opposite walls foreshorten the width of the room. The enclosure becomes narrower; the compression of the space is haptically registered. Very specific decisions have to be made to determine size and directionality, horizontality

71 Pieter Jansz. Saenredam, *The Interior of the Grote Kerk, Haarlem*, 1636–7, oil on oak.

72 Gerrit Berckheyde, *The Interior of the Grote Kerk, Haarlem*, 1673, oil on oak.

73 Richard Serra, *Diamond*, 1974/2001, paintstick on Belgian linen.

and verticality of a drawing in a given space. How much surface is actually needed in order to hold the shapes as weights in relation to the size of a given space? Which are the cuts that have to be made in order to destabilize the experience of space? The process of decision-making is similar to the conceptualization of site-specific sculpture in that the site determines how I think about what I am going to do.[52]

For many people the idea of a diamond shape evokes neither architecture nor painting but the playing card and the harlequin. Harlequin was originally a character in the sixteenth-century *commedia dell'arte* – Arlecchino – whose clothes were covered with patches, but gradually the patches were replaced with a regular diamond pattern. In the eighteenth century he is a popular figure of the *Comédie Italienne* and is immortalized in paintings by Jean-Antoine Watteau, Paul Cézanne, Pablo Picasso (illus. 74) and others in which the figure, sometimes with his trademark half masque but often without, touches the viewer with a melancholy aspect at odds with the brightly coloured diamonds of his costume. The characteristic multicoloured diamond patterning of the harlequin costume remains popular today for fancy dress parties for both sexes. In French, the ace of diamonds is *l'as de carreau*, a *carreau* meaning a 'tile' (though also used for a windowpane, a diamond and a check, as in checked shirt). This suggests that the diamond shape is culturally embedded in concepts of material forms as a fundamental part of European visual vocabulary. Everyone knows what is meant by diamond-leaded windowpanes, whether they are found in an English country house (illus. 75), in a Bavarian *Weinstube* or in replica at a DIY store. Playing cards have a complex history but it is generally agreed that the familiar figures and emblems (or *enseignes*) that we know today originated in the fifteenth century when they became distinct from Tarot cards, with which they shared a root. There has been much debate about what the *enseignes* might mean, with the diamond being associated on the one hand with the bourgeois on account of its similarity to the paving stone, and on the other as deriving from the *carré* or cube, considered by the ancients as a symbol of wisdom and constancy and introduced under this heading into heraldry.[53]

For today's artists, it is not only the shape of a diamond but its symbolic values that resonate. Knowledge that diamonds are pure carbon and that they are unimaginably old in geological terms, combined with their inordinate financial value, has made them attractive to artists both as medium and as theme. These artists have studios that are like laboratories and their artworks are achieved through combining media that may be animal, vegetable and mineral. One journalist, interviewing Marc Quinn (b. 1964) in his Hoxton studio in London in 2003, described finding it 'modern, functional – not like a lab, not quite, but rather clinical'.[54] Quinn is known for using DNA in

74 Pablo Picasso, *Acrobat and Young Harlequin*, 1905, oil on canvas.

portraiture. Moreover, in 2003 he made a self-portrait titled *Now I'm Perfect* for which he burnt some of his hair, reducing it to carbon; this he gave to a chemist in the USA who turned it into a diamond. Quinn has rejected this work – though it is known from photographs – because the man who transformed the carbon into the diamond subsequently turned his process into a commercial concern.[55] It is now possible to go to any one of a number of companies who offer to create 'a certified, high-quality diamond created from a lock of hair or the cremated ashes of your loved one as a memorial [or 'cremorial'] to their unique life'.[56] Whereas the Florentine academicians and Antoine Lavoisier tried to break down diamonds, the chemists in the laboratories of these companies are reversing the process and making diamonds from carbon. In fact, as a BBC science programme *Bang Goes the Theory* demonstrated in August 2011, it is possible to make diamond crystals from nothing using the heat of an oxyacetylene welding torch, though it takes many hours to achieve the result.[57] The cloying testimonials from those who have paid large sums to these companies to secure stones generated from the ashes of their pets or their relatives fail to recognize that there is no way of ascertaining precisely where the carbon comes from that goes into the making of these diamonds.

75 Leaded window, iron frame, late 19th century.

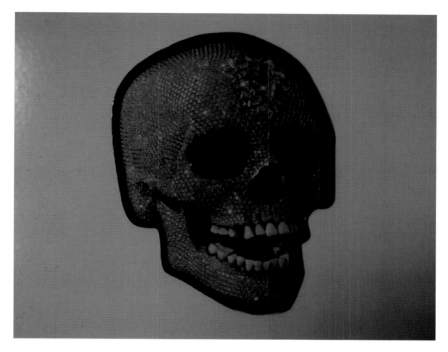

76 Fridge magnet replica of Damien Hirst's *For the Love of God*.

The publicity of the memorial diamond business carefully avoids any linkage between diamonds and the ending of lives in violent conflict of the sort explored elsewhere in this book. It is the mantra of 'diamonds are forever' that is invoked ('The memory of your loved one lives on with you forever'), with the diamond standing in metonymic relation to the deceased.[58] By contrast, when Damien Hirst (b. 1965) first exhibited *For the Love of God* in 2007, he was exploiting a rich and macabre set of cultural associations linking diamonds and cadavers. His diamond-studded human skull set with real teeth became a popular icon; when exhibited at Tate Modern in 2012 the gallery shop sold all kinds of Hirst-connected memorabilia, including a fridge magnet of the diamond-studded skull (illus. 76) – its appeal stemming from the contradictory presence of a traditional memento mori and 8,601 glittering (ethically sourced) diamonds, symbolic of what is excessively expensive and understood to be superfluous. Of course, we know that diamonds do have uses but these are brilliant multi-faceted diamonds, pavé set (meaning each diamond comprises a series of very small diamonds arranged closely together so the effect to the non-specialist eye is of a single stone); their only use could be in jewellery or as investment. Hirst had evidently already been thinking about minerals and their characteristic shapes, as a screenprint in the *London* portfolio of 1992 shows rows of ordered minerals on a pink ground, including a diamond (illus. 77).[59] But the move into actual diamonds was a big investment, and not merely of money. 'I just thought "what can you pit against death," the artist is reported to have declared.[60] This is by no means the first work of art to use the unchangeable and seemingly indestructible properties of diamonds as a way of drawing attention to the decay and degradation over time of the human organism, though it may be the most spectacular.[61] *For the Love of God* has been exposed at a number of solo exhibitions, always under maximum security and in special lighting conditions. The skull tends to appear diminished in size under its vast weight of 1,108.16 carats. Hirst is a consummate showman and this melding of Gothic horror and cupidity has resulted less in a twenty-first-century memento mori – a reminder that death awaits us all – and more in a challenge to the global marketing of diamonds as gifts for beautiful young women suggesting love and devotion divorced from the mundane realities of life (illus. 78). The sight of all those diamonds en masse subverts the very idea of the diamond as unique that is so carefully fostered by jewellers to the rich and famous. At the final count it is the wealth of the artist with sufficient means to source such a large number of stones that is on show in *For the Love of God*.

Anselm Kiefer's (b. 1945) claim to an interest in diamonds predates Hirst's conjunction of mortal remains and mineral wealth and is a great deal more interesting. Kiefer states:

In 1989, as part of an action filmed by the BBC, I made a sacrifice to the earth. Not long before, I had made money for the first time selling my paintings and I had converted part of this amount into diamonds. Around this time I learned of the existence of an unfinished tunnel, which had been dug in the late 19th century to link Calais to Dover. Conceived by two British engineers, this project had been interrupted after a while. Two tunnels remained, one on the French side and one on the English side of the Channel. It

77 Damien Hirst, *Untitled*, 1992, screenprint from *London* portfolio, Tate, London.

occurred to me that this was the ideal site for my action. I scattered
the diamonds in the damp earth of one of the tunnels and forgot
about them. The diamonds are still there, covered over by the silt
that accumulates below the vertical shafts. By means of this sacrificial
act, I gave back to the earth what had been taken from the earth.[62]

This ceremonial and dedicatory act differs from that of someone concealing their wealth, protecting it from theft. The diamonds are not buried but scattered: they are an abiding presence as real as those that are seen embedded into the surfaces of Kiefer's images. These stones in Kiefer's work are meaningful as part of the cosmological order of the universe and on account of their origins at great depths under the surface of the earth consequent upon volcanic action. Here the diamond forges a philosophical link between the perception of time and the material evidence of the effects of time. Although it is hard to verify both the precise materials used and when they were used, it seems that Kiefer introduced diamond-like material into his work as early as 1992.[63]

The oldest extant work by Kiefer is a small book titled *Die Himmel* (The Heavens) made in 1969 and containing cloud and sky pictures cut out of magazines and pasted onto pages. Sky and earth and the interplay between microcosm and macrocosm are an abiding preoccupation. In 1999 he produced the starry effect of a galaxy viewed from earth using emulsion, acrylic, shellac and broken glass in a work entitled *Falling Stars*.[64] From the late 1990s Kiefer increasingly used what are regarded as 'precious materials' (gold, silver and diamonds), referencing alchemical mysteries and the properties of minerals like lead and diamonds. The implied opposition here between what is toxic and malleable and what is bioinert and superlatively hard is striking. To a viewer of these works, whether or not it is Swarovski crystals, powdered glass or diamonds that generate the glitter might appear not to matter. However, the integrity of the work and the conviction that materials and meaning are one require that the diamonds are real. It remains perhaps puzzling that Kiefer chooses to deploy cut and polished diamonds rather than rough stones in their natural state – that is, stones that would avoid the powerful associations with privilege and consumerism. On the other hand, rough stones (difficult to source in large numbers) do not glitter and the work would thus be robbed of the important connection with stars, only a very small proportion of which we see from earth but which nonetheless we know to exist. *The Secret Life of Plants for Robert Fludd* (1987/2014) is a triptych made up of three panels of lead, the lower sections of which bear encrustations of thick fracturing pigmentation like the surface of the moon while above the heavens are studded with different sized diamonds and, on one panel, the lines that mark out the constellations in astronomical diagrams.[65] At around the same time, Kiefer made another enormous work of lead studded with diamonds of varying sizes, *For Ingeborg Bachmann: The Renowned Orders of the Night* (1987/2014).[66] The lead provides a great sense of weight, depth and impenetrability while the diamonds seem to pulsate like the stars in the milky way – at least if viewed from sufficient distance so as not to notice the claws securing stones that also appear to be set pavé; here they must surely be attached to pins that penetrate the lead, securing them and presumably allowing their retrieval during storage and transport. For all the nursery-rhyme-like quality of diamonds in the sky, these two works with their crumbling and cracking surfaces invite sombre thoughts of dissolution. But what is perhaps most interesting is how they demonstrate the impossibility of looking into, and making sense of, refracted light. This may be why the diamonds have to be cut and polished: the consequence of studding a surface with hundreds of faceted diamonds is that the work can never be completely accessed but must always remain, however the viewer struggles, to some degree alien and other, remote and unattainable.

78 'What kind of man would give his wife a vacuum cleaner for their anniversary?',
De Beers advertisement, *Harper's and Queen* (May 1977).

FOUR

A GIRL'S BEST FRIEND? DIAMONDS AS LUXURY AND NECESSITY

Women Acquiring Diamonds

FOR MANY OF US, THE WORD DIAMOND conjures up an extremely expensive piece of jewellery such as a Tiffany ring, a brooch by Van Cleef & Arpels or a Cartier tiara (see illus. 9) – a work of the finest craftsmanship that endures and is valued as possession and heirloom. And it is certainly true that many pieces made by jewellers working for these famous companies are extraordinarily beautiful. Like Old Master paintings or antique coins, they are collected, as well as occasionally worn, and at the owners' deaths they are auctioned, arousing huge public curiosity. The individual pieces become famous in their own right. Elizabeth Taylor's jewellery collection, when sold by Christie's in 2011, fetched $116 million and included the 33.19 carat diamond ring given to the actress by Richard Burton.[1] The sale of jewellery that had belonged to Wallis Simpson, wife of the Duke of Windsor, in 2009 included a diamond-studded panther bracelet made by Cartier (illus. 79).[2] These women were commissioning jewellers to make pieces to their own particular specifications. Women who may not, like Taylor and Simpson, have had access to limitless funds have also found in collecting jewellery a means of personal expression and of agency – of the power to make a point non-verbally and in some instances to affect an outcome. Madeleine Albright, former U.S. Secretary of State, amassed a collection of jewellery, some of which was deliberately witty, like the diamond-studded bug made for her by Iradj Moini that

139

she wore to a meeting with the Russian foreign minister after a listening device had been found by the U.S. State Department (illus. 80). Asked in 2010 about her use of jewellery as a diplomatic tool, she stated:

> I had an arrow pin that looked like a missile, and when we were nego-
> tiating the Anti-Ballistic Missile Treaty with the Russians, the Russian
> foreign minister asked, 'Is that one of your missile interceptors you're
> wearing?' And I responded, 'Yes. We make them very small. Let's
> negotiate.'[3]

The self-conscious and deliberate use of precious stones to impress and make a point is as old as the wearing of diamonds themselves. What might be termed the sublime effects of diamond jewellery, the 'Wow!' factor, was

79 Panther bracelet designed by Cartier from 1952 formerly belonging to the Duchess of Windsor, sold at Sotheby's, London, on 23 September 2010.

80 Iradj Moini, diamond-studded bug made for Madeleine Albright, 1997.

registered in what has been thought of as the first consumer age by a public in every way as voracious as that which lines up to see the diamond-wearing Oscar nominees. Observers writing in the newly established newspapers as well as individuals writing letters to their friends reporting on court and fashionable society in eighteenth-century London gave detailed accounts of precisely how many diamonds were being worn. In 1729 Mary Delany, who was of relatively modest means but very well connected, attended court in her 'best array' and, as she told a friend, 'borrowed my Lady Sunderland's jewels, and made a tearing show'.[4] As Hannah Greig has pointed out, the lower classes who came out (and probably waited a long time) to witness the public appearance of the nobility and aristocracy in their finery expected to see diamonds and rated the event accordingly.[5]

Diamonds were analysed by the German sociologist Georg Simmel, who proposed that 'the wearer of a piece of unique jewellery – and it must be unique to carry esteem – receives pleasure from it only indirectly, that is through the envious looks of those whose eyes are drawn to it.' He refers to a kind of 'radioactivity' around someone wearing precious jewels, which creates 'an extension of the personality and an intensification of the jewel's sphere'.[6] The eighteenth-century economist Adam Smith was interested in diamonds, describing them as commodities whose use had yet to be discovered. He ruminated on the purchase of the Regent diamond for the French crown in 1717 and remarked: 'If for every ten diamonds there were ten thousand, they would become the purchase of everybody, because they would become very cheap, and would sink to their natural price.'[7] In his 'Essay on the Imitative Arts', written around 1780, Smith uses the example of a woman in jewellery known to be fake precisely to make the point about the relationship between appearance, knowledge and worth:

> The difference between real and false jewels is what even the experienced eye of the jeweller can sometimes with difficulty distinguish. Let an unknown Lady, however, come into a public assembly, with a headdress which appears to be very richly adorned, and let a jeweller only whisper in our ear that they are all false stones. Not only the Lady will immediately sink in our imagination from the rank of a princess to that of a very ordinary woman, but the headdress from an object of the most splendid magnificence will at once become an impertinent piece of tawdry tinsel finery.[8]

Smith was writing at a time when diamonds from Brazil had flooded the market and when cleverly deceptive paste diamonds were widely available. As a Lady of Fashion confesses in a poem of 1778 in the form of a letter from Lady Maria Modish to Lady Belinda Artless:

> My diamonds are most of them gone, here and there;
> A few with false stones now assist in the Glare.
> Thus, what with my Gaming, my Tradesmen and Bets,
> Twenty thousand, I think, would not clear off my debts.

When we think historically about women in relation to diamond jewellery, it is important to take account of factors that have little or no relevance to a Wallis Simpson or an Elizabeth Taylor, both of whom were commoners. It is helpful to understand family jewellery as a temporary arrangement of precious stones, recycled but seldom sold. In the case of crown jewels, as is immediately apparent to anyone visiting the Tower of London where a room contains a collection of 'skeleton' crowns, important gems are regularly reset. The jewels of the crown are, through moral burden and tradition rather than through legislation, precisely that; they adhere to the crown, not to the monarch, and are therefore inalienable. However, things are seldom so clear-cut. There was in the French crown jewels a particular parure that Marie Antoinette liked and wore a great deal at the start of her reign; this she enhanced by the addition of some of her own diamonds, thus creating a confusion between her own gems and those of the crown. She then asked the king to attribute all the jewels mounted in this piece to her personal property, an assignment that was approved in 1785, the year of the scandal of the Affair of the Diamond Necklace discussed in the next chapter, and ratified in 1788.[9] The same is true of families who observe the law of heirloom: the wearer has the diamonds for their lifetime only. Of course there are attempts to subvert the practice. Anthony Trollope's novel *The Eustace Diamonds* (serialized in 1871, published in 1872) tells the story of a beautiful and wily young woman who persuades the elderly and wealthy Sir Florian Eustace to marry her. He soon dies and she is left with a substantial income and, so she contends, a diamond necklace worth £10,000. The Eustace family lawyer, however, asserts that this piece of jewellery is an heirloom and if Lizzie marries again, which she is intent upon doing, the necklace must return to the family.

The relationship between men and women and diamonds is by no means defined by the simple equation in which men purchase diamonds for women who then wear them in a display that signals men's wealth as well as other abstract investment values like love, devotion, longevity, succession. While the fashion for men's diamonds has fluctuated, it is clear that through long periods of history, men have worn diamonds in rings and hat jewels, on pins attached to cravats, on ceremonial sword hilts (illus. 81), in accessories like snuff boxes and most extensively on shoe buckles. The advent of paste imitation diamonds in the eighteenth century probably spared men the loss of diamonds from their shoes when attending crowded social events such as the Queen's Drawing Rooms where theft was also a risk despite the apparent exclusivity of the occasion. Dancing proved hazardous for men's jewels: in 1775 Lord Belamont is reported to have said that his diamond shoe buckles 'very seldom lasted him above two or three *minuets*'.[10] The following year the Earl of Mexborough had a magnificent diamond order 'of immense value' cut from his ribbon in the presence chamber at St James's during the Queen's birthday celebrations.[11] 'One heard nothing but screams and women carried out in fits. The whole ground was strewed with different coloured foil, and pearls and diamonds crumbled to pieces,' reported Lady Duncannon to Lady Spencer on 26 March 1789 after attending the Queen's Drawing Room celebrating the recovery of George III.[12] In our own time, high-profile male sports figures like cricketer Kevin Pietersen (who wears diamond studs in his ears) and footballer David Beckham (who has been photographed wearing a variety of large diamond earrings) have publicized their personal wealth in this way.

The idea of women consuming men's resources in the form of gifts of diamonds (with all the sexual connotations attached to this image) is nonetheless deeply embedded in Western culture. When I have mentioned to people that I am writing a book about diamonds, their immediate response has often been to reference Marilyn Monroe and the song 'Diamonds Are a Girl's Best Friend' from the movie *Gentlemen Prefer Blondes* (1953), based on the novel by Anita Loos (1925).[13] Because luxury presupposes expenditure, debates about luxury since the eighteenth century have been fought over the ground of gender difference.[14] When a blogger named 'Glaw' wrote in response to an article on diamonds posted on the web from the *Atlantic Magazine* in 1982: 'bitchez [sic] will always want the diamonds bitchez',[15] he (as I presume it was) is merely articulating in crude language what is expressed in countless advertisements by upmarket jewellers. That women have themselves ironized in popular culture the association between diamonds and luxurious female consumption is a measure not only of women's own ability to appropriate but also of just how pervasive that connection has been and remains. Marilyn Monroe famously articulated the idea that, though a kiss may be elegant, it will not pay the rent.[16] She has been followed by others, including Amanda Lear, who sings about eating diamonds for breakfast.[17]

The double entendre that characterizes the dialogue in Anita Loos's novel is lost in these songs. In the fourth entry of her entertainingly semi-literate

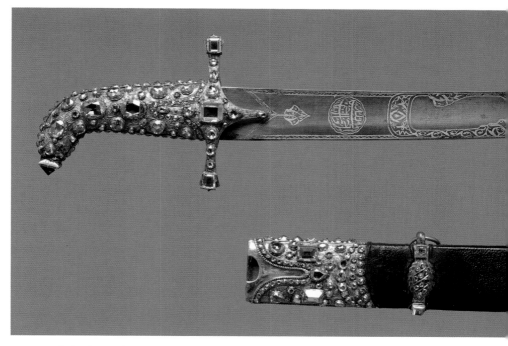

81 Turkish sabre, 16th century, with diamonds added to the hilt and scabbard in 1712.

diary, dated 22 March, Lorelei Lee recounts her disappointing birthday when Gus Eisman, a gentleman who, if he really has an interest in educating a girl, 'would want her to have the biggest square cut diamond in New York', arrived with 'a little thing you could hardly see'. Lorelei continues: 'I told him I thought it was quite cute, but I had quite a headache and I had better stay in a dark room all day and I told him I would see him next day.' Gus, a button manufacturer who complains the Bolsheviks are ruining his business, clearly got the message as he 'came in at dinner time with really a very beautiful bracelet of square cut diamond so I was quite cheered up'.[18] On the other hand, there is much historical evidence to suggest that women have for centuries recognized that owning diamonds in their own right accorded them a degree of financial independence they would not otherwise have possessed. Gifts of diamonds were made to married women at rites of passage, especially but not exclusively on marriage. In the great diamond age of the eighteenth century, young women coming out were given jewels. Lady Anne Strafford recounted to her friend in 1735:

Many things have happened to me since I came here [to London] viz: the borring of my Ears, Papa's giving me a pair of £100 Earrings, a pink Diamond ring, & a pair of gold buckles ... with 4 guineas for my pocket. Mama is giving me a pair of star Earrings, a set of stay buckles, & an Ermine muff. So I think I came to town to some purpose.[19]

Although spending the fashionable season in London was the practice of many established and aspiring families of the nobility and aristocracy, it was by no means a prerequisite for acquiring costly diamond jewellery. The extensive family archive of the Delaval family of Northumberland contains correspondence with both male and female members of the family from London jewellers who were more than ready to send examples of their work on approval. Invoices reveal that cut and polished diamonds owned by the Delavals were incorporated into new jewellery or accepted as part payment for new pieces the jewellers had constructed. There are scraps of paper containing memoranda written by members of the family listing diamonds set in jewellery and their values.[20] Jewellery was constructed with an eye both to the fashion and to economics; importantly account was taken of the fact that the owner might at some point wish to dismantle it. There was significant division of labour and good stones had to be searched for. Recommendations ensured patronage.

In 1772 James Fog, a London jeweller, wrote to Sir John Delaval (a great industrialist and entrepreneur) apologizing for the delay in sending him the jewels intended for his wife, Susanna. Having failed to find a suitable courier, he was now sending them by wagon from the White Horse in Cripplegate in a box in which he had put a piece of rock crystal to give it weight (and presumably discourage robbers, who might have been curious about a small, lightweight package). The letter is valuable evidence of how jewellers working with precious stones managed their business.[21] The jewels exceeded in weight what Fog had anticipated as they are 'set very close with great nicety and care' but, he is at pains to point out, he has charged no more than the workman's charge for the setting, and the cost of the diamonds. If Her Ladyship should wish to alter or part with them, the jeweller would 'take them at the same price only deducting the fashion'. It seems that Sir John had recommended the jeweller to the Duke and Duchess of Cumberland and he had therefore taken the liberty of showing them the jewels he had set for Sir John, and was now making a 'very rich pair of diamond Bracelets with ten rows of large pearls to each' for them. Fog then goes on to describe the jewellery he has made for Lady Delaval, making sure to refer to other prestigious clients:

> The Necklace I have made in three rows, in the middle are all my large Roses tapering off to the end with a Row of small on each side, which has very striking effects & round the neck makes as rich an appearance as one I made for the Empress of Russia @ £2200. It is so contriv'd that her Ladyship may if she pleases take off the sides to brade in her hair occasionally which is now much the taste. The Sleeve knots are as light as if tyed with a ribband and set in such a manner that no more silver than what is absolutely necessary to secure the diamonds is seen.

Fog concludes by expressing the hope that Sir John would 'remit me soon for them' as he has done his best 'to render them price-worthy'. He had been 'obliged to hunt about for 20 Carats of the Diamonds' and he is 'certain were the Stones to be at any time taken out they would always sell to advantage'.

Susanna Delaval, recipient of the diamonds, had also purchased diamond jewellery on her own account from the London jeweller Charles Belliard.[22] A receipt for 458 diamonds removed from various pieces of jewellery, including several brilliants from rings, a large rose and 116 smaller diamonds 'out of the stars', 44 roses and thirteen brilliants from an egrette (hair ornament), a rose 'out of a hook' and 41 roses 'in one star' was sent to 'Mrs Delaval', probably in 1753. On 28 February 1754 the jeweller sent her an invoice for work that included twelve brilliants added in the esclavage (part of a necklace), mending six brilliants in a cross, mending some roses in the esclavage, setting a necklace esclavage and cross and supplying a large case for this evidently elaborate piece of diamond jewellery.[23] Unlike many Delaval creditors, he was paid immediately.[24] From the 1750s to the 1770s every woman, it has been said, aspired to a necklace of brilliants and Susanna Delaval's was evidently very grand indeed.[25] A similar order was made in 1772 by Sir John, who paid a well-known London jeweller, James Cox, £620 for a rose diamond necklace set with 175 diamonds, all of which are listed in the invoice, and a pair of sleeve knots set with rose diamonds, the relatively low price probably reflecting the fact that the purchaser supplied many of the stones.[26]

Unusually, we know something about the jeweller that Susanna Delaval used. Charles Belliard's name is listed at a business address in Pall Mall but not until 1762–93, so either he was established much earlier than previously thought or there was a father and a son of the same name.[27] Belliard purchased diamonds from James Dormer in Antwerp, whose business was discussed earlier.[28] His position as the provider of luxurious jewellery is confirmed not only by his address in Pall Mall – the home of the best jewellers – but by the fact that in April 1787 he insured the contents of his house: household goods, wearing apparel, plate, china and glass, were covered for the considerable sum of £500.[29] Susanna died in 1786 and Sir John remarried in 1803 after the death of his 23-year-old mistress.[30] His wife was Susannah Knight and it was for her, we may assume, that he was purchasing between 1803 and 1807 diamonds from Rundell & Bridge of Ludgate Hill, Goldsmiths and Jewellers to Their Majesties.[31] On 28 January 1803, a watch, bracelets, a seal and topaz earrings were sent north by the Newcastle Mail.[32] Unfortunately there was some confusion about where the parcel should be left in Newcastle, and a further letter was sent three days later regretting the delay in receipt – an indication nonetheless of how quickly commodities could be transported from London to Newcastle.[33] In February 1806 there were further orders, this time for two diamond bracelets and small ornaments to make into a brooch 'which with the pair of brilliant top earrings' will be completed within a week.[34] It is intriguing to think of these packages of diamonds being regularly transported up the Great North Road by coach. In a letter of 1807, the year before Lord Delaval died at his breakfast table aged eighty, the jewellers (by now Rundell, Bridge & Rundell) sent 'for approbation' a watch and bracelets and two sets of coral 'with the price of each annext'. These were, as usual, sent by coach but had been entered 'value thirty pounds' (presumably an underestimate) 'for greater safety'. Lady Delaval evidently approved of the bracelets because they were sent back to Rundells to be shortened.[35]

Women also purchased diamonds on their own account as an investment and a way of securing a degree of personal independence in a period when everything else a married woman had was her husband's by law. Women whose fathers secured a marriage settlement in their favour might keep control over some personal items like jewellery; others might spend their sometimes-generous pin money to secure jewels that were theirs to control. The Letter Books of the Cholmley diamond merchants give several instances of women on their own account sending an 'adventure' to India for the purchase of a stone. On a grander scale altogether was the extremely wealthy Duchess of Marlborough, who was exceptional in that her husband, who was away commanding the English army in the War of the Spanish Succession, made her responsible for their finances. She did remarkably well by investing in diamonds. She bought them at sales and probably also directly from dealers like the Cholmleys, and then used them to manipulate the complex relationships within her extended family and across her network of political and social associates.[36]

Diamonds and Luxury

The Duchess of Marlborough (1660–1774), whose origins were relatively humble and who rose by court and political intrigue, purchased diamonds not in the main in order to wear them herself, though she was quite able to appear splendidly decked out when circumstances demanded. She would not have understood diamonds as luxurious but rather as a necessity for a person of her class, a required form of agency given the station in life she had acquired through her own efforts rather than through birth, and the means to independent action whether through bribery or liquidation. The question this raises is that of the complex relationship between luxurious consumption and what is regarded as a prerequisite for the maintenance of position in the social order. Luxury is always relative. What is luxurious is that which is in addition to those things accounted the necessaries of life. But the relationship between necessity and luxury is forever fluid, since what is one person's luxury might be another's necessity. The owner of a luxury yacht doubtless comes to see it as a necessity to their way of life. Luxury therefore might be said to be in the eye of the beholder. In other words, it is less a question of what something costs than of how it is valued by the people who buy it and own it. Nor does the quality of luxury belong to the item itself, so that something purchased as a luxury might come to be a necessity and, equally, something that was acquired for its basic functionality might in certain circumstances come to be a luxury. If you have a fully functioning bathroom, having a bath is seen as belonging more to the side of necessity than that of luxury, but if you have no bathroom it might seem luxurious to be able to have a bath.

If luxury is widely understood to be constituted by what is excessive, by expenditure on what is not useful, it is inevitable that the purchase and wearing of diamonds generates moral criticism and that diamonds recur with frequency in satirical discourse. Voltaire's biting satirical story *Candide* (1759) has many revealing diamond episodes, as for example that in which the old woman tells how a boat she was on was overtaken by Moors who stripped her and her companions 'as bare as ever we were born', thrusting their fingers into 'that part of our bodies where we women seldom admit anything but ---- to enter.' Afterwards she discovers it was to see if they had any diamonds concealed. Albeit fictional, this is further evidence of that investigative pathology through which the precious stone is envisaged as one with the biological body that we have remarked in relation to the body searching of miners (see pp. 46–9). Other episodes offer moral instruction: in chapter XVIII Candide and his companion Cacambo find their way to El Dorado, a country whose geographical position behind an impenetrable barrier of mountains has protected it from 'the rapacious fury of the people of Europe' with their 'unaccountable fondness for the pebbles and dirt of our land, for the sake of which they would murder us all to the very last man'. Despite their recognition of the peace, prosperity and happiness of this land, Candide and his companion cannot resist returning whence they came with their pockets full of diamonds which were soon stolen from them.

Novelists in the eighteenth century like Maria Edgeworth and Fanny Burney described heroines who were bedecked with precious stones but were 'cold and empty within'.[37] Burney, in *Camilla* (1796), could rely on her readers appreciating the irony when Ensign Macdersey says of the exquisite but frivolous Indiana: 'O what a beautiful creature she is! Her outside is the completest diamond I ever saw! And if her inside is the same, which I dare say it is, by her smiles and delicate dimples, she must be a paragon upon earth!'[38] In fact Indiana turns out to be utterly cold-hearted and without moral compass. In his short story 'The Necklace', the nineteenth-century novelist Guy de Maupassant gave an account of the catastrophe that befell a vain young woman with ambitions above her station. Invited with her husband (a small-time clerk) to a grand party, she borrowed a diamond necklace from a wealthy former schoolfriend only to lose it on the way home. The couple borrowed a large sum of money and bought a replacement without telling the lender what had happened. They worked themselves to death to pay back the money. Ten years later, the young woman met her friend again and on her remarking that she looked very worn, was told finally about the loss and the replacement. The shocking revelation was then made that the borrowed diamonds had been paste all along.[39]

With the establishment of press advertising in the eighteenth century, and the extension to mass media in the nineteenth, anything with the potential to be viewed as a luxury became subject to extreme forms of marketing and advertising. The conundrum is that advertising aims to persuade us both that something that is expensive is luxurious (better than other similar things and unavailable to anyone without a great deal of money) *and* that something that is not necessary is nonetheless a 'must have' in today's parlance – in other words, a necessity. Thus luxurious objects participate in the creation and circulation of myths. Jewellery – ornamental, decorative and non-functional – is an obvious example of what most of us would regard as a luxury. The tenuousness, the fragility, of this category 'luxury' is illustrated by the story of Gerald Ratner who transformed his family's struggling business into the biggest jewellers in the world with over 2,500 shops. He learned the importance of myth in the marketing of luxury when, in 1991, in a speech to the Institute of Directors, he quipped that one of his products was 'total crap' and boasted that some of Ratner's earrings were cheaper than a Marks & Spencer prawn sandwich but probably would not last as long. The speech was splashed across the tabloids and wiped an estimated £500 million from the company's shares.[40] He was bankrupted.

'All girls want an engagement ring, you know'

Until very recently the engagement ring was uniquely purchased by men and given to women; this piece of jewellery is now ubiquitous in the English-speaking

Treasures of the heart   Where is the storehouse strong enough to store the treasures of the heart—the soaring joy of a love-enchanted world—the first intent awareness when soul calls to soul? Her engagement diamond is a drop of magic flame fashioned through eons to preserve such scenes and memories in its shining lights. Safe from all harm, clear to her eyes, there she will see them always.

Remember, color, cutting and clarity, as well as carat weight, contribute to a diamond's beauty and value. A trusted jeweler is your best adviser. Extended payments can usually be arranged.

¼ carat (25 points) $80 to $205
½ carat (50 points) $190 to $455
1 carat (100 points) $455 to $1155
2 carats (200 points) $1225 to $3270

In April, 1955, jewelers throughout the country were asked for the prices of their top-grade engagement diamonds (unmounted) in the weights indicated. The result is a range of prices, varying according to the qualities offered. Exceptionally fine stones are higher priced. Add Federal tax. Exact weights shown are infrequent.

Love Scene—painted for the De Beers Collection by Pierre Ino

a diamond is forever

De Beers Consolidated Mines, Ltd.

82 Pierre Ino, *Love Scene*, *c*. 1947, in De Beers's advertising campaign 'A Diamond Is Forever'.

world and Japan, something that would have baffled eighteenth-century enthusiasts of luxurious diamond jewellery like the Delavals. The diamond engagement ring is a triumph of marketing – a luxury that has become a necessity. According to an American writer in 1926, 'the solitaire diamond as large and as perfect as [the bridegroom] could afford has for many years been the standard engagement ring.'[41] It was not always so. Certainly betrothal and marriage had long been the occasion for an exchange of tokens, whether a broken gold or silver coin, a rush ring or a posy ring on which were inscribed names, initials or terms of endearment. It was not, however, until the second half of the nineteenth century that the engagement ring as such makes an appearance in popular literature, invoices and receipts, trade catalogues and advertisements. These are arguably a more reliable measure of trends than surviving examples, since the sale and recirculation of engagement rings is generally embargoed by their associations with love and marriage, something allegedly encouraged by the diamond cartels in order to maintain sales. According to Edward Jay Epstein, through the 1970s De Beers, in tandem with N. W. Ayer, their advertising agent, concentrated on keeping a conservatively estimated 500 million carats of gem diamonds 'in safe hands' (illus. 82).[42] Diamonds never wear out; therefore if sales are to be maintained each couple must be persuaded that a new diamond ring is a prerequisite and that 'diamonds are forever'. It is a measure of the success of De Beers's campaign that it overcame the long-standing association of newness with brashness and vulgarity, as well as the caution of a couple starting out on life together who might more sensibly have put the money towards buying a house. In research published in 2010 in the USA on attitudes to expenditure on weddings, it was found that the average spent on a wedding in 2009 was $28,385, including $5,847 for an engagement ring. It also found that hypotheses about gender attitudes that posited women as romantics and men as pragmatists were not borne out, with women favouring spending less money on weddings and rings and more on setting up home.[43]

The emotive and class-related nature of these issues is longstanding and embedded in English-language culture. It is epitomized in Edith Wharton's novel *The Custom of the Country* (1913). Undine Spragg, surely the most obnoxious heroine of any novel, is the only daughter of a dubious entrepreneur and his vulgar and ignorant wife. She is also extremely beautiful. Having ensnared Ralph, only son of an old Boston family, she is given an engagement ring of sapphires. A manicurist who is also the purveyor of gossip remarks that the stones are old and the setting quaint and she wouldn't be surprised if the ring had come down from the Dagonet side of Ralph's family, whereupon the following exchange takes place between Undine's mother and the manicurist:

'Why, don't you s'pose he bought it for her, Mrs Heeny? It came in a Tiff'ny box.'

The manicurist laughed again. 'Of course he's had Tiff'ny rub it up. Ain't you ever heard of ancestral jewels, Mrs Spragg? In the Eu-ropean aristocracy they never go out and *buy* engagement rings, and Undine's marrying into our aristocracy.'

Mrs Spragg looked relieved. 'Oh, I thought maybe they were trying to scrimp on the ring —.'[44]

On an extended honeymoon, Ralph gradually realizes the terrible error he has made; a key moment occurs when he discovers via a jeweller's bill that Undine has had reset two items of jewellery:

> The pearl and diamond pendant was his mother's wedding present; the ring was the one he had given Undine on their engagement. That they were both family relics, kept unchanged through several gener-ations, scarcely mattered to him at the time: he felt only the stab of his wife's deception.[45]

Wharton's story was published in 1913, shortly after the engagement ring begins to appear as an important ingredient in a life story for all classes of women. 'The hardest thing in the world for a young woman to do is to look unconcerned the first time she comes out in a handsome engagement ring,' declared one writer.[46] The lover's quarrel and the returned engagement ring feature both in historical fiction and in popular poetry:

> 'Yes! All is over between us now!'
> He groans, with a blighted air.
> 'The tokens are here of a broken vow –
> Ah! Fickle and false, as fair!'
> And again he lifts with a trembling touch
> The engagement ring returned.[47]

Court cases in the USA generate precise definitions of the engagement ring, as for example with the following statement:

The diamond ring on a woman's left index finger puts the world on notice that she is spoken for. That little piece of metal and stone symbolizes a great deal, and the meaning is so much greater than just a gift. Just as the name implies, the engagement ring is a symbol and carries the connotation that 'marriage [will] occur'.[48]

However, litigation over the ownership of an engagement ring when the engagement has been broken off reveals how what was high in symbolic value can become merely another valuable piece of property for the ownership of which the couple vies. In 1999 the Pennsylvania Supreme Court adopted a no-fault approach in a case that involved a $17,500 ring, and decided that the donor should be entitled to the return of the ring or its equivalent in value, regardless of which party broke the engagement.[49] By contrast, Ogletree's 2009 research found that a majority of women believed that in the case of a break-up the woman should be entitled to retain the ring.[50] In an early reported case of litigation, in 1885 a Jewish couple from the labouring classes in the British city of Sheffield disputed ownership of a ring of little financial value. But in this instance the decision was in favour of the recipient. Levi Franks, a tailor, had given Esther Goldsmith a ring that she said was an engagement ring. He asked to borrow the ring but failed to return it to her, so she sued him. He claimed that he broke off the engagement because he was going away for three years and placed the responsibility on her. Esther told the judge that she 'had not been engaged to other gentlemen and kept their presents. Nor had she taken the ring to the defendant's lodgings, thrown it at him, and said that she neither wanted him nor his ring.' Judgement in this case was given to the plaintiff for the restoration of the ring or payment of £2 10s. to her.[51]

Cases like this demonstrate the importance of the engagement ring – even when it does not include a precious stone – as property that a woman might call her own, and on which a price can be put. However, it was not until circa 1900 that diamond engagement rings began to be produced for the mass market, many of them in Birmingham (illus. 83). By 1930 the engagement ring with a diamond had become de rigueur. In England, the firm of Bravingtons, based in King's Cross, became so closely associated with the area that it gave its name to Bravingtons Walk. It commanded a large section of the lower-end market with advertisements on the Tube and on the back of the Green Line Coaches timetable (illus. 84). Bravingtons produced a handbag mirror (now selling on eBay) as an advertisement – perhaps given away by estate agents. The reverse side (illus. 85) pictures a woman touching a sequence of three diamonds mounted on a ring that encircles a substantial detached house, its chimney cheerfully smoking, and the motto: 'Every Woman sees a home through her engagement ring.' Around the perimeter is inscribed the jeweller's name and address.

Bravingtons went into receivership in 2007 but the popularity of low-cost diamond engagement rings remains undiminished today, as may be seen from the website of H. Samuel, where you can buy a solitaire diamond ring for £199. Jewellery stores in London, New York and other cities display huge numbers of diamond engagement rings at relatively modest prices (illus. 86). Tiffany also has a website advertising engagement rings but the prices are available only on request. In 2007 it was calculated that 80 per cent of American brides received

83 'Diamond Mounting Shop', from *Modern Jewels*, trade catalogue, B. H. Joseph, Birmingham, *c.* 1900.

84 Advertisement for Bravingtons, 'The Cash Jewellers', 1937.

a diamond engagement ring, while a book of advice titled *The Groom* advises: 'Plan to spend between one and two months' salary on the engagement ring. Consider financing options if you don't have the money up front, but don't get buried in debt.'[52] My request to access the H. Samuel archive was refused

– post-Ratner, the low end of the diamond market is understandably nervous. But it is interesting to note that the department store John Lewis decided in 1973 that its strength was 'inexpensive accessory jewellery' and that 'it would be inappropriate . . . to aim at the sort of investment market or engagement ring market which will always be the prerogative of specialist jewellers.'[53]

The dilemma of the groom who, according to convention, cannot get engaged without a ring but who in order to get a ring must expend a sum of money that may risk his financial stability is illustrated in an early silent film released in 1912 (illus. 87). In *The Engagement Ring* an ardent suitor wins a young woman only to lose her to his rival when he fails to keep up with the payments on the ring he has purchased and the vendor comes to her house and seizes it. The young woman prefers the first suitor but mercenary considerations (backed up by her fierce-looking mother) mean that she takes whoever can provide the ring. Fortunately for him, the first suitor is knocked over by a motor car – surely one of, if not the, first car accidents on film – and the driver produces a bundle of dollar bills to compensate the victim, who is then able to limp to the jeweller, retrieve the ring and re-engage the young woman, much to the rage of his rival, who is a classic stage villain in a bowler hat, waving a walking stick and snarling, and who then beats a retreat, leaving the happy couple under the eye of the mother.[54]

85 'Every Woman sees a home through her Engagement Ring,' back of lady's compact mirror, *c.* 1930, Bravingtons, London.

86 Display of diamond engagement rings, West 47th Street, New York, 2011.

If the engagement ring were merely a symbol, any ring would do in a world where jewels on women's fingers connoted a high-end lifestyle (illus. 88). The financial investment – that is, the luxury element of it – is paramount. Rings are traditionally thought to connote eternity (through a form which has no beginning and no end).[55] While it might seem common sense for a woman to look after what may be the most valuable piece of jewellery she possesses, there is something fetishistic about 1960s images of women showing off and caring for their diamond engagement rings (illus. 89). These scenes, redolent of the fascination with luxury objects, contrast sharply with the utilitarian layout of jewellers' trade catalogues, with their repetitive rows of almost identical settings, and with the practices of jewellers in New York's West 47th street as they compete for trade at the lower end of the market (illus. 90). Edward Jay Epstein has described the notion that an engagement ring must contain a diamond as the greatest marketing coup of all time. Although at times overstated, his account is nonetheless useful. It argues that because the value of diamonds depends on their scarcity, once diamonds were discovered in South Africa in 1870 financiers realized that without some controls on the

87 Mack Sennett's 1912 silent film *The Engagement Ring*: from top: the courting couple; the ring purchased on credit by the fiancé; the ring repossessed as the fiancé is behind with his payments and the rival moves in; the original fiancé is knocked over by a car after which he is offered a wad of dollar bills with which he will retrieve the ring from the jeweller; the couple reunited while the angry rival is shown off the premises by the fiancée's mother.

88 Trade catalogue, Ascott, Birmingham, *c.* 1935.

89 'The new fiancée modestly shows off her ring. The diamond tells the rest of the story,' from Joan Younger Dickinson, *The Book of Diamonds: Their History and Romance from Ancient India to Modern Times* (1965).

90 Dream Gems, Jeffrey Staub, West 47th Street, New York, 2011.

91 'The Richest Diamond Mine in the World',
from the *San Francisco Sunday Call* (21 March 1909).

market, diamonds would become at best semi-precious stones. While other commodities fluctuated wildly in response to economic conditions, diamonds have by and large continued to gain in value, and after its creation in 1888, De Beers Consolidated Mines went on to become the most successful cartel in the annals of modern commerce. However, after the end of the First World War, the market in Europe was depressed. Although about three-quarters of the cartel's diamonds were sold for engagement rings in the USA, these stones were small and of poorer quality than those sold in Europe.[56] Something needed to be done to boost trade and in 1938 Harry Oppenheimer, son of the founder of De Beers, met a representative of the advertising agency N. W. Ayer and the 'diamond forever' connection was sealed.

The relationship between diamonds and a desire for luxury that was understood to be intrinsically feminine was framed in arguments about national and global economies. An article published in the USA in 1909 entitled 'The Richest Diamond Mine in the World' (illus. 91) proclaims that: 'the American woman is the greatest consumer of diamonds. When money was scarce in the United States the South African mines all but closed down.' The piece is headed by an image of a glamorous woman in a Stars and Stripes evening gown holding a huge tray into which 'kaffirs' (black miners) who are emerging from the earth pour baskets full of diamonds.[57] De Beers's advertising agent stressed the need to strengthen the association in the public's mind of diamonds with romance. Young men in particular needed to be inculcated with the idea that diamonds were a gift of love and that the larger and finer

92 Window display, De Beers jewellery store, Old Bond Street/Piccadilly, London, 2016: 'De Beers – for you, forever – Discover our new personalised service enabling you to create your unique De Beers diamond ring, individually crafted for you, forever.'

93 Ianelli Diamonds Inc., West 47th Street, New York, 2011.

the diamond, the greater the expression of love and of the ability to provide. The show goes on today: De Beers's London flagship store at the corner of Piccadilly and Old Bond Street offers diamond rings 'individually crafted' by the jeweller 'for you, forever' (illus. 92). In New York's diamond alley, jewellers at the lower end of the market with their displays of photographs sent by happy customers (illus. 93) purvey the myth that the right diamond ring will ensure a successful marriage and beautiful offspring.

Size, as Lorelei Lee knew, matters; it is also the source of a wealth of smutty innuendo in a well-established strain of diamond humour. In a George Burns and Gracie Allen show aired on TV on 13 March 1952, Gracie appears searching for her diamond engagement ring which she has lost – and not for the first time. Asked how big it is she makes a large circle with her finger and thumb. Her interlocutor misunderstands and thinks this refers to the diamond. 'It was my engagement ring,' she says, 'It was a white gold ring and it had a diamond in it. It was about that big.' 'Wow,' says her interlocutor, 'that big?' (illus. 94). 'And the diamond was a small tiny one,' she goes on. 'Did you have it at lunch?' 'No, I had a Swiss cheese sandwich . . .'. The ring is found and George appears alone on stage holding up a ring. 'The cleaning woman

165

94 'Gracie's Engagement Ring', an episode from the CBS sitcom *The George Burns and Gracie Allen Show*, originally aired 13 March 1952.

found it in the powder room. Wish she could see the diamond. Wish I could see the diamond . . '. He then tells how when he proposed he got down on his knees; Gracie then got down on her knees as she thought the diamond had fallen out. And many more gags.[58]

The diamond engagement ring was the focus of the N. W. Ayer advertising campaign that included film stars wearing big diamonds, portraits of engaged socialites and lectures to students. The slogan 'A Diamond is Forever' was devised in 1947 by Frances Gerety, a copywriter for the agency (see illus. 82). The previous decade had already seen a 55 per cent increase in diamond sales in the USA. Towards the end of the 1950s, N. W. Ayer reported to De Beers that twenty years of advertising and publicity had had a profound effect on the American psyche: 'Since 1939 an entirely new generation of young people has grown to marriageable age . . . To this new generation a diamond ring is considered a necessity to engagements by virtually everyone.'[59] The rhetoric was effective but it was just that – a form of inflated but eloquent language designed to persuade people that what was in fact a luxury was really a necessity. Human subjects find ways of subverting and turning to their own account the norms and conventions of social decorum. The diamond engagement ring meant different things to different people and was recycled and put to use in the twentieth century in ways that N. W. Ayer and De Beers were unlikely to have envisaged. Certainly it did seem that propriety demanded a ring, but wars and personal circumstance seldom impeded those who lacked means or time for this expensive material acquisition. Although women were supposed to be the passive recipients of diamond engagement rings, these items of jewellery could be turned to practical use, demonstrating that the stereotypical gendered roles adhered to and promoted by the advertising industry and the jewellers did not reflect reality.[60] The diamond engagement ring could morph from symbol into agent when required.

Twentieth-century Stories

To conclude this chapter I shall turn to some oral testimonies of those who bought and those who owned engagement rings in England during the twentieth century. These first-person narratives were recorded by the BBC as part of the creation of the Millennium Memory Bank. Expenditure on an engagement ring, and attitudes to it, reflect class and social position. The poet Anthony Thwaite OBE (b. 1930) tells how he got engaged to a fellow student at Oxford and gave her a ring which he was able to buy because his father provided him with an allowance of £500 per annum. 'It was', he says, 'a ridiculous thing to do'. By that time he had met someone else so the engagement was called off amid 'rage, tears and things'. He was given back the ring that was 'quite expensive' and went and threw it off Magdalen Bridge.[61] For most, the purchase of a ring is a serious matter.

Carroll Sullivan (b. 1958), who describes herself as from a working-class background, met her husband at their workplace in Hull and they started going out. When the relationship became serious and they talked of getting engaged, he told her: 'I want to get you a nice ring.' They began looking in jewellers' shops but found everything 'so expensive', 'so much money for what they were'. The rings were like Gracie's in the comedy series mentioned earlier, with a tiny diamond in the middle that you could hardly see and costing £50. The solution for Paul and Carroll came through a golfing contact who arranged for them to meet a man in a pub. The man put a hand in his back pocket and pulled out a dirty handkerchief and a cascade of rings fell onto the bar. They chose one containing 'fantastic diamonds' for which the vendor wanted £75 and took it to a jeweller who valued it at £250 so they bought it. The man in the pub claimed to have got the ring from a pawnshop. But Carroll thinks it was 'knocked off from somewhere' and claims it has brought them luck as a family. At the time of the interview she was running her own interiors and soft furnishings consultancy.[62] What is common to all the accounts I have read is the absolute necessity of having a ring if you are going to get engaged. Only war, hastening marriage to a soldier leaving for the front, was reason to omit this ritual; as Gladys Ellis (b. 1916) recounted, she married because of the war and had no engagement ring.[63] John Ayling, a clergyman (b. 1902), having vowed to remain celibate, fell in love with Winifred and proposed to her. 'All girls want an engagement ring, you know,' he told his interviewer, and 'it cost me everything I'd got.' The ring had three stones and he told his fiancée: 'Look dear – those two small diamonds are you and me and the big one in the centre is Our Lord . . . this is the pattern of our lives . . . and the gold band is what binds us all together.'[64]

The business of the engagement ring, as we have seen, is a male responsibility and men are often recorded as spending all their available resources on it. Harold Crowe (b. 1927), a retired bank manager, spent the only £27 he had on his fiancée's engagement ring.[65] Patricia Fern (b. 1929) was courted on the back row at 'the pictures' (the cinema) by Norman, who joined the navy when he was nineteen. When he came out of the service two years later he brought a ring with him. Patricia showed it to her father who told her: 'You're not getting married. You're too young,' to which she replied: 'Yes I am, I've got the ring.' She adds: 'Me dad liked him when he got to know him.'[66] Sometimes the expense of any kind of ring is beyond the means of those who wish to marry. But one couple in Sheffield struck lucky when they won the lottery. Interviewed in 1999, Derek Moore (b. 1947), a bus driver, described how he and his partner had been living together with their children for eight years in great hardship, arguing about money and wondering how they would survive. Having won, they immediately decided to get married and Derek bought his partner an engagement ring, a wedding ring and an eternity ring, all in the space of three months.[67]

In these personal accounts, real-life issues of value for money intersect with sentiment, and necessity with luxury. With the advent of synthetic diamonds that are hard even for gemmologists to distinguish from real gemstones, couples may not only avoid the moral hazard posed by the possibility of inadvertently buying non-certificated stones that have been part of the trade in 'conflict diamonds', about which I wrote in Chapter Two, but may also effectively for the first time disconnect the financial from the symbolic. The scenario with fake diamonds projected by Adam Smith and described earlier is unimaginable today when, it seems, there is a split between the financial worth of jewellery and its social function. Fake diamonds are no longer greeted with uncertainty. Quite the contrary: rapper Jay Z proposed to singer Beyoncé in 2011 with an 18-carat flawless diamond ring worth an estimated $5 million, but also gave her an imitation version to wear in public.[68] The production of the fake here serves as a guarantee of just how valuable the original is. In the gap between the valuable diamond flashing on the finger of a celebrity and the imitation worn on occasions when there might be a risk of theft lies a vast terrain of material and representational strategic manoeuvring driven by cupidity, desire and emulation. However, in wartime in Europe in the twentieth century, there was good reason to cherish an engagement ring with an authentic diamond that might, if need arose, constitute a vital source of exchange value.

David Solomon was born in 1916 into a wealthy, strict Jewish family who owned a large furniture business in Liverpool. At the age of twenty he fell in love with Babette, whom he met at the Jewish Club. He bought her an engagement ring ('similar to my mother's') with two large diamonds. The Second World War was imminent. David was about to be called up so he gave the following instructions to Babette. If it looked as though the Allies were going to lose the war, she should get a jeweller to take one stone out of the ring and give that stone to a ship's captain in return for passage to New York. Once in New York she should take the ring to one of the many Jewish pawnbrokers in the city and ask him to remove the other stone. With the proceeds of the sale of that stone she would be able to live and every six months she should go to the Waldorf Astoria Hotel and ask for poste restante mail. That way the couple would be reunited should he survive. Happily, Babette's engagement ring remained intact; David returned to Liverpool after serving in the British Expeditionary Force in France and the couple went on to enjoy a 58-year marriage.[69]

The word 'luxury' derives from two Latin words: *luxuria* and *luxus*. From the first come the connotations of reprehensible indulgence, and from the second comes the more neutral sense of luxury as descriptive of certain kinds of commodities. Diamonds are always luxurious in the first sense – they suggest 'over-the-top' worldly ostentation on the part of the wearer or the purchaser. But the engagement ring reconciles these differences. Functioning as a necessary demonstration of commitment to the religious sacrament of marriage (the binding together), the engagement ring legitimates what in other contexts might appear mere vulgarity. It is a triumph of compromise.

FIVE

THEFT

W HERE THERE ARE DIAMONDS there is criminality: the immense value invested in these precious stones has made them above all others the object of greed and larceny. Stealing something valuable and convertible purely for financial gain (like copper metal theft, described in 2013 in the U.S. as an epidemic) is unromantic.[1] However, on account of the aesthetic qualities of diamonds and what, in the case of famous stones, is often understood as their individual character, diamond theft has attained a unique position in the history of Western fiction. There is a disconnect between the notions of fascination, fear and compulsion that shape novels like Wilkie Collins's *The Moonstone* (1868) or films like *Rififi* (1955), and the generally sordid and petty history of most diamond theft.[2] The fictional versions omit the horrific punishments meted out in the past to those convicted, whether the young man indicted in 1715 for robbing the Bishop of Norwich of plate, apparel (clothing) and other items including a pair of diamond earrings and sentenced to death, or what might befall the hapless 'kaffir' labouring in a South African mine allegedly found with a diamond concealed on his person (see illus. 23).[3]

Woven into myth and history, the theft of big, famous diamonds like the Koh-i-noor, discussed in Chapter One, becomes part of the identity of a named stone, enriching its value by association.[4] When a large diamond is stolen, the diamond itself rapidly ceases to matter, except to those who have an investment in its financial value. Rather, it is the methods used to purloin the stones that are recorded, imagined and narrated. Stolen diamonds often vanish and are never heard of again, but that does not prevent speculation and sightings; among the most famous 'missing' stones are the Mirror of Portugal, taken from the French treasury during the robbery at the Garde Meuble on the night of 16 September 1792, and the Pigot diamond, which was sold to the pasha of Egypt in 1822 and has never been seen since.[5] The very absence of the gem creates a vacuum into which imaginary events and characters are poured. Few have any idea of the mineralogical values (203.4 carats) or the financial worth (£200 million) of the Millennium Star diamond, but the way robbers used a JCB digger to get through the perimeter fence and into the 'money zone' of the exhibition at the Millennium Dome in Greenwich on 7 November 2000, and how they were foiled by the Flying Squad of the Metropolitan Police, who had been tipped off and were there in the Dome, many dressed as cleaning staff, is well known. Had they succeeded, the robbers would have been responsible for what would have been then the biggest diamond heist in history.[6] Most diamond theft, however distressing for the owner, has generally been small-scale and has involved the loss of personal jewellery. Because ownership of a small quantity of diamond jewellery – and more especially a diamond ring – became the norm even for tradespeople and those of relatively modest means in the eighteenth century, when diamonds became very plentiful and fashionable, this is the era in which we find domestic and small-scale theft first regularly recorded.

As well as telling us what happened, the proceedings at the Old Bailey offer remarkable insights into people's attitudes to property, to how jewellers worked and, coincidentally, to how people lived. Pre-twentieth-century thefts of diamonds fall into a number of categories: thefts within the jewellery trade; highwaymen holding up travellers at gun point; confidence tricks or 'scams'; shoplifters; opportunists who find items dropped by accident and appropriate them; servants stealing from masters and mistresses; fraudulent jewellers deceiving clients. Receivers of stolen diamonds are also indicted: the chain of disposal often involves accomplices, jewellers and pawnbrokers. Punishments for those found guilty in England have ranged historically from death or transportation to branding, hard labour and confinement in Newgate Prison.

The Old Bailey in the Early Modern Period

A typical case is that of Mary Hubart of the Parish of All Hallows, Barking, who was indicted for stealing a diamond ring worth £4 from the house of her employer. When the lady of the house, a Mrs Alkorne, was washing her hands on 26 December 1701, she took off her ring and laid it down. Afterwards, missing it, she suspected her maid and had her brought before a magistrate (in this case the Lord Mayor), and the diamond ring was found sewn into the stomacher (bodice) of the accused. Mary was found guilty and branded, which would have made it very difficult for her to find further employment.[7] Further up the social scale, 58 diamonds worth £250 were stolen from the Hon. Lady Catherine Herbert a couple of years later. Again the accused was one of her servants, a coachman. Samuel Davis had allegedly got the keys to a closet where Lady Catherine kept her jewels. When she missed them, she advertised their loss and offered the very considerable reward of £80 to anyone with information.[8] Where she did this we do not know but by 1703, when this theft occurred, newspapers were already carrying offers of rewards for the restitution of property. Her offer seems to have succeeded since she then heard that a diamond had been sold on London Bridge. The vendor was described and eventually tracked to East Ham, where he was found 'with all his goods bundled up and ready to be gone, and in his Trunk found all the Diamonds but one, which was found upon him in the Role of his Stocking, when serarcht [sic] before the Justice'. Men's stockings were rolled above the knee and held in place by the close-fitting leg of knee breeches. As with Mary Hubart, owning little and living in his employer's house, it was the clothing Samuel was wearing that furnished the most obvious temporary hiding place. He was found guilty and branded.[9] Because of the importance of precisely describing a unique item of jewellery, advertisements placed by people who had lost them, whether through accident or theft, can often tell us a great deal about how diamonds were set and worn, which is some compensation for the fact that almost no jewellery from this period survives.

Transportation for fourteen years was the punishment meted out to a confidence trickster named in court as Margaret Scarlett after she had conned a gunsmith's wife into giving up her diamond earrings in 1743. As she was aged

72 at the time of the crime, it is very unlikely she would have seen England again. John Segalas and his wife Winifred lived and worked in Green Street by Leicester Fields. In 1743 Scarlett came to their door asking if they had any old clothes to sell. When Winifred replied in the negative, Scarlett told her that she had 'a lucky Planet' in her face, and that she would tell her fortune. Invited into the house, she asked for coffee but there was none so she then said she had to go and sort out a lawsuit but would return. On her second visit she told Winifred, in a conversation overheard by her husband who was 'at work in a little closet', that there was a great treasure buried in the house by a deceased person and that the soul of the person would not rest until Winifred Segalas had recovered the treasure. A sum of money was needed to start the spell but as Winifred did not have it she was persuaded to bring out her diamond earrings, worth three guineas. These were wrapped up in a parcel with salt which would, when she went on her knees and said the Lord's Prayer three times, cause 'the mould in the cellar to rise' and she should find the treasure. Scarlett gave the plainant a parcel made of a handkerchief which purported to contain the earrings Winifred had given her and said it should not be opened until she came again. Fortunately John Segalas was watching and intervened and in the package was found a pair of brass buttons; in the ensuing skirmish, during the course of which Scarlett swore and cursed a great deal, one of the earrings was dropped and broken and the other John found in her hand. Scarlett insisted the earrings had been planted on her but she was found guilty.[10]

The case against James Lockart, who seems to have taken advantage of his less-than-careful employer, concerned the theft on 22 June 1785 of eighteen diamonds, a string of pearls, a ring set with hair and diamonds, two sapphire rings, a gold buckle and two linen handkerchiefs. It offers us evidence of rough diamonds brought back from India by men of relatively modest means, of the extreme difficulty of identifying these once they were stolen, and of the working of jewellers. Major Ewen Bailey, who lived in rented rooms in London, stated in court that he had brought back from India early in June 1784 'diamonds and pearls to a certain amount', which were shown to a broker. The latter sold them but pointed out to Bailey that the number he had sold did not correspond to the quantity on the invoice and that therefore some must have been stolen before they reached him. Handbills were circulated 'in the usual form' but these produced no result. It was then that the Major's servant, Lockart, came under suspicion, after evidence was taken from another jeweller who had purchased pearls and diamonds from the servant, describing him as 'a mulatta, a genteelish looking man'. Questioned 'Do you frequently buy diamonds in the rough state?', the jeweller replied: 'Not very often, I cannot say that I bought any others, I believe not.' Asked 'How many strings of pearls might you buy besides these?' he replied: 'I have bought diamonds ready wrought, and strings of pearls; I really cannot say, but I believe half a dozen or a dozen in that state.' After Major Bailey discovered his possessions were missing he began to suspect people in the house in which he was living, both of the theft of the original rough diamonds and pearls and of the other items. So he moved to new lodgings and reported the thefts. His servant's boxes were then searched and all the items were found except the diamonds and pearls already sold, which had by then been dispersed.

When identifying the goods in court, Bailey stated:

> This ring I purchased of Mr Gray in Bond-street; I am clear it is the same, the form of the ring is particular, I have no doubt of its being mine from the hair in the inside; it was made by my particular directions; this is the stone of a ring that I wore, when I lost it it was set; I have had it several years, I have no doubt of this being the same.

Gray of Bond Street was a well-known jeweller and the ring was evidently a mourning ring. Bailey's servant, it is revealed, never wore livery and when he offered the jeweller the diamond and pearls he made 'a very genteel appearance' and the jeweller took him for 'a dealer coming from India'. The background to this sad story is revealed when the prisoner makes his own defence, claiming that it was a servant the Major had had before him who had taken the valuables, at which point the Major was asked to describe the prisoner's character. Bailey alleges that he had taken Lockart into his household at seven years of age at the time of the general famine in Bengal when millions were starving, brought him back to England and educated him, transferring him to a family of his particular acquaintance, that of General Lockyer. It was there, we may guess, that this Bengali boy was given his Scottish name. Upon Bailey returning from India, he took Lockart again into his employment and five or six days later missed his valuables. The jury found the prisoner guilty and he was sentenced to death.[11]

Two Early Modern Diamond Heists

In all likelihood Major Bailey's diamonds and pearls were among the large quantities imported unofficially from India either about the persons of returning East India Company personnel, through the offices of ships' captains or as a consequence of the easing of Company rules governing independent traders. Having got them safely back to London, the theft must have been especially galling for him. It is undoubtedly in transit that diamonds were and still are most vulnerable to theft, Brink's-Mat notwithstanding, as the recent Brussels airport heist of diamonds worth £32 million demonstrates.[12] It is all the more extraordinary to think of all the diamonds that were, as established in the previous chapter, generally without incident, transported from the capital to far-flung areas of England where the nobility and aristocracy had their country estates. It is in the early modern period in Europe, with the development of global networks of trade in diamonds and increasing levels of extraction, that major losses of diamonds and other precious stones are recorded.[13] One such robbery took place in autumn 1629 in Madrid when over 7,600 diamonds were stolen in one go, including 'a stone with a diamond of great value' (suggesting that the gem was still in its matrix).[14] This rough octahedron diamond was said to be larger than any that had been seen exported from India in many years, and its estimated value was more than twenty thousand ducats. A complete list of all the diamonds (illus. 95), with weights listed in the Spanish *quelato*, was included in the deposition lodged with the governor of Rome on 12 July 1631 by a lawyer acting on behalf of the merchants Balthazar and Ferdinand de Groot. They were established in Antwerp in the early years of the seventeenth century and rapidly became immensely wealthy (illus. 96).[15] The diamonds were imported into Lisbon from India and sent by mule train across the mountains to Madrid; they were wrapped in linen cloths in small bags, some of which were sealed.[16] One of the muleteers, Simone Gonzalez

l'estratto è copia d'una l[ette]ra scritta de Paulo Sanvio in n[ost]... @ 5 Novembre
l'anno 1629, diretta à s[igno]r Balthasar è Ferdinando de Groote —

Per designarvi la persona ilquale ha rubbato li bassoli in Madril è un giovene
d'anni 22 in 24 in circa, de nahoria un portugese nom[e] Manuel Alua...
de mediocre statura, magro, è pallido nel viso, con una bocca larga, ilquale
alhora era vestito de seta verde con la spada indorata et con centigl...
d'oro bisognerà essaminarlo in quella persona s'aveua conoscente con Don
Fabritio de Valguarnera Siciliano quale de puta s'è trova in Italia ...
et doue l'ha conosciuto, et doue ultimamente gli ha parlato dopo che s'è ...
...stato con li diamanti quando et doue, et si ancor sapessedare quale ...
doue il s'i retroua, et s'i la persona s'è trovato ilquale ha fatto il furto che si ...
perdonarebbe è donarli qualche cosa recompensa mediante lo restitui...
diamanti è principalm[en]te de queste, l'acquette del s[ud]d[ett]o ... doue sono ...
N° 21 più picol'acquette de N° 1 @ 21 — In qual'si acquette sono
à queste sorte de diamanti come segue —

N° 1 : 1 Diamante molato è pesa ___ 11 3/4 quelado
N° 2 : 9 Diamanti molachi pesa ___ 45 quelat
N° 3 : 10 Diamanti come sopra ___ 40 quelat
N° 4 : 11 Diamanti come soprapesano ___ 43 1/2 quelat
N° 5 : 111 Diamanti quelati d'antiquo ___ 43 1/2 quela
N° 6 : 500 Diamanti lasques è molach ___ 111 quelat
N° 7 : 500 Diamanti come sopra ___ 111 quelat
N° 8 : 636 Detti — pesano ___ 127 quela
N° 9 : 610 Detti pesano ___ 127 quela
N° 10 : 732 Detti pesano ___ 153 quela
N° 11 : ___ Detti pesano ___ 103 quelat e ... quelat
N° ... : ___ Detti pesano ___ 167 quelat e ... quelat
N° 13 : ___ Detti come sopra ___ 164 quelat e ... quelat
N° 14 : ___ Detti pesano ___ 127 quela e 9 in quelat
N° 15 : ___ Detti come sopra pesano ___ 126 quela e 9 in quelat
N° 16 : 0101 Diamanti pesano ___ 96 1/2 quela
N° 17 : 137 Diamanti pesano ___ 75 quela
N° 18 : 17 Diamanti pesano ___ 51 1/2 quela
N° 19 : 16 Diamanti pesano ___ 43 1/2 quela
N° 20 : 16 Diamanti pesano ___ 50 quela
N° 21 : 400 Diamanti pesano ___ 120 quelat
     144 Diamanti ___ 59 quelat ___ 101 1/2 quelat
     15 Diamanti ___ 22 1/2 quelat

95 List of diamonds stolen in the Valgaurnera case.

96 Page from account listing Balthazar de Groote's assets, October 1647 (total 824,518.01 guilders).

97 Miniature of Tsar Alexander I (1801–25) mounted in a bracelet and covered by a lasque, or portrait-cut, diamond.

Barigello, described in evidence in Madrid sixteen of the bulses containing raw diamonds as worth a thousand ducats.[17] There is some evidence that European diamond cutters worked in India but it is generally assumed that importers favoured rough stones, as Indian styles of cutting did not appeal to European markets.[18] However, the diamond haul that was stolen in Madrid contained not only rough stones but 'Diamanti molachi' (polished diamonds) and 'Diamanti lasques e molachi'. The lasque was a diamond cut along its cleavage, producing a thin, flat stone and losing less overall weight in the process. Unlike the Cholmleys who, as we have seen, avoided lasques, the importers of the Madrid haul appear to have been happy to accept the bulk of their consignment in that form. Lasques were sometimes called 'portrait diamonds' as they could be used to cover a portrait miniature, as with the example shown here (illus. 97), in which it is likely that the miniature was made to fit the diamond, rather than vice versa.[19]

The owners of the diamonds were a joint stock company or consortium of merchants, come together to purchase and import this large consignment of stones. Some were evidently Jewish. Diego de Crasto, 'assistente in quella banda', was based in India and shipped the stones to Lisbon. In addition to the de Groots, members included Domenico Fernandez Vettorino from 'Hebbas' and Alfonso Rodriguez Pazarigni; these two were in Lisbon and took delivery. They and Martino Alfonso della Palma were responsible for arranging transfer of the diamonds from Lisbon to Madrid. Also involved was the latter's friend or brother ('fratello') Luigi de Freytes, who was resident in Antwerp.[20] The consignment travelled by mule train from Lisbon to Madrid into the care of Manuel Alvarez Carapetto, cashier to a banker named Mendez de Boito. It appears to have been in Madrid that the diamonds were to be apportioned between members of the consortium. However, before that could happen they disappeared, and Carapetto with them. The key investigator in the search precipitated by this theft was another investor named Paulo Zonis (or Zonnio or Sonnio), described as a Fleming resident in Madrid. An 'amico grande' of the absconded cashier and, it subsequently transpired, his wife's lover, was a Sicilian nobleman named Fabricio Beltrano et Valguarnera, who had been in Madrid for some time dealing porcelain, relics and paintings he had imported from Italy. It was to him that Zonis turned for assistance, but Valguarnera himself then disappeared and it was the failure to find either man that eventually led to the formal accusation received by the Rome prosecutor on 12 July 1631. By the time it arrived, most of the diamonds had been laundered: many were given to jewellers and set in rings that were easier to dispose of than rough diamonds and many were exchanged for paintings.[21]

Once the diamonds were missed, the merchants sent out searches to many cities in Spain and Italy including Valguarnera's home town of Palermo, spending considerable amounts of money and offering rewards for the restitution of the stones. Although none of the handbills issued by the merchants has survived, it is evident that within about fifty years the European print market was being utilized by victims of major jewel thefts. News of a jewel heist in Austria in 1684 was published in German and Dutch (illus. 98) and included full-scale diagrams of some of the stones lost. The Lisbon merchants in 1629 focused on Valguarnera who, as a gentleman, would have found it very difficult to change his identity, and it was in any case suspected that he might have eliminated Carapetto. Certainly, when he was finally apprehended and appeared in court, he was very well dressed in his cloak of Spanish wool and silk, silk stockings, shoes of black chamois with knotted black ribbons, sleeves of black watered taffeta, a bodice of turquoise damask trimmed with black lace, and breeches of black watered taffeta. At first, Valguarnera admitted to being knowledgeable about jewels and to knowing jewellers but claimed he was not a professional (a 'maestro') and denied any responsibility for the theft. He was able to account for all the diamonds that had been found at his residence. Describing himself as a gentleman not a merchant, Valguarnera was at pains to distinguish himself from a dealer. The evidence all pointed to the opposite as he had sold many works of art in Madrid before the theft. Back in Italy it was difficult to disguise the fact that he was using diamonds as currency in his investments in cultural objects. In Naples, for example, he traded two diamonds worth 300 scudi for two paintings worth 260 scudi and accepted the difference in the form of an agate vase and a medallion worth 49 scudi.[22] Finally he confessed and made a detailed statement to the court on 21 July 1631.

Valguarnera told how he had become intimate with a certain Dona Giovana in Madrid and when she married Carapetto he remained friendly with them both. After the cashier had fled with the diamonds, he remained in contact by letter and then returned to Madrid one night for a meeting with Valguarnera, who agreed to remain in Madrid to deal with the merchants while Carapetto made his way to France. Valguarnera had unwisely kept Carapetto's letters addressing him as brother ('hermano mio') which, along with a great deal of other incriminating correspondence, as well as letters from his long-suffering wife in Sicily, were sequestered from his lodgings in Rome at the time of his arrest.[23] However, the merchants became suspicious and when an attempt was made to ambush Valguarnera, he fled with the help of a Palermitan priest in

SPECIFICATIE,

Van eenige Juweelen, Diamanten;
Peerlen en andere Gesteenten en gemaeckte
Juweelen, die den eersten May, 1684. des
avonts tusschen 4 en half 5 uuren zijn gestoo-
len tot Lints in Oostenrijck alwaer sijne Key-
serlijcke Majesteyt sijn Hof tegenwoordigh
is houdende.

1. En Hairnaelt van 24 Diamanten Dunsteen, wegen t'samen 1½ Craat in de mid-
del is een Orientael Granaet in silver geset, en den bodem vergult.
2. Twee Hairnaelden van 32 Diamanten Roosen, wegen ½ Craat in silver geset en den bodem vergult, daer in sijn 18 Knop Peerlen.
3. Twee gelijcke Hairnaelden van Diamanten in silver geset met goud verbodemt, daer in sijn als volght twee Rosen, wegen 2½ Craet hooge spitse stenen by na vierkah-
tigh, 16 Rosen wegen 5½ Craet, groote en kleyne garnisset stenen, wegen 4½ Craat aan silver en goud 14 Engelsche.
4. Een Spinnekop in't midden een Orientalen Safier achtkantigh met ruyten oversneden
met 71 Diamanten gegarnisseert, daer in drie stucken Diamant Roosen wegen ¾ Craat, ende
68 stucken kleyne Diamanten 2 Craat, is met Pluym aedje gearbeyd.
5. Een Hairnaald Spinnekop met een achtkantige Safier, in't midden met ruyten oversneden en met 44 Diamante Roosen gegarnisseert en met groen loofwerck geamiljeert.
6. Een paar Pendanten van 106 Diamant Roosen, en 10 stucken Amaraude, daer by zijn 4
Diamanten gelijck Peren, wegen 3½ Craat, noch 2 stucken wegen ¾ Craat, kleyne Diamanten 11½ Craat, 6 Pere Amaraute met ruyten oversneden, boven in de print doorboort, vier
stucken vierkantige Amaraute, wegen t'samen 44 Craat aan silver en goud over de 14½ Engelsche.
7. Twee Pendanten in gout gewerckt, daer in 128 kleyne Diamant Roosen, wegen 3½
Craat aan goud over 2½ Engelsche, zijn 2 Peer Pendanten.
8. Twee Pendanten van 198 Diamant Roosen in silver gewerckt en met goud verbodemt
met 2 Oorringe, daer in is 1 Diamant Roos, weeght 3½ Craat, een ander stuck daer by
weeght 3½ Craat lanckachtigh, noch 4 stucken wegen 2½ Craat is een Peere, een ander stuck
daer by weeght 1½ Craat als een Peer, 4 stucken bier van wegen t'smen 3 Craat oock als een
Peer, 5 ander stucken wegen 1½ Craat lanckachtigh te samen, noch 2 stucken wegen 1½
Craat, in de Oorringe ronde steene en kleyne Diamantjes, wegen 12½ Craat aan silver en
goud 17 Engelsche.
9. Twee Pendanten van 94 Diamante Roose, en 2 Peerle mooy in silver en met goud verbodemt, namentlijck ses Diamante Roose, wegen 1½ Craat sijn vier Peirkens, en
A   2 ronde

98 Handbill (in German and Dutch) announcing the theft of diamonds and other jewels
in Linz, 1 May 1684, between 4 and 5 o'clock.

March 1630, and joined Carapetto in Bayonne. In June 1630 the pair reached
Genoa via Lyons, trading diamonds en route and defending themselves against
the predations of other thieves. From there they went to Livorno and then to
Naples, where they sold nine diamonds for 1,100 scudi, most of which, by the
end of two weeks, Carapetto had spent on clothes and whores, according to

Valguarnera, who by this time had despaired of his accomplice's profligacy and been tempted to kill him. In January 1631 Carapetto was persuaded to return to Spain with the remaining diamonds (thirteen bulses), make restitution of them and request clemency. He was never heard of again.

During the following six months Valguarnera stayed in Rome at the house of a priest and systematically exchanged diamonds for paintings. The evidence given to the court by many well-known artists has been analysed from the point of view of identifying the works of art bought and sold.[24] By contrast, little attention has been paid to the detailed descriptions of the diamonds that were exchanged. Calculating relative values of different currencies is notoriously problematic and I shall not attempt it here but simply point out that both Valguarnera and the artists who were selling their work were evidently not unaccustomed to trading in diamonds.[25] One example will suffice. Giovanni Lanfranco (1582–1647) testified to the court on 27 July 1631.[26] The artist described how the previous December the accused had come to his house in the company of a priest called Meniatore and asked him to show him some paintings. Valguarnera chose a sketch ('abbozzato') of the Magdalen and returned a few days later to collect the finished work. This was paid for in Spanish doubloons ('a pretty stable currency with us') and Valguarnera on this occasion asked Lanfranco to complete a Crucifixion for him. Lanfranco also retouched a portrait of his family for the buyer. Returning about a month later he was offered payment in the form of loose diamonds, two ultramarines and a pair of girl's earrings set with little diamonds. Some of the diamonds Valguarnera gave him were described as faceted in a heart shape and set into a gold ring;[27] he had no means of valuing any of them but trusted the purchaser, though he guessed the small stones in the earrings were not worth very much. He accepted payment in diamonds even though, as he told the court, he was in need of cash. Lanfranco managed to liquidate the diamond jewellery fairly rapidly. The court heard he no longer had the diamonds in his possession, having sold the earrings to jewellers in Trastevere and used the money to pay what he still owed on the purchase of a vineyard, and having given another diamond to his wife, who had disposed of it. He also testified that on one occasion when visiting Lanfranco's house, Valguarnera showed him four other diamonds set into rings, one of which was very large and was said by Valguarnera to be worth 2,500 scudi. Another ring was set with a ruby surrounded with diamonds and was said to be worth 400 scudi. He finally declared that while he knew Valguarnera had given diamonds to other painters in Rome he had no idea where they had come from.

The ruby described by Lanfranco is unlikely to have been part of the theft from the Lisbon merchants as, according to their deposition, that comprised exclusively diamonds. Or perhaps Valguarnera was unusually wily and mixed stones he had acquired legitimately from other sources with his share of the diamond booty to discourage identification. What is clear from the court proceedings, which offer invaluable evidence for the commercial and artisanal processing of diamonds in early modern Europe, is that although rough diamonds were commonly used (as Voltaire's Candide uses them) as currency, equally acceptable – and less likely to arouse suspicion – were diamonds set into jewellery. Included in the material seized from Valguarnera's lodgings was a small box covered with velvet and trimmed with gold, in which were three rings set with diamonds and two tickets for others taken by a pawnbroker described only as 'Isaace Tedescho Hebreo' (Isaac, German Jew).[28] The Rome jewellers and pawnbrokers must have welcomed the business provided by Valguarnera's diamonds. Then as now, once dispersed, diamonds are virtually impossible to identify and the best way of ensuring that they could not be traced was firstly to disguise them by cutting and polishing them and secondly to 'launder' them by exchanging them for valuable but non-incriminating goods, in this case works of art, which were luxury commodities readily available in Rome's thriving artist's community. What went wrong was probably the fact that not only did Valguarnera run around Rome dressed in Spanish fashion but too many diamonds were released onto the market in this way and people (jewellers and artists) talked. In September 1631 the hearing ceased owing to the illness of the prisoner and on 2 January 1632 the court was given notice of the death of Valguarnera in prison after several days of fever, witnesses having been shown his unmarked body dressed and nude.[29] We may take it that, despite some inconsistencies and uncertainties, the case against Valguarnera was proven. The same cannot be said of the theft of the diamonds set in the so-called *collier de la reine* that occurred 155 years later in France and which has been regarded as one of the great unsolved mysteries of diamond history.

The Valguarnera diamond theft was what we would now call a heist – the stones were lifted from under the noses of the proprietors and made to disappear. The theft in 1785 of what was then the most valuable piece of diamond jewellery ever made in Europe depended on an ingenious fraud, or a scam, through which the owners were persuaded to part voluntarily with their diamonds. They were set in a necklace in the form of a *rivière* or stream, now known only from replicas and from the widely disseminated engraving the jewellers had had made, most probably to circulate as part of a sales initiative (illus. 99), and which was eventually used as evidence in court. An incomparable collection of diamonds, the necklace was the work of the crown jewellers Charles Auguste Bohmer and Paul Bassange, Jews who had probably come to Paris from Dresden.[30] They had made it some time prior to 10 May 1774, the day Louis xv died. The necklace, according to Mme Campan, Marie Antoinette's confidante and wife of her librarian, a woman who had been at court since the age of fifteen, had been intended as a gift for Mme du Barry, the king's mistress, but it had not been delivered at the time of the king's death and was therefore left on the jewellers' hands.[31] It is likely that it would have taken them a very considerable time to assemble this remarkable collection of stones if, as seems the case, they were all of high quality and closely matched in colour.

This immense piece of jewellery consisted of gradated stones, many very large (the pear-shaped central stone was 45 grains, that is, over 14 carats), set in clusters with festoons dropping onto the breast and braids of diamonds hanging down the back, while the neck itself would have been encircled by a string of single diamonds from which hang – independently or attached to loops of diamonds – a series of massive stones between 7 and 10½ carats.[32] These were known as *esclaves* (slaves), a technical jewellers' term to describe a dependant appendage. The necklace, which would have been extremely heavy, has been described as the ugliest piece of jewellery ever made and as 'if not the beautifulest the dearest necklace in the world'.[33] The jewellers themselves described it as 'a large diamond necklace comprising a unique and rare collection of this type [of stones]'; they valued it at 1,600,000 livres (nearly £216,000 or, today, equivalent to around £15 million).[34] The disappearance of this necklace generated a scandal that swept up a number of what we would now call celebrities, including the immensely wealthy and influential Cardinal de Rohan, a popular trickster who went by the name of Comte de Cagliostro, various bankers and, most disastrously, the queen. To the events that unfolded around the theft of this collection of diamonds has been widely attributed the fall of the Ancien Régime in France. So many writers have explored and speculated on the unsolved mystery of this theft that the London Library devotes an entire section (under History) to the diamond necklace affair.

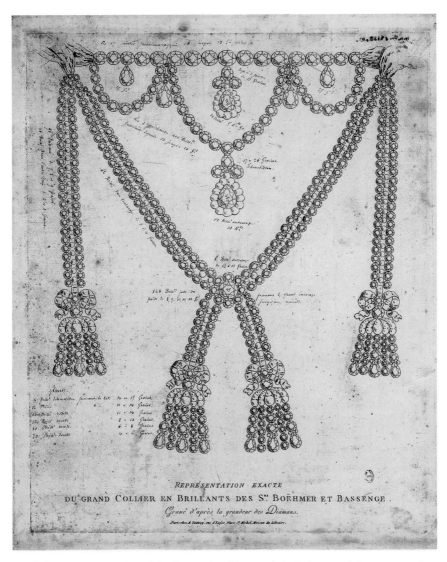

99 Life-size representation of the diamond necklace made by Bohmer and Bassange, c. 1785.

Authors range from Thomas Carlyle and Johann Wolfgang von Goethe to Alexandre Dumas and the Cardinal de Rohan's 'grand vicaire', the Abbé Jean-François Georgel. The spell has held through to the present day with many modern expositions both in English and French, most recently by Jonathan Beckman in 2014, and films including *The Affair of the Necklace* starring Hilary Swank, directed by Charles Shyer in 2001.[35] Accounts of the affair, including Beckman's, concentrate on the romance inherent in the events and have little or nothing to say about the importance of diamonds per se.[36]

We cannot be sure who was responsible for the theft, as neither the necklace nor its diamonds were ever found. But certain things are beyond doubt.[37] The scam was instigated in 1784 when an attractive but penniless young woman called Jeanne de St Rémy, who claimed to descend from the House of Valois and who lived on the fringes of the court of Versailles, realized that several people were politically vulnerable and therefore open to persuasion. The Cardinal de Rohan – the most senior cleric in France – had offended Marie Antoinette's mother, Empress Maria Theresa of Austria, and was consequently not welcome at court in France – an immense disadvantage to a man of his birth and distinction. He needed to regain the queen's favour. The two jewellers were desperate to dispose of their necklace and had hoped that the queen, who was known to love diamonds, would purchase it. But by 1785, Marie Antoinette was unpopular and regarded as a spendthrift (she was nicknamed Madame Déficit in libellous tracts of the period).[38] The king had already refused to buy the necklace and when Bohmer who, as court jeweller, had access to the queen and had provided many personal diamonds for her jewel collection, begged her to purchase the necklace he had failed to sell to other European rulers, she promptly dismissed him. Jeanne meanwhile had married an equally impecunious former soldier called Nicolas de la Motte and the two went by the names of the Comte and Comtesse de la Motte. The cardinal was a womanizer and was intimately acquainted with Jeanne. Taking advantage of this acquaintance, she devised an enormously bold plan that included all the classic ingredients of grand opera: impersonations, forged letters and assignations in gardens by night.

With the help of an accomplice who, as well as being able to act the part of a courtier, was an excellent forger, Jeanne convinced the cardinal that the queen truly wanted to buy the necklace but did not wish her purchase to be public. Jeanne's husband had picked up a prostitute in the arcades of the Palais Royal. The couple dressed this young woman *en chemise* in the manner of Vigée Le Brun's portrait of the queen, which had created such a scandal at the Salon of 1783 on account of its informality that it was removed from the exhibition.[39] A series of forged notes bearing the signature 'Marie-Antoinette de France' (a form of words that was a serious rupture of protocol and which should have aroused suspicion) was produced to convince the cardinal, who was then lured to a night-time enactment in a dark corner of the garden at Versailles. Here the prostitute, Nicole le Guay, impersonated the queen. In the darkness, the cardinal was sufficiently persuaded by this charade that purchasing the necklace on the queen's behalf would be his route to restoration that he agreed to act as surety.

Despite his vast income the cardinal, like so many members of the elite in Paris at the time, was seriously in debt, but this did not deter him. He witnessed delivery of the necklace to the queen's valet (actually the handy forger in appropriate costume) on 1 February 1785. By 1 August, when the first of several staggered payments was due and when the queen had neither worn the necklace nor referred to it, alarm bells began to ring. Of course, by that time the necklace's diamonds had been extracted from their settings and were in the process of being dispersed. A diamond necklace, as Thomas Carlyle points out in his essay on the affair, is merely an agglomeration of minerals, each with their own global history to tell.[40] With the theft of the necklace, the stones were again 'released into commerce' to participate in new histories.[41] On 15 August the Grand Almoner of France, Cardinal de Rohan, was arrested as, clad in his vestments, he prepared to celebrate mass in the chapel at Versailles.[42] He was sent to the Bastille, followed rapidly by Jeanne de la Motte, Cagliostro (who was regarded as altogether suspicious on account of his masonic activities and his connections with the cardinal), Nicole le Guay and other assumed accomplices who, unlike Jeanne's husband, who had made for Amsterdam and London in order to sell the diamonds, had lacked the foresight to leave Paris.

The cardinal's crime was the theft not of a necklace but of the royal name. The offence was most clearly set out in the Lettre-Patente du Roi, made at

Saint-Cloud on 5 September 1785: 'We have not seen without legitimate indignation that one has dared to use such an august name dear to us for so many reasons and so to violate with such an unheard of temerity the respect due to Royal Majesty.'[43] Carlyle described the necklace as having throttled the cardinal. As events transpired, it would have been much better for the royal family if the king, urged on by his minister Breteuil (an enemy of the cardinal) and by the queen, had not prosecuted the affair through Parlement and the courts between September 1785 and May 1786, since the dirt displayed in the process adhered to the queen, who was already the butt of libellous humour. Though clearly innocent, the association of the queen's name with low intrigue and, particularly, with diamonds, irreparably damaged her position. The actual theft of the necklace and the consequent losses to the jewellers and their creditors is overshadowed in histories by the political losses. The verdict, announced on 31 May, was applauded by the wildly excited crowd: the cardinal was acquitted, as were Cagliostro, upon whom Jeanne de la Motte had cast blame, and Nicole le Guay, who claimed herself to be a dupe. Jeanne de la Motte was found guilty and was to be branded with a hot iron and incarcerated for life in the Salpêtrière, from where she escaped in 1787 only to meet with an extremely unpleasant end a few years later in London. As one observer remarked, she paid the price for all of the accused in the case.[44] The cardinal was subsequently, at the king's command, relieved of his responsibilities as Grand Almoner and exiled to the Auvergne. Cagliostro was banished and took himself and his wife to London, where he continued his activities as a high-class thief and rogue. The cardinal was required to repay the jewellers in full but since within a couple of years the revolutionary government sequestered his property this never happened.[45] So, what of the diamonds?

The French chargé d'affaires was in London in the autumn of 1785, on the track of Mme de la Motte's husband and attempting to discover what had become of the jewels from the necklace. He interviewed William and Robert Gray of 13 New Bond Street, and Nathanial Jefferys of Piccadilly, jeweller to the Prince of Wales and the Duke of York. Jefferys's dealings with the stolen diamonds were slight by comparison with those of the Grays and he claimed to have been convinced that the diamonds had been dishonestly secured.[46] In a deposition on 25 October 1785, Gray the younger recounts how he first met de la Motte the previous April and that he showed him and his father, during a number of visits, diamonds of an immense value, all of which he wished to sell, saying that they came from a stomacher belonging to his mother, who had recently died. De la Motte (calling himself de Valois) was in a hurry and Gray decided to purchase some of the stones he was offered, for which he paid more than £10,000, in part with silver and in part in kind with various luxury items. It was also agreed that the Grays would mount some of the remaining diamonds as a necklace and earrings for Mme de la Motte; Gray later recognized these as the 41 brilliants from the three festoons of Bohmer's necklace. Having been sent a copy of the engraving, Gray was able to state:

> The stones that I received from M. de Valois resemble in some respects so exactly, and in all general respects are so nearly the same as the stones of a necklace made lately in Paris (a necklace that I know through a drawing and some details which have been recently given to me in trust) that I had no doubt whatsoever that the stones had been taken away from this necklace... All these diamonds were taken out of their mounts when Mr de Valois brought them to me and their cut was so damaged that I understand someone must have stripped them down from the settings with a knife or another similar tool.[47]

The point of greatest risk for any diamond heist is at disposal; it is then that perpetrators give themselves away. Mme de la Motte aroused suspicion when she tried to change her diamonds for cash, so she laundered them for consumer goods (just as Valguarnera laundered his for paintings and art objects); with these she transformed herself briefly into a grand lady. She already owned, in the spring of 1785, a gift she had received from the jewellers for facilitating the disposal of the necklace, which the jewellers believed was now with the queen, namely a pair of earrings, two watches, two chains enriched with diamonds, two solitaires (worth 9,000 and 15,000 francs) and a medallion.[48] Now, the same summer, she went with her hands full of diamonds to purchase for the house in Bar-sur-Aube, which she and her husband now owned, all kinds of fashionable furnishings, tapestries, marbles, stucco-work and knick-knacks.[49] While there, the de la Mottes were seen driving around in a coach-and-six while flashing their diamonds.[50] It did not take long for the finger of suspicion to be pointed.

The losses sustained by those touched by the diamond necklace affair were enormous and extensive, and virtually everybody involved (lawyers apart) was a loser. Historians stress these events as an epistemic shift, which indeed it was. However, looked at from the point of view of jewellers, the picture is rather different. The sum Bohmer received from the sale in 1788 to Paul-Nicolas Menière of his by now surely shaky position as crown jeweller, including the accommodation in the Louvre that went with the post, was a mere drop in the ocean of the firm's debts. The bankruptcy papers read like a roll call of Parisian aristocratic society interwoven with the names of probable jewellers, diamond dealers and moneylenders (D'Elezenne, Blatzer, Crose). The diamond necklace affair was the culmination of a series of financial disasters to affect Bohmer and Bassange, disasters symptomatic of the economic disintegration of the Ancien Régime, whose ancient feudal families had been living beyond their means. The crown jewellers had been badly hit by the bankruptcy in 1782 of the Prince of Guémené, at a time when they were owed huge sums for diamonds supplied on the occasion of the marriage of the Prince and Princess of Rochefort, as well as for diamonds supplied to the Cardinal de Rohan's elder brother, the Duc de Montbazon.[51] However, also outstanding were unpaid debts for money or goods attributed to the Manufacture Royale d'Horlogerie, Counts Potocky (a leading Polish family) and Tomatis (who appears in Casanova's memoirs) in Warsaw, the merchants Richard and Bernaud and Mietzkousky, and one in 'Gzodno en Pologne'. Money was owed by an Officer of the Guard, a man at the Comédie-Italienne, the famous Mme Vestris at the Comédie-Française (who owed the jewellers for two diamond bracelets and other objects), Count Lebereria in Madrid, the Duc de Villeroy, the director of the Variétés (for two diamond rings and a silver medal) and Count Bieniowsky in London.

Some Classic Diamond Thefts in Fiction and Film

The novel as a medium for representing the world in the framework of moral and social imperatives, that had evolved in the writing of authors such as Henry Fielding and Samuel Richardson, was established in the nineteenth century throughout Europe as the major genre of naturalism, first in serial form and then in novels, many of which were instantly translated: Charles Dickens, George Eliot, Honoré de Balzac, Émile Zola, Giuseppe Mazzini, Fyodor Dostoevsky, Theodor Fontane . . . the roll call is long and familiar. The century is the age of the realist novel, enshrining characters battling their fates and torn by moral dilemmas. It is also the age of ever more accessible newsprint spreading the latest scandals and crimes from city to country and across nations. In Wilkie Collins's *The Moonstone*, originally published as a serial with the first episode appearing early in 1868, a newspaper cutting is a crucial clue as to the whereabouts of the missing diamond.[52] Court cases like those heard at the Old Bailey attracted huge public interest. Although Arthur Conan Doyle's Sherlock Holmes did not appear in print until 1887, the professional detective, a man who was not only brilliant at problem-solving but invariably a being of exemplary moral rectitude, if also of eccentric habits, was born with Sergeant Cuff of *The Moonstone*. The detective story and the thriller became fully fledged genres in their own right and, on account of all those qualities that characterize diamonds that have been set forth in this book, a diamond often lies at the heart of these stories.

As we move into the twentieth century and the advent of the moving image, stories of thefts of precious stones feature in films, where the most successful in the genre are based on novels such as *Diamonds Are Forever* (Ian Fleming, 1956, filmed 1971) or *Topkapi* (based on Eric Ambler's novel *The Light of Day*, 1962, filmed 1964), in which the object of the heist is an emerald-encrusted dagger. In the thefts that unfold in these stories, diamonds act as a kind of moral prism; their unparalleled light is cast upon the moral weaknesses of the characters involved with them, revealing through their refractive brilliance hypocrisy, greed, cruelty, envy. Diamonds represent the irresistible allure against which men struggle despite themselves while women, whose proverbial desire for glittering jewels has caused them to be brought to the surface of the earth and into circulation, generally stand for resistance to temptation and moral uprightness. At the end of the day, everybody is by and large better off without them.

In *Rififi* (1955, directed by Jules Dassin), the group of four criminals are all lovable and sympathetic rogues, from the hardened Tony le Stéphanois just out of prison and Jo, the devoted father of a small child, to the two Italians Mario and César. They are stereotyped as charming but unreliable 'macaronis'. César is the weak link through which their audacious theft from the Paris Mappin & Webb store is exposed, but even he is presented as human, declaring that he intends to devote his share of the haul to setting up his four good but 'not beautiful' unmarried sisters. They are contrasted with the 'bad' criminal gang who are into drugs and kidnapping. The film is misogynistic: women are generally either faithless or stupid and regularly expose their men to danger. The heist succeeds but then unravels when two of the robbers are unable to resist giving the women they sexually desire gifts from the stolen 'ice'. Shot in black and white on the dark and wet streets of Paris, the film is a classic; the moment after le Stéphanois, the mastermind, releases the drawstring of the bag containing the diamonds that spill onto Jo's sitting-room table is unforgettable (illus. 100). *Rififi* is a film about diamond jewellery, not about the lure of a single diamond, but as with all these narratives, it is suffused with the conviction that diamonds can change lives for the better, whereas what always happens is that they change lives for the worse. In the end, the thieves pay the ultimate price, though not before le Stéphanois has rescued Jo's kidnapped little boy and disposed of the bad guys in the process. The final shot shows the child's mother sweeping him up from the car in which le Stéphanois has managed to bring him home and is now dying of gunshot wounds.

The idea of a diamond that is cursed has a long history and almost certainly originates in an invention on the part of an owner to protect it from theft. In the children's classic *Moonfleet* (1898) by the poet, antiquarian and successful businessman John Meade Falkner, set in Dorset in the middle of the eighteenth century, young John Trenchard is warned by the saintly Grace to 'have a care how you touch the treasure; it was evilly come by and will bring a curse with it.'[53] She turns out to be right and John is only able to live happily ever after with Grace as his wife by spending every penny of the proceeds of the sale of the cursed diamond on good works and never touching 'a penny piece' on his own account.[54] It is no accident that both works I take here as exemplary of the genre of the novel of mystery and detection have 'moon' in their titles. It is the pearl that has been traditionally associated with the moon (the light of which shining upon the sea was thought to engender the stone),

100 Tony (Jean Servais) examines the stolen diamonds in the presence of his three associates
in Jules Dassin's film *Rififi* (1955).

but two of the most celebrated diamonds put before the public at the Great
Exhibition of 1851 were named by invoking metaphors of light: the Daria-i-
noor, meaning in Persian 'ocean of light', part of the Iranian crown jewels and
presumed to be stored in the Central Bank of Tehran, and the Koh-i-noor,
meaning 'mountain of light', now in the British crown jewels. This connection
between the otherworldly light of the moon and the light a diamond appears
to emit is exploited in naming what astronomers call the diamond-ring effect
that occurs at the beginning and end of totality during a total solar eclipse
(illus. 101). As the last bits of sunlight pass through the valleys on the moon's
limb, and the faint corona around the sun is just becoming visible, the highly
transient effect resembles a ring with a glittering diamond.[55] Moonfleet is
the name of a fictitious village on the Dorset coast that we are told derives
from Mohune, the name of the now defunct landowners, but as much of
Falkner's tale of mystery and suspense takes place by moonlight, the novel's
title is redolent also of the sense of an ungraspable light source. For its part,

101 Diamond-ring effect during a solar eclipse, Hawaii, July 1991.

the moonstone that gives Wilkie Collins's novel its title takes its name from the diamond that rightfully belongs on the forehead of a statue of the Indian God of the Moon.

The Moonstone has an intricate plot, the construction of which is highly innovative and much influenced by the kind of witness statement heard in this period on a daily basis at the Old Bailey. There are in all eleven narrators, each responsible for a different section of the book, describing events that commenced, we are told, in 1848, as a group assembled in a country house in Yorkshire. Collins's story is elaborate and many-stranded; the perpetrator of the crime is the least likely of all the possible suspects and the reader is held in such suspense that crowds gathered around the offices of *All the Year Round* (the periodical in which it first appeared) on the day of publication and placed bets on how and where the diamond would be recovered.[56] The narrative is preceded by a prologue which makes it clear that the author had in mind the Koh-i-noor, the legitimacy of whose ownership by Queen Victoria, as well as its contentious recutting following the Great Exhibition, were still much discussed at the time. Classic lapidaries were reprinted in the nineteenth century and there were also several important studies of gems, at least one of which Collins had certainly read.[57] He had also read various accounts of the history of India and it has been suggested that the theft is a symbol of the rape of a nation.[58] The novel tells how the 'adventures' of a large yellow diamond – the true protagonist of the story – began in the eleventh century and how the diamond had survived to that day in a shrine guarded night and day by three Brahmins. A prophecy forewarned that the moonstone, as the diamond is called, must be watched night and day for ever and that any presumptuous mortal who laid hands on the gem would suffer certain disaster. The moonstone eventually entered the possession of Tippoo Sahib, still guarded by the Brahmins, but at the Siege of Seringapatam the dissolute and shady Colonel John Herncastle murdered the treasury guards and seized the moonstone. Collins was the son of the painter William Collins, who named him in honour of another painter, the Scot David Wilkie. So the novelist must surely have known Wilkie's enormous painting of 1839 titled *General Sir David Baird Discovering the Body of Sultan Tippoo Sahib after Having Captured Seringapatam, on the 4th May, 1799.*[59]

Colonel Herncastle is cast out by his family, including his widowed sister Lady Verinder and her only daughter Rachel, and lives under the diamond's curse, unable to spend more than one night beneath the same roof for fear of being robbed. A parallel in Collins's mind might have been Thomas Pitt who, having acquired his 410-carat diamond in India around 1702 for £20,400 (a quarter of its asking price), spent many years of wanderings and anxiety and only managed to rid himself of it by selling it in 1717 to Phillippe II, Duc d'Orléans, the Regent of France.[60] The curse on the moonstone, we are told, would only be lifted once it was restored to the Moon God's shrine. The possibility of sending it to Amsterdam to be cut is, however, held out as a course of action to be taken in extremis.[61] Herncastle engages in a complex series of legal manoeuvres to ensure his and the diamond's safety, and in an act of vengeance on his deathbed, he leaves the moonstone to Rachel, who receives it on her birthday. And it is at this point that the story proper opens and the reader is introduced to the three mysterious Indians who are found lurking around the Verinders' Yorkshire residence. The moonstone immediately exerts its fascination, as the faithful household steward Betteredge recounts:

> Lord bless us! It *was* a Diamond! As large, or nearly, as a plover's egg! The light that streamed from it was like the light of the harvest moon. When you looked down into the stone, you looked into a yellow deep that drew your eyes into it so that they saw nothing else. It seemed unfathomable; this jewel, that you could hold between your finger and thumb, seemed as unfathomable as the heavens themselves. We set it in the sun, and then shut the light out of the room, and it shone awfully out of the depths of its own brightness with a moony gleam, in the dark. No wonder Miss Rachel was fascinated.[62]

Diamond's phosphorescence had been recognized by Robert Boyle and was still able to impress, as is evident here. The display of the moonstone also provokes a member of the company to retort 'mere carbon, my good friend, after all'; this is just one component within a novel that features various aspects of contemporary popular science and medicine. But for all the scepticism betrayed in these words, this moment when the eye of the diamond (Collins's original intended title was 'The Eye of the Serpent') establishes a kind of subjection, and in which the moral compass of those drawn into it is threatened, is a familiar trope in fiction. We shall meet it again when John Trenchard in *Moonfleet* finds the hidden diamond, the search for which has already brought him and his companion close to death. The very night on which Herncastle's gift is delivered it disappears, but not before the devoted Betteredge expresses his dismay that 'in the nineteenth century . . . in an age of progress, and in a country which rejoices in the blessings of the British constitution' a quiet English house should be 'invaded by a devilish Indian Diamond'.[63]

The Moonstone is a gripping story that brings into play forensics, the law (in the person of Mr Bruff, the family solicitor), religious proselytizing, love, narcotics, greed, suicide, murder, medicine and the expertise of an exotic traveller with fluent Hindi. The tenacious high-caste Brahmins who, as the reader is several times reminded, have made the extreme sacrifice of their caste are bent on retrieving the diamond and returning it to the God's shrine. Rachel's bizarre behaviour when the theft is discovered (illus. 102) is only explained right at the end of the novel. An 'experiment' conducted by the Anglo-Indian doctor's assistant, Jennings, reveals that the thief, who was seen by Rachel but whose identity she had suppressed through her love for him, was in fact her cousin who, having been given a dose of laudanum without his knowledge, has sleepwalked. It is not until the final pages that the diamond – all the more authentic for containing a flaw – is located in the possession of the hypocritical Godfrey Ablewhite. By the time he is discovered, in disguise in a London lodging house as he prepares to leave for Amsterdam, Ablewhite is a corpse, having been smothered by the Indians. But by the bed an empty box is found, certified to have contained the moonstone by the jeweller who had taken it in pawn. By that time the Indians are on their way back to their native country where the traveller, Mr Murthwaite, witnesses the moonstone restored to the statue of the God. Directly or indirectly the Indian Diamond (as it is often called) has been the cause of the death of Lady Verinder, the near-fatal nervous breakdown of Rachel Verinder, the nearly disastrous rupture of the relationship between Rachel and Franklin Blake, the suicide of the servant Rosanna who throws herself into the quicksands, the murder of Ablewhite and a scandal that threatened the whole family and its immediate associates. The

"*'You villain, I saw you take the Diamond with my own eyes.'*"—*p.* 317.

102 'You villain, I saw you take the Diamond with my own eyes,'
illustration by Francis Arthur Fraser for Wilkie Collins, *The Moonstone* (1894).

sinister, quivering surface of the 'Shivering Sands', ostensibly different from the ungraspable light of the hard, glittering diamond, is nonetheless also an image for the diamond itself, which swallows up those who venture too close to it.

Moonfleet is on an altogether smaller scale, but as an explanation of the capacity of a diamond to corrupt and destroy, it is unbeatable. John Trenchard, a poor orphan, is gripped by the tale of Colonel John Mohune (Blackbeard), who had 'deserted the allegiance of his house' during the Civil War, joined the rebels and been made Governor of Carisbrook Castle, and thereby the king's jailer. Mohune heard that the king always kept on him a very valuable diamond, a gift of the king of France, and so promised Charles I that he would arrange his escape in exchange for the diamond. He took the diamond but prevented the escape. Suspicion fell on him and he was removed from his post and lost favour with both royalists and parliamentarians. He retired to Moonfleet and lived a life of seclusion. It is Blackbeard's diamond that John sets out to find. The back story, one of contraband smuggling along the Dorset coast, provides a cast of generous-hearted local sea-faring villains, chief of whom is Elzevir, who becomes a father figure and companion to John, against which the inhumane cruelty of the local magistrate (father of the motherless Grace) and the posse stand in contrast. John finds a clue in the coffin of Bluebeard, which he accidentally discovers while almost fatally trapped in the flooded crypt of the parish church. It leads him and Elzevir, after a terrifying cliff climb to escape their pursuers, to Carisbrook Castle, where John, lowered in a bucket down an exceptionally deep well, discovers the diamond after taking measurements to identify the precise spot given in the coded message from Blackbeard's coffin (illus. 103). Finding a little bag behind a brick in the well wall, he opens it:

> into my hand there dropped a pure crystal as big as a walnut. I had never in my life seen a diamond, either large or small – yet even if I had not known that Blackbeard had buried a diamond, and if we had not come hither of set purpose to find it, I should not have doubted that what I had in my hand was a diamond, and this of matchless size and brilliance. It was cut into many facets, and though there was no light in the well save my candle, there seemed to be in

103 John Trenchard finds Blackbeard's diamond hidden in the wall shaft
in Fritz Lang's film of *Moonfleet* (1955).

this stone the light of a thousand fires that flashed out sparkling red
and blue and green as I turned it between my fingers.[64]

Elzevir and John have bribed the turnkey with a promise of a part of their
prospective fortune in order to gain entry to the castle, which is full of French
prisoners of war. The two men shout impatiently from the top of the well,
but John is mesmerized by the diamond and crouches in the bottom of the
bucket, obsessed with the diamond and with thought of how he and Elzevir
would get rich and live happily ever after.

> I was, as it were, dazed by its brilliance, and by the possibilities of
> wealth that it contained, and had, perhaps, a desire to keep it to myself
> as long as might be; so that I thought nothing of the two who were
> waiting for me at the well-mouth.[65]

As with *The Moonstone*, once in the hand, the diamond wreaks its disastrous influence: the turnkey, struggling to seize the diamond for himself, falls
down the well, and John and Elzevir escape and cross on a boat to Amsterdam,
but they are cheated by a dealer, Aldobrand, who tells them the stone is worth-
less and takes it from them. Realizing they have been cheated, John frantically
seeks to retrieve it, but wise Elzevir advises: 'Perhaps there may be after all
some curse that hangs about this stone, and leads to ruin those who handle
it.'[66] This turns out to be true: the two are convicted in court on the evidence

of Aldobrand and committed to forced labour. Many years later, the ship on which they are being transported to the Dutch sugar plantations is wrecked in a terrible storm. They find themselves the last two men on board as the dismasted brig, head to sea, is carried towards a lee shore. Peering through the rain and murk they recognize that it is toward Moonfleet Bay they are drifting. Only those who know the sea, as John remarks, know that in such circumstances the ship will be shattered to pieces and anyone on board will never make it to shore because of the terrible undertow of the pounding waves.[67] On the strand are men waiting with ropes, but though only 100 ft away from them, they knew that no one had ever survived a wreck on Moonfleet beach. John in fact does survive because Elzevir selflessly uses his great strength to ensure he catches the rope, while he himself perishes. In the aftermath it turns out that the diamond has also poisoned the life of Aldobrand who, after selling the stone, found that both his health and his fortune declined until he had nothing left but profits of the sale of the Mohune diamond. On his deathbed he left the proceeds of this cursed diamond to John who, as we have seen, never touched a penny piece.

REFERENCES

Introduction

1 See, for example, DeeDee Cunningham, *The Diamond Compendium* (London, 2011).

2 On the history of ornamental diamond glass engraving see Wilfred Buckley, *Diamond Engraved Glasses of the Sixteenth Century* (London, 1929), introduction.

3 S. Tolansky, in *The History and Use of Diamond* (London, 1962), p. 16, reports that several such rings, with the diamond point worn, are preserved in the Victoria and Albert Museum. There are indeed early pointed diamond rings (for example M. 188–1975, *c.* 1400), but whether they were used for this purpose is unclear. See www.oldbaileyonline.org.

4 *Theophrastus on Stones*, trans. and ed. Earle R. Caley and John F. C. Richards (Columbus, OH, 1956); The *Natural History* comprises 37 books, covering a very wide variety of topics, completed in 77 CE. It has been described as in essence 'a series of extended "essays" on topics within the major fields of "applied science"', John F. Healy, *Pliny the Elder on Science and Technology* (Oxford, 1999), p. 40; there is an online translation of the *Natural History* by John Bostock and H. T. Riley at www.perseus.tufts.edu.

5 Healy, *Pliny the Elder on Science and Technology*, p. 190.

6 Georges-Louis Leclerc, Comte de Buffon, in *L'Histoire naturelle des minéraux* (1783–8), vol. I, pp. xxxv–xxxvi. www.buffon.cnrs.fr.

7 See Tolansky, *The History and Use of Diamond*, pp. 54–5, 67–8.

8 T[homas] N[ichols] of J. C. in Cambridge, *Gemmarius Fidelius or the Faithful Lapidary* (London, 1659), p. 46. Nichols draws heavily on the work of Boetius de Boodt, *Gemmarum et Lapidum Historia* (1609).

9 Origen, *Homilies on Jeremiah and 1 Kings 28*, trans. John Clark Smith (Cambridge, 1998). I am indebted for the exegesis to Evelien Chayes, *L'Éloquence des pierres*

précieuses de Marbode de Rennes à Alard d'Amsterdam et Remy Belleau, sur quelques lapidaires du XVIe siècle (Paris, 2010), p. 137.

10 Marbodei Galli, *De lapidus pretiosis enchiridion*, ed. Pictor de Willigen (Fribourg, 1531). This is one of several editions published in different places in that year.

11 Camillus Leonardus, *The Mirror of Stones . . . Now Translated into English* (London, 1750), pp. 62–3.

12 Remy Belleau, *Les Amours et nouveaux échanges des pierres précieuses: vertus et proprietez d'icelles* (Paris, 1576), no. 2.

13 Ibid., line 175.

14 Ibid., lines 127–50.

15 George Frederick Kunz in *The Curious Lore of Precious Stones* [1913] (New York, 1971), p. 157, quoting an early Scottish ballad.

16 'There followed no effect.' Francis Bacon, *Sylva Sylvarum; or, A Natural History in Ten Centuries* (London, 1676), pp. 2, 84.

17 Robert Boyle, 'The Origin and Virtues of Gems', in *The Philosophical Works of the Honourable Robert Boyle Esq., Abridged, Methodized, and Disposed under the General Heads . . . by Peter Shaw* (London, 1725), vol. III, p. 99. See also pp. 101, 102–3.

18 Galileo published his findings in *Lettera al Principe Leopoldo di Toscana* in 1642.

19 Michael Bycroft, 'Wonders in the Academy: The Value of Strange Facts in the Experimental Research of Charles Dufay', *Historical Studies in the Natural Sciences*, XLIII/3 (June 2013), pp. 334–70, 343.

20 Charles Dufay, 'Notes sur l'électricité', in *Archives de l'Académie des Sciences*, Dufay dossier, 'Donner à l'Abbé Nollet': 'Le Diamant jaune de Mr Délery exposé à l'ombre est plus lumineuse que . . . 86 brillans' (Mr Délery's yellow diamond exposed in the dark is more luminous than 86 brilliants). I am grateful to Michael Bycroft for making available to me his scans of this material as well as allowing me to read his PHD dissertation, 'Physics and Natural History in the Eighteenth Century: The Case of Charles Dufay', University of Cambridge, 2013.

21 See H. Guerlac, *Lavoisier – The Crucial Year: The Background and Origin of His First Experiments on Combustion in 1772* (Ithaca, NY, 1961), pp. 78–91.

22 Industrial diamonds are now largely manufactured stones. The first artificial diamonds were produced in the 1950s by crushing graphite in conditions similar to a volcano. They are expensive to make and though now used also in jewellery are difficult to detect without specialist equipment such as that produced by De Beers.

23 David Jeffries, *A Treatise on Diamonds and Pearls: In Which Their Importance Is Considered: And Plain Rules Are Exhibited for Ascertaining the Value of Both:*

And the True Method of Manufacturing Diamonds [1750], 2nd edn with large improvements (London, 1751).

24 The *Oxford English Dictionary* gives for pinchbeck, definition two, 'Contemptuously, as a type of what is counterfeit or spurious'. For more details of pinchbeck see Marcia Pointon, *Brilliant Effects: A Cultural History of Gem Stones and Jewellery* (New Haven, CT, and London, 2009), pp. 34–6.

25 Jeffries, *A Treatise on Diamonds and Pearls*, dedication.

26 Ibid., p. 66.

27 See www.kimberleyprocess.com and 'The Kimberley Process', www.globalwitness. org, 1 April 2013.

28 'Diamonds: Miners' Best Friend', *Financial Times*, 29–30 November 2014. Although figures are not available it seems likely that demand from China has also had a significant effect. Robert N. Proctor argues that diamonds are over-valued socially and economically and that De Beers are responsible for creating the equivalent of the McDonald's Big Mac. See R. N. Proctor, 'Anti-agate: The Great Diamond Hoax and the Semiprecious Stone Scam', *Configurations*, IX/3 (2001), pp. 381–412.

29 R. E. Raspe, *Account of the Present State and Arrangement of Mr James Tassie's Collection of Pastes and Impressions from Ancient and Modern Gems with a Few Remarks on the Origins of Engraving on Hard Stone, and the Methods of Taking Impressions of Them in Different Substances* (London, 1786), p. 7.

30 Paul W. May, 'Diamond Thin Films: A 21st-century Material', *Philosophical Transactions of the Royal Society of London*, Series A (2000), 358, pp. 473–95. These and other abstracts and papers are available electronically from the Bristol CVD group website, www.chm.bris.ac.uk. I am grateful to Paul May for allowing me to visit his laboratory and for explaining so lucidly to me, a non-scientist, the work in which he and his colleagues are engaged.

31 See www.e6.com, accessed 12 January 2014.

32 John Cholmley to Mr John Aelst Whitby, 19 November 1683, MS. North Yorkshire County Record Office, ZCG V 2/3, f. 31.

33 A Google search under 'diamond inclusion mantle' takes one to many scientific papers and images on this subject.

34 Vladimir Nabokov, *Speak Memory: An Autobiography Revisited* (New York, 1989), pp. 143, 253.

35 Gary Shteyngart, *Little Failure: A Memoir* (London, 2014), p. 79.

36 This weight is given in old French carats, a unit similar to, but slightly smaller than, the metric carat that was widely adopted in 1914. The modern equivalent would

therefore be more like 115 carats. Diamonds were also measured in grains in the early modern period; one grain was equivalent to one-third of a metric carat. See http://mineralsciences.si.edu.

37 Jean-Baptiste Tavernier, *Les Six voyages de Jean-Baptiste Tavernier, ecuyer Baron d'Aubonne en Turquie, en Perse et aux Indes* (Paris, 1676), part II, p. 337.

38 I have in general adopted the terminology proposed by François Farges (François Farges, 'Les grands diamants de la Couronne de François Ier à Louis XVI', *Versalia: Revue de la Société des Amis de Versailles* (2014), p. 75, n. 3), who points out that lapidary in the early modern period referred to cutters of all gems as opposed to the present time when 'diamantaires' is used to describe diamond cutters. Nonetheless, it is worth noting also that Tavernier specifically referred to 'deux Diamantaires Hollandais' working in Ispahan, in *Les Voyages de Jean-Baptiste Tavernier*, vol. I, p. 484; John Francillon's obituary, *Gentleman's Magazine*, 23 June 1816, p. 92. The drawing and memo are now in the collection of the United States Geological Survey; see http://mineralsciences.si.edu.

39 Muséum National d'Histoire Naturelle, Paris.

40 This paragraph draws on François Farges, John Vinson, John J. Rehr and Jeffrey E. Post, 'The Rediscovery of the "French Blue" Diamond', *Europhysics*, XLIII/1 (January–February 2012), pp. 23–5 (quotation from p. 25), and Farges, 'Les grands diamants de la Couronne de François 1er', pp. 64–6. I am grateful to Michael Bycroft for drawing my attention to the work of Farges.

ONE   Diamonds and Empire

1 Jean-Baptiste Tavernier, *Les Six voyages de Jean-Baptiste Tavernier, ecuyer Baron d'Aubonne en Turquie, en Perse et aux Indes* (Paris, 1676), pp. 293–4.

2 'de meilleur tître', suggesting the supremacy of Dutch trading, ibid., pp. 313, 316–17.

3 *The Travels of Marco Polo*, amended and enlarged by Hugh Murray (New York, 1845), p. 265. The author is Rustichello da Pisa, reporting stories told to him by Marco Polo, who travelled in Asia, Persia, China and Indonesia between 1276 and 1291.

4 On Borneo as a source for diamonds see Jack Ogden, 'Diamond, Head Hunters and a Prattling Fool: The British Exploitation of Borneo Diamonds', Gem-A online library, 2013, p. 3 (downloaded from www.academia.edu) and Hazel Forsyth, *London's Lost Jewels: The Cheapside Hoard* (London, 2013), pp. 93–6.

5 *Arabian Nights' Entertainments*, ed. Robert L. Mack (Oxford 1995), p. 148.

6 John Ruskin, *The Ethics of the Dust* [1866], in *The Complete Works of John Ruskin*, ed. E. T. Cook and A. Wedderburn (London, 1903–12), vol. XVIII. For a discussion of

Ruskin's attachment to the *Arabian Nights* see Marcia Pointon, *Brilliant Effects: A Cultural History of Gem Stones and Jewellery* (New Haven, CT, and London 2009).

7 John Mawe, *Travels in the Gold and Diamond Districts of Brazil* [1812], revd edn (London, 1821), p. 319.

8 Louis Rousselet, *L'Inde des Rajahs: Voyage dans L'Inde Centrale et dans les présidences de Bombay et du Bengale par Louis Rousselet* [1875], 2nd edn, *317 gravures sur bois déssinés par nos plus celebres artistes* (Paris, 1877), pp. 440–41.

9 Ibid., p. 443.

10 Ibid., p. 442.

11 Tijl Vanneste draws attention to the myths surrounding the discovery of diamonds in Brazil but has established that Bernardo was a real person. Tijl Vanneste, *Global Trade and Commercial Networks: Eighteenth-century Diamond Merchants* (London, 2011), p. 50. *Faiscadors* were poor miners who looked for gold in already explored mines.

12 Carlos Prieto, *Mining in the New World* (New York, 1973), p. 49.

13 Hubert Bari, *Diamants: au coeur de la terre, au coeur des étoiles, au coeur du pouvoir* (Paris, 2001), p. 102.

14 For examples, see Pointon, *Brilliant Effects*, p. 180; Marcia Pointon, 'Material Manoeuvres: Sarah Churchill, Duchess of Marlborough, and the Power of Artefacts', *Art History*, XXXII/3 (June 2009), pp. 485–515; Hannah Greig, *The Beau Monde: Fashionable Society in Georgian London* (Oxford, 2013), pp. 47–60.

15 Boris Fausto, *A Concise History of Brazil*, trans. Arthur Brakel (Cambridge, 1999), p. 49.

16 Prieto, *Mining in the New World*, p. 47.

17 Ibid., p. 50.

18 Fausto, *A Concise History of Brazil*. p. 53.

19 An excellent summary of the complicated history of this period in relation to Brazilian diamond mining is provided in Vanneste, *Global Trade and Commercial Networks*, pp. 50–57.

20 Ibid.

21 Prieto, *Mining in the New World*, p. 103.

22 See Bari, *Diamants: au coeur de la terre*, pp. 102–5.

23 George Beet and Thomas Laurent Terpend, *The Romance and Reality of the Vaal Diamond Diggings*, printed and published by the Diamond Fields Advertiser Ltd, (Kimberley, 1917), p. 102, 'Life on the Orange River'.

24 For the history of famous diamonds see Ian Balfour, *Famous Diamonds* (London, 1997).

25 On Kimberlite in South Africa see see www.princeton.edu/geosciences/people/
    schoene/pdf/FlowersSchoene_HeKaapvaal_G10.pdf, accessed 23 June 2016. For
    a thorough but accessible account of diamond properties, formation and excava-
    tion, including geographical occurrence and diamond processing, see DeeDee
    Cunningham, *The Diamond Compendium* (London, 2011).

26 Balfour, *Famous Diamonds*, p. 64.

27 Trevor Nace, '1,111-Carat Diamond, World's Second Largest, Found in Botswana',
    20 November 2011, www.forbes.com.

28 For a detailed analysis of the debate leading up to the gift see Bill Guest, 'The
    "Row about the Great Diamond": The Presentation of the *Cullinan Diamond* to
    the British Crown, 1907', *Historia*, LII/2 (November 2007), pp. 112–24.

29 *The Times*, 19 August 1907, quoted in Balfour, *Famous Diamonds*, p. 69.

30 For a full account see Claude Blair, ed., *The Crown Jewels: The History of the
    Coronation Regalia in the Jewel House in the Tower of London* (London, 1998).

31 Joan Younger Dickinson, *The Book of Diamonds* (New York, 1965), pp. 18–19.

32 Stefan Kanfer, *The Last Empire: De Beers, Diamonds, and the World* (London,
    Sydney and Auckland, 1993), p. 110.

33 Bari, *Diamants: au cœur de la terre*, p. 110.

34 Beet and Terpend, *The Romance and Reality of the Vaal Diamond Diggings*, p. 86.

35 Anthony Trollope, quoted in Martin Meredith, *Diamonds, Gold and War: The Making
    of South Africa* [2007] (London, 2008), p. 55. Trollope was at Kimberley in 1887.

36 Lord Randolph Churchill, quoted in Kanfer, *The Last Empire*, p. 110.

37 Edwin W. Streeter, *Precious Stones and Gems* (London, 1898), p. 88.

38 Meredith, *Diamonds, Gold and War*, p. 161.

39 On eighteenth-century London diamond dealers, see Gedalia Yogev, *Diamonds
    and Coral: Anglo-Dutch Jews and Eighteenth-century Trade* (Leicester, 1978).

40 'Sightholder Directory', at www.debeersgroup.com/globalsightholdersales/en/
    directory.html, accessed 23 June 2016. The sight-holder events were transferred to
    Botswana in 2013; Kanfer, *The Last Empire*, chap. 19.

41 The rise of the Oppenheimer dynasty and their involvement in De Beers business
    practices is charted in Janine Roberts, *Glitter and Greed: The Secret World of the
    Diamond Cartel* [2003] (New York, 2007), see especially chap. 4.

42 Franziska Bieri, *From Blood Diamonds to the Kimberley Process: How NGOs Cleaned
    Up the Global Diamond Industry* (Farnham, 2010), p. 4.

43 Ibid.

44 'Nicky Oppenheimer and Family', www.forbes.com, accessed 10 March 2016,
    where Oppenheimer is alleged to be worth $6.7 billion; report in *London Evening*

Standard, 8 September 2014, p. 22, which also claims that Oppenheimer did not cut off all his ties with the firm at this time and that he kept his rights to land his helicopter on the roof of the diamond firm's HQ in Charterhouse Street, the only person granted permission to land a helicopter within the Square Mile.

45   Nils Pratley, 'Anglo American: Big Problems, Only Some Solutions', 26 October 2012, www.theguardian.com; Rupert Neate, 'Miner Dies as South African Industrial Unrest Continues', 5 October 2012, www.theguardian.com.

46   See www.worlddiamondcouncil.com.

47   See www.debeersgroup.com/en/building-forever/our-issue-areas/ethics.html and www.debeersgroup.com/content/dam/debeers/corporate/documents/BuildingForever/BPP%Contractor%20Workbook%202016.pdf, accessed 23 June 2016.

48   See 'Partnership Africa Canada', www.pacweb.org, and 'Conflict Diamonds', www.globalwitness.org.

49   The Lupin ice road runs 350 miles from Yellowknife to the Diavik mine, over 85 per cent of lakes and 15 per cent of land porterage; see 'Ice Roads and Runways', http://nunalogistics.com, accessed 10 March 2016.

50   Bieri, *From Blood Diamonds to the Kimberley Process*, p. 104.

51   Bieri, in chap. 4 ibid., explains how KPCS works. Further information, constantly being updated, can be found on the Global Witness site listed above.

52   Aryn Baker/Tshikapa, 'Dirty Diamonds', TIME, 7–14 September 2015, p. 29.

53   Extractive Industries Transparency Initiative, http://eiti.org/CentralAfricanRepublic.

54   Baker/Tshikapa, 'Dirty Diamonds', p. 30.

55   'Diamond Watchlist', www.pacweb.org.

56   See 'The Case for Human Rights Due Diligence', Global Witness's comments for tripartite meeting on responsible sourcing of precious stones, 26 May 2016, www.globalwitness.org.

57   See www.kimberleyprocess.com.

58   The World Federation of Diamond Bourses, www.wfdb.com.

59   For an exemplary analysis of one particular instance see David De Vries, *Diamonds and War: State, Capital, and Labor in British-ruled Palestine* (New York and Oxford, 2010).

60   'Trading Partners', *Financial Times*, 4 January 2014, Analysis, p. 7. Diamonds have been mined in Siberia since the late 1940s.

61   Kanfer, *The Last Empire*, pp. 298–9.

62   V. L. Allen, *The History of Black Mineworkers in South Africa*, vol. 1: *The Techniques of Resistance, 1871–1848* (Keighley, 1992), pp. 109–29. Allen records on p. 21 his

fruitless attempts to get access either to the mines or to crucial data during the course of his research, and points to the influence of the mining houses on the availability of evidence for this aspect of South African history.

63 John M. Smalberger, 'I.D.B. [illicit diamond buying] and the Mining Compound System in the 1880s', *South African Journal of Economics*, XLII/4 (December 1974), pp. 398, 399.

64 Beet and Terpend, in *The Romance and Reality of the Vaal Diamond Diggings*, illustrate on p. 87 diamonds swallowed by and recovered from one worker.

65 Smalberger, 'I.D.B. and the Mining Compound System', p. 413.

66 See John M. Smalberger, 'The Role of the Diamond-mining Industry in the Development of the Pass-law System in South Africa', *International Journal of African Historical Studies*, IX/3 (1976), pp. 419–34.

67 Harris had premises on Donkin Street, Port Elizabeth, in 1880–90, and then with a photographer called McNaught in 1891–4; A. D. Bensusan, '19th Century Photographers in South Africa', *Africana Notes and News*, XV/6 (June 1963), p. 236.

68 One such album published in 1888 and titled *South Africa Illustrated by a Series of One Hundred and Four Permanent Photographs* was published in Port Elizabeth in 1888 and is now in Cambridge University Library (Y305C). Another is in the library of the Wellcome Institute in London. A further collection of Harris's photographs including figure subjects was sold at Bonham's, London, on 5 October 2010, lot 290.

69 Prints of one of these photographs and of another not included in the Yale collection were sold tipped into an album of Harris's work by Dreweatts Bloomsbury, New York, on 24 October 2007 (lot no. 188). The entry remains on the web at www.dreweatts.com, but the two photographs that were on the site have been removed. They were, however, copied and may be see on a blog: 'A Digger's Lament: A Soul Safari Compilation', https://soulsafari.wordpress.com, 21 September 2012. The eight Yale photographs can be seen at http://images.library.yale.edu.

70 Smalberger, 'I.D.B. and the Mining Compound System', pp. 412–13, quoting S. Ransome, *The Engineer in South Africa* (London, 1903), pp. 66–7.

71 Gareth Hoskins, 'Geo-centric Histories of Diamond Mining in Kimberley South Africa', paper presented at the Visuality, Materiality and Mining Symposium, University of Brighton, 26 June 2015, downloaded from www.academia.org (unpaginated).

72 Dipti Bhagat, 'Buying More Than a Diamond: South Africa at the Colonial and Indian Exhibition, 1886', MA dissertation, V&A/RCA, May 1996, p. 55.

73 Sir Sydney Cowper reporting to the Governor of the Cape, quoted ibid., p. 80.

74 *Westminster Review*, July 1886, p. 46, quoted ibid., p. 74.

75 Kanfer, *The Last Empire*, p. 265.

76 Ben Macintyre, 'A Glittering History of Rulers and Rough Diamonds', *The Times*, 6 April 2002, p. 26.

77 Balfour, *Famous Diamonds*, p. 172.

78 Natural History Museum, report from 11 January 1888, in *Reports, Letters* etc., vol. XXVI, NHM Library.

79 See Pointon, *Brilliant Effects*, pp. 345–7.

80 *The Baburnama* is quoted in Balfour, *Famous Diamonds*, p. 157.

81 Ibid.

82 Ibid., p. 158.

83 Streeter, *Precious Stones and Gems* (London, 1877), and *The Great Diamonds of the World* (London, 1882) (his accounts in these two works are contradictory); James Tennant, *On Gems and Precious Stones* (25 March 1852) in *Lectures on the Results of the Great Exhibition of 1851, delivered before the Society of Arts, Manufactures, and Commerce*, 2nd series (London, 1853), pp. 75–104. Tennant used actual gems loaned to him and from his own collection to illustrate his lecture, as well as diagrams of the Koh-i-noor and its faceting.

84 Jean Baptiste-Tavernier, *Travels in India by Jean-Baptiste Tavernier . . . translated from the original French by Valentine Ball . . .* (London, 1889).

85 Balfour, *Famous Diamonds*, p. 165. There are also allegations that the Daria-i-noor is in a Bangladeshi bank; see Shyam Bhatia, 'Meet Daria-i-Noor, the Koh-i-Noor's Little-known Sibling', www.tribuneindia.com, 28 March 2012.

86 Balfour, *Famous Diamonds*, p. 167.

87 WG [William Gaspey] *Tallis's Description of the Crystal Palace: Illustrated* (London and New York, 1851), division I, p. 31.

88 Ibid.

89 Edward Concannon, *Remembrances of the Great Exhibition* (London, 1852), quoted by Lara Kriegel in 'Narrating the Subcontinent in 1851: India at the Crystal Palace', in Louise Purbrick, ed., *The Great Exhibition of 1851: New Interdisciplinary Essays* (Manchester, 2001), p. 164.

90 Transcribed in Stephen Howarth, *The Koh-i-noor Diamond: The History and the Legend* (London, 1980), pp. 126–7.

91 N. B. Sen, *Glorious History of Koh-i-noor* (Delhi, 1974), p. 109.

92 Dalhousie to Sir George Cooper, August 1849, quoted in Balfour, *Famous Diamonds*, p. 167.

93 Queen Victoria's journal, quoted in C. A. Bayly, ed., *The Raj: India and the British, 1600–1947* (London, 1990), p. 182.

94 'A Chapter on Diamonds', in *The New Monthly Magazine and Humorist*, ed. Harrison Ainsworth, vol. LXXXIX (London, 1850), p. 439. For the subsequent life of Duleep Singh see Kevin Rushby, *Chasing the Mountain of Light: Across India on the Trail of the Koh-i-noor Diamond* (London, 1999), epilogue.

95 WG, *Tallis's Description of the Crystal Palace*, division 1, p. 32.

96 'A Lady's Glance at the Great Exhibition', *Illustrated London News*, 23 August 1851, p. 242.

97 Quoted in Iradj Amini, *Koh-i-Noor* (New Delhi, 1994), p. 238. On the display of the stone at the exhibition, see Judy Rudoe, 'Jewellery at the Great Exhibition', in *The Great Exhibition and Its Legacy*, ed. Franz Bosbach and John R. Davis (Munich, 2002), pp. 67–80.

98 Tennant, *On Gems and Precious Stones*, pp. 80–81.

99 Paul Young, '"Carbon, Mere Carbon": The Kohinoor, the Crystal Palace, and the Mission to Make Sense of British India', *Nineteenth-century Contexts: An Interdisciplinary Journal*, XXIX/4 (December 2007), p. 346.

100 Isobel Armstrong, *Victorian Glassworlds: Glass Culture and the Imagination, 1830–1880* (Oxford, 2008), pp. 230–31.

101 *Great Exhibition of the Works of Industry of All Nations 1851: Official Descriptive and Illustrated Catalogue* (London, 1851), vol. II, section 23, 'works in precious metals, jewellery etc.'

102 *Illustrated London News*, 17 May 1851, p. 426.

103 Quoted in Armstrong, *Victorian Glassworlds*, p. 231.

104 This is the gist of Paul Young's argument, in '"Carbon, Mere Carbon"', p. 353.

105 Jeanette Greenfield, *The Return of Cultural Treasures* (Cambridge, 1989), p. 148.

106 Ibid., p. 149.

107 Helen Lawson, 'The Koh-i-noor Diamond Will Stay in Britain, Says Cameron As He Rules Out Returning Gem on Final Day of Visit', www.dailymail.co.uk, 21 February 2013.

TWO **Diamond Business**

1 Ordnances, declarations and other documentation on the Natie is in the Antwerp Stadsarchief, GA 4477.

2 Antwerp Stadsarchief, GA 4477, no. 13.

3 For a full account see Veerle Vanden Daelen, 'Negotiating the Return of the Diamond Sector and Its Jews: The Belgian Government during the Second World War and the Immediate Post-war Period', *Holocaust Studies: A Journal of Culture*

and History, 18 (Autumn/Winter 2012), pp. 231–60. I am grateful to Dr Vanden Daelen for making time to discuss her work with me.

4 Promotional film, Antwerp World Diamond Centre, and information from Barbara Descheemaecker, Public Relations and Protocol Officer, whose help I gratefully acknowledge.

5 See www.diamondbourseantwerp.com.

6 See the information provided by the World Federation of Diamond Bourses, www.wfdb.com.

7 Henricus Arnoldus drew one in his sketchbook; see W. von Stromer, 'Modell der Edelstein-Schleifmaschine des Heinrich Arnold aus Zwolle von 1439', *Aus den Schatzkammern der Welt: Mythos Kunst Wissenschaft* (Darmstadt, 1992), pp. 120–21, quoted in Annibale Montana, 'Italian Gemology during the Renaissance: A Step towards Mineralogy', in *The Origins of Geology in Italy*, ed. Gian Battista Vai and W. Glen Caldwell, Geological Society of America, Special Paper 411 (Boulder, CO, 2006), p. 2.

8 There is continuing debate about the origins of the rose-cut diamond, known as an 'à la mode' in the seventeenth century. François Farges claims that the earliest reference to this cut occurs in 1667 when the French royal jeweller, Pittan, uses it; see François Farges, 'Les grands diamants de la Couronne de François Ier à Louis XVI', *Versalia: Revue de la Société des Amis de Versailles* (2014), p. 77, n. 162.

9 Karin Hofmeester gives an authoritative account of Indian and Western diamond cuts, including the irregular so-called Mughal cut, though she does not discuss lasques and her reliance on the evidence of one person, John Fryer, for the assumption that most diamonds exported from India were in the rough may be incorrect. As I discuss in Chapter Five, there is evidence of lasques being imported in considerable quantities in the sixteenth century. See Karin Hofmeester, 'Shifting Trajectories of Diamond Processing: From India to Europe and Back, From the Fifteenth Century to the Twentieth', *Journal of Global History*, VIII/1 (March 2013), pp. 31–3.

10 Montana, 'Italian Gemology during the Renaissance', p. 3.

11 For an authoritative account of diamond cuts, see Herbert Tillander, *Diamond Cuts in Historic Jewellery, 1381–1910* (London, 1995).

12 John Cholmley to Nathaniel Cholmley, 3 January 1678, transcribed in Rosalind Bowden, *The Letter Books of John and Nathaniel Cholmley, Diamond Merchants*, North Yorkshire County Record Office Publication no. 67, *Review 2001* (Northallerton, 2002), pp. 42–3. The following discussion of the Cholmleys draws both on Bowden and on a reading of the manuscripts, not all of whose contents she transcribed. North Yorkshire County Record Office ZCG V 2/3.

13 Iris Kockelbergh, Eddy Vleeschdrager and Jan Walgrave, *The Brilliant Story of Antwerp Diamonds*, trans. Gilberte Lenaerts (Antwerp, 1992), p. 71. Caution is needed as this book is badly translated and the footnotes are unreliable. In earlier periods wax was also used for this purpose according to Marjolijn Bol, paper delivered to 'Gems in Transit' workshop, University of Warwick, Department of History, May 2015.

14 Esther Kreitman, *Diamonds* [1944], trans. Heather Valencia (London, 2010), pp. 88–9.

15 I am grateful to Elke Verhoeven, anthropologist and adviser on diamond history in the Kempen to the Antwerp Provincial Department of Culture, for the invaluable information she provided and also for taking me to see Nijlen and Grobbendonk.

16 There is a paucity of detailed studies of diamond trading and smuggling but one noteworthy book, based on a detailed reading of the records of several Jewish firms, is Gedalia Yogev, *Diamonds and Coral: Anglo-Dutch Jews and the Eighteenth-century Trade* (Leicester, 1978). Joseph Salvador was the alleged author of a pamphlet and of a booklet published in 1753 entitled *Further Considerations on the Act to Permit Persons Professing the Jewish Religion to be Naturalized by Parliament in a Second Letter from a Merchant in Town to his Friend in the Country*. Salvador's mercantile and political activities are recounted in Maurice Woolf, 'Joseph Salvador, 1716–1786', *Transactions and Miscellanies of the Jewish Historical Society of England*, 21 (1962–7), pp. 104–37.

17 Yogev, *Diamonds and Coral*, p. 67.

18 Tijl Vanneste, *Global Trade and Commercial Networks: Eighteenth-century Diamond Merchants* (London, 2011), p. 49.

19 On Nabobs see Tillman W. Nechtman, 'A Jewel in the Crown? Indian Wealth in Domestic Britain in the Late Eighteenth Century', *Eighteenth-century Studies*, XLI/1 (2007), pp. 71–86, and Marcia Pointon, *Brilliant Effects: A Cultural History of Gem Stones and Jewellery* (New Haven, CT, and London, 2009), pp. 190–92.

20 Nils Büttner, 'Aristocracy and Noble Business: Some Remarks on Rubens's Financial Affairs', in *Minuscula Amicorum: Contributions on Rubens and His Colleagues in Honour of Hans Vlieghe*, ed. Katlijne van der Stighelen (Turnhout, 2006), vol. I, pp. 69–70.

21 '. . . après douze ans de négoce ensemble l'expérience demonstre que la meilleur merchandise est de mon côté l'or et l'argent, du votre Diamants. Il faudra y tenir a l'avenir', Sir John Chardin to Daniel Chardin, 2 January 1700, MS, Beinecke Library, Yale University, GEN MSS 216, Box 1 (8).

22 Vanneste, *Global Trade and Commercial Networks*, p. 48.

23 John Cholmley to Nathaniel Cholmley, 3 January 1677.

24 Labradores are not as Bowden (*The Letter Books of John and Nathaniel Cholmley*, p. 57) states 'a kind of feldspar' but are Portuguese-worked, block-shaped stones. I am grateful to Jack Ogden for explaining this.

25 John Cholmley to Nathaniel Cholmley, 13 March 1674.

26 John Cholmley to Nathaniel Cholmley, 3 December 1669.

27 John Cholmley & Co. to Daniel Chardin and Salvadore Rodriguez, London, 30 March 1687. Mangelin was the weight used in southern India for measuring stones. The collett is the base of the stone.

28 John Cholmley to Nathaniel Cholmley 3 December 1669.

29 Raisin is mentioned in Sir John Chardin's correspondence, 1686–1706, Yale University, Beinecke Library GEN MSS 216, series II, folder 12. I am grateful to Tijl Vanneste for drawing my attention to these references. The business relations of Chardin and Raisin and the latter's death and its aftermath are discussed in Dirk Van der Cruysse, *Chardin Le Persan* (Paris, 1998), pp. 42, 348–53.

30 Jean Chardin, *Journal du Voyage du Chevalier Chardin en Perse et aux Indes Orientales...* (London, 1686). Also published in English the same year.

31 John Cholmley to Nathaniel Cholmley, December 1670. Bowden reads 'prizes' for 'sizes'. There is no entry for Cholmley in the index of Van der Cruysse, *Chardin Le Persan*.

32 John Cholmley to Nathaniel Cholmley, 13 December 1672.

33 John Chardin to Daniel Chardin and Salvador Rodriguez, undated draft letter, Beinecke Library GEN MSS 216, Box 1 (6).

34 See Van der Cruysse, *Chardin Le Persan*, pp. 348–53.

35 Colin Campbell to James Dormer, 29 April 1741, Antwerp Stadsarchief MS. IB 1159.

36 See www.felixarchief.be; the collection is in what is known as 'Insolvente Boedelskamer', an official body that conserved the records of Antwerp firms that went bankrupt. Some of the riches of this UNESCO archive are briefly summarized at http://www.antwerpen.be/nl/overzicht/felixarchiev/geschiedenis/insolvente-boedelskamer, where there are two downloadable pdfs, accessed 23 June 2016. Two of James Dormer's notebooks are shown and described at p. 59.

37 'Ayant apris que vous avez apporté de votre voyage de la Chine quelque partie de curiosités assez bien choisies et de bon gout, j'ai voulu vous ecrire celle ci, Monsieur, pour vous demander, sçavoir si vous voudriez me faire l'amitié de m'envoyer une petite liste de ce que vous avez apporté de joli ou de curieux, et si vous voulez y ajouter le prix, vous m'obligerez et je le garderai seulement pour moi, je vous félicite, au reste, sur votre heureux retour et sur la part que vous avez à la bonne et prompte

expedition des affaires de la Compagnie.' Comte de Calenburg to James Dormer, 30 October 1733, Antwerp Stadsarchief, MS. IB 1159.

38 Two dissertations present studies of Dormer and his second wife: Joris Smeets, *James Dormer, 1708–1758*, Katholieke Universiteit Leuven, 2002, and Eva Louwette, *Joanna Theresia Goubau (1710–1781) en dochter. Een blik in de leefwereld van twee achttiende-eeuwse dames*, Katholieke Universiteit Leuven, 2002.

39 Information from Tijl Vanneste, personal communication, June 2015.

40 Dormer was exporting paintings by Rubens and Snyders in 1737 and 1738 (Antwerp Stadsarchief, MS. IB 1223) and in 1741 he bought pictures for Sir Marmaduke Constable (IB 1223), but he also purchased on his own account (IB 1186).

41 Antwerp Stadsarchief, MS. IB 1222.

42 Antwerp Stadsarchief, MS. IB 1171.

43 Antwerp Stadsarchief, MS. IB 1223, IB 1175, IB 1175, IB 1117.

44 A letter to Madame Düfone in Paris in 1747, 'marchande joailliere & courtier de Diamants', is at Antwerp Stadsarchief, MS. IB 1222.

45 Vanneste, *Global Trade and Commercial Networks*, chap. 3, including an excellent diagram on p. 68.

46 George Clifford & Sons to James Dormer, Amsterdam, 7 September 1747, Antwerp Stadsarchief, MS. IB 1747, quoted in Vanneste, *Global Trade and Commercial Networks*, p. 65.

47 Berthon & Garnault to James Dormer, 24 June 1749, Antwerp Stadsarchief, MS. IB 1652, quoted in Vanneste, *Global Trade and Commercial Networks*, p. 65: 'en veut du blanc tant en rozes quen brilliants & en surplus en ces derniers on les recherche parfaits bien taillées et surtout bien estendus.'

48 Vanneste, *Global Trade and Commercial Networks*, p. 65.

49 Naomi Weaver, 'Naomi Campbell's "Blood Diamond" Testimony at War Crimes Trial: Live Updates', www.theguardian.com, 5 August 2010.

50 See, for example, Simon Meisenberg, 'The Final Judgement in the Trial of Charles Taylor', http://blog.oup.com, 23 September 2013.

51 For a full account of the *affaire du collier* see Pointon, *Brilliant Effects*, chap. 5.

52 Franziska Bieri, *From Blood Diamonds to the Kimberley Process: How NGOs Cleaned Up the Global Diamond Industry* (Farnham, 2010), p. 1.

53 'Tainted Love: Blood Diamonds Still Cast Shadow over Valentine's Day', press release, www.globalwitness.org, 8 February 2010.

THREE Diamond: Shape, Pattern, Symbol

1 See also Rihanna, 'Diamonds' (2014).

2 Horace Walpole to Lady Mary Coke, Paris, 22 August 1771, *The Yale Edition of Horace Walpole's Correspondence* ed. W. S. Lewis (London and New Haven, CT, 1961), vol. XXI, p. 158.

3 See www.diamondresorts.com; Diamond Supply Company, at www.zumiez.com.

4 Diamond Light Source, 'About Us', at www.diamond.ac.uk, accessed 10 March 2016.

5 *Diamond Sutra*, British Library Or.8210, www.bl.uk.

6 King James Bible (KJV 2000), The New International Bible (NIV, 1968, revd 2011) gives the line as: 'I will make your forehead like the hardest stone, harder than flint. Do not be afraid of them or terrified by them, though they are a rebellious people.' Quotations are from www.kingjamesbibleonline.org.

7 King James Bible, Ezekiel 28:13–17.

8 King James Bible, Exodus 28:1–21. Commentators are undecided about 'ligure', unknown in modern mineralogy, but it may be tourmaline or jacinth. There is general agreement on the names of the other stones.

9 I am indebted in this discussion to Jennifer O'Reilley, 'Patristic and Insular Traditions of the Evangelists: Exegesis and Iconography', in *Le Isole Britanniche e Roma in Età Romanicobarbarica*, ed. A. M. Luiselli Fadda and É. Ó. Carragáin (Roma, 1998), pp. 49–94.

10 'After this I saw four angels standing at the four corners of the earth, holding back the four winds of the earth, that no wind might blow on earth or sea or against any tree', Revelation 7:1.

11 At www.bl.uk/catalogues/illuminatedmanuscripts/ILLUMIN.ASP?Size=mid& IIID=28259, accessed 23 June 2016.

12 Peter Pomerantsev, 'Forms of Delirium', *London Review of Books*, 10 October 2013, p. 5.

13 Teresa of Avila, *The Interior Castle* in *The Collected Works of St Teresa of Avila*, 2nd revd edn, ed. Kieran Kavanagh and Otilio Rodriguez (Washington, DC, 1987), p. 412.

14 Teresa of Avila, *The Book of Her Life*, ibid., p. 249.

15 Ibid.

16 Teresa of Avila, *The Interior Castle*, ibid., p. 289.

17 Teresa of Avila, *The Book of Her Life*, ibid., p. 358.

18 Gerard Manley Hopkins, 'That Nature is a Heraclitean Fire and of the Comfort of the Resurrection', 1918, stanzas 21–4, *Gerard Manley Hopkins: Selected Poems*, ed. Peter Feeney (Oxford, 2006), p. 64.

19 George Withers, *A Collection of Emblemes, Ancient and Moderne* (London, 1635), book III, no. 37, p. 171.

20 'Haec amat obscurum; volet haec sub luce videri, judicis argutum quae non formidat acumen; haec placuit semel; haec decies repetita placebit.'

21 'Caesar Laurentius ex nostra Societate, alteri eum honorem declinati partier, dedit pro tesserae pyxidem, quibusdam intus gemmis instructam, quae lucem in Sole hauriunt, & seruant, egeruntque; si pyxis eadem, ubi clausa fuerit, recludatur in tenebris.' Silvestri a Petrasancta, *Symbola heroica* (Amsterdam, 1682), book IX, p. 464.

22 Oleg Grabar, *The Formation of Islamic Art* (London and New Haven, CT, 1973), p. 192.

23 Alfred Gell, *Art and Agency: An Anthropological Theory* (Oxford, 1998), p. 77.

24 Grabar, *The Formation of Islamic Art*, p. 202.

25 George Puttenham, *The Arte of English Poesie* [1589], facsimile edn (Menston, 1968), pp. 75–7.

26 Eva Baer, *Islamic Ornament* (Edinburgh, 1998), p. 43.

27 Hans Eworth, *Margaret Dudley, Duchess of Norfolk*, 1562, oil on panel, 1,118 x 864 mm, from the private collection of Lord Braybrooke, Audley End, English Heritage.

28 Unknown artist, *Katheryn of Berain*, 1568, oil on panel, 972 x 686 mm, National Museum of Wales, Cardiff. Both these portraits are discussed by Tarnya Cooper in *Elizabeth and Her People*, exh. cat, National Portrait Gallery, London (London, 2014), nos. 17b and 48.

29 Finger Ring Collection, Ashmolean Museum, WA 1897. CDEF. F818.

30 E.J.W. Barber, 'On the Antiquity of East European Bridal Clothing', in *Folk Dress in Europe and Anatolia*, ed. Linda Welters (Oxford, 1999), pp. 13–31. The motif 'is generally thought to represent the female vulva', p. 16.

31 Sigmund Freud, 'The Sense of Symptoms', Lecture 17 [1917] in *Introductory Lectures on Psychoanalysis*, trans. James Strachey (London, 1963), vol. XVI, pp. 264–9, 268.

32 John Mitchell, 'Ways of Seeing: Eyes and Minds in the First Millennium', inaugural professorial lecture, School of World Art Studies, University of East Anglia, 2014; personal communication.

33 Jacques Derrida, *Dissemination* [1972], trans. Barbara Johnson (Chicago, IL, 1983).

34 Zoë Opačić, *Diamond Vaults: Innovation and Geometry in Medieval Architecture* (London, 2005), p. 10.

35 Ibid., p. 4.

36 Juan Arfe y Villafañe, *Quiltador, de la plata, oro, y piedras, conforme a las leyes reales, y para declaracion de ellas* [1572] (Madrid, 1598); *De varia commensuracion para la esculptura y architectura* (Seville, 1585).

37 For the definitive discussion of the building of Audley End see P. J. Drury, 'No Other Palace in the Kingdom Will Compare with It: The Evolution of Audley End, 1605–1745', *Architectural History*, 23 (1980), pp. 1–39, accessed on JStor, 11 July 2016.

38 Other examples can be seen on the porch at Gorhambury, Sissinghurst Castle, and Cranborne Manor, illustrated in Mark Girouard, *Elizabethan Architecture: Its Rise and Fall, 1540–1640* (New Haven, CT, and London, 2009), pp. 154, 172, 397.

39 'In der Architecture, beneffens den ouden ghemeenen wegh der Antijcken en *Vitruvij,* heeft hy ander nieu ordenen opgebrocht, van Cornicen, Capitelen, Basen, Tabernakelen, Sepultueren, en ander cieraten, waerom alle naevolgende Architecten hem te dancken hebben, dat hy hun van d'oude banden en stricken verlost heeft, en ruymen toom, en verlof gegheven, van yet beneffens d'Antijcken te versieren: Doch om de waerheyt te segghen, is desen toom so ruym, en dit verlof by onse Nederlanders so misbruyckt, dat metter tijdt in de Metselrije een groote Ketterije onder hun ghecomen is, met eenen hoop raserije van cieraten, en bre-kinghe der Pilasters in't midden, en op de Pedestalen voeghende hun aenghewende grove puncten van Diamanten, en derghelijcke lammicheyt, seer walghelijck om aen te sien.' Karel van Mander, *Het Schilderboek* (Haarlem, 1604), facsimile edn (Utrecht, 1969), f. 168v. I am grateful to Paul Taylor, Lucy Gent and Christine Stevenson for their advice about this passage.

40 Personal communication, 28 October 2014.

41 'Les Livres d'architecture', http://architectura.cesr.univ-tours.fr, accessed 10 March 2016.

42 'Et cosi di età in età si è venuto variando tal opera: quando ad imitation di diamante in tavola piana, & quando con maggior rilievo, si come si vede qui sotto disegnato.' Sebastiano Serlio, *D'Architettura* (Venice, 1566), p. 138. English translation published in 1611.

43 Sebastiano Serlio, *The First Book of Architecture* (London, 1611), book IV, chap. 5, f. 15.

44 Gedalia Yogev's useful tables of diamond imports from India to England cover only the period 1711–96. Gedalia Yogev, *Diamonds and Coral: Anglo-Dutch Jews and Eighteenth-century Trade* (Leicester, 1978), appendix 1. See, however, the letter books of the Cholmley brothers from 1664 – when John Cholmley was already a well-established merchant – to 1694, for evidence that extremely large quantities

were imported during the seventeenth century. MS. North Yorkshire County Record Office, CRO ZCG V. Literature on the wealth and international reach of Flemish dealers can be found in Bert Timmermans, *Patronen van patronage in het zeventiende-eeuwse Antwerpen* (Amsterdam, 2008).

45 See Diana Scarisbrick, 'Seventeenth-century Diamond Jewellery and the Ornamental Print', *Een Eeuw van Schittering: diamantjuwelen uit de 17 de eeuw* (Antwerp, 1993), pp. 23–36.

46 Madeleine C. Viljoen, in an interesting article, draws attention to the theme of hot air and its importance for ornament printmakers, 'The Airs of Early Modern Ornament Prints', *Oxford Art Journal*, XXXVII/2 (2014), pp. 117–33. She does not, however, comment on the plethora of diamonds in these prints, nor on the importance of bellows and hot air for the 'philosophers' experimenting at this time on diamonds by placing them in hot furnaces.

47 See article on Saenredam by Walter Liedtke in Grove Art Online, www.oxfordartonline.com.

48 George Evans, 'Hatchments', at www.theheraldrysociety.com, accessed 10 March 2016.

49 Paint stick is oil paint but mixed with wax and formed into a stick; unlike oil paint it never oxidizes and therefore never fully dries. Allegedly Serra melts several sticks to form a large pigment block.

50 Many of the drawings in the series remain in his own collection and were first seen in exhibition in 2012 at the Metropolitan Museum of Art, New York.

51 The quote is from Richard Shiff, 'Drawing Thick: Serra's Black', in *Richard Serra Drawings: A Retrospective*, ed. Bernice Rose, Michelle White, Gary Garrels (Houston, TX, London and New Haven, CT, 2011), p. 34.

52 First published in 1988, quoted ibid., p.22.

53 I am indebted here to Jean-Pierre Séguin, *Le Jeu de Carte* (Paris, 1968), especially pp. 35, 41–8.

54 Miranda Sawyer, 'Flower Show: Miranda Sawyer Has a Lesson in Art from Marc Quinn', *The Observer*, 25 May 2003, at www.theguardian.com.

55 Ibid.

56 See www.lifegem-uk.com.

57 'Making Diamonds with a Blowtorch', video at www.bbc.co.uk, 15 August 2011.

58 See www.phoenix-diamonds.com.

59 The portfolio includes the work of eleven artists based in London. It was commissioned by Charles Booth-Clibborn and published under his imprint, The Paragon Press, London. See 'Untitled (1992): Damien Hirst', www.tate.org.uk, accessed 10 March 2016.

60 Damien Hirst cited in 'Conversation', Gordon Burn, 'Beautiful Inside My Head Forever' (Sotheby's, 2008), sale catalogue, vol. III, p. 21, cited from www.damien hirst.com, accessed 10 March 2016.

61 See the discussion in Marcia Pointon, *Brilliant Effects: A Cultural History of Gem Stones and Jewellery* (New Haven, CT, and London, 2009), pp. 45–6.

62 Anselm Kiefer, in a lecture given at College de France while Chaire de Création Artistique, 2010–11, 7 February 2011, 'Trois Oeuvres', www.college-de-france.fr. The 'action' was cited without the details in the text panel to room 9 of the Anselm Kiefer retrospective at the Royal Academy, 2014.

63 Anselm Kiefer, *Silvan Solitude*, 1992, 183.5 x 106.7 cm, private collection, was exhibited at 'Masterpieces: Art and East Anglia', The Sainsbury Centre, University of East Anglia, 2013.

64 Anselm Kiefer, *Falling Stars,* Museum of Old and New Art, Hobart, Tasmania, 508 x 285 x 48 mm.

65 The date is given as 2001 in Matthew Biro, *Anselm Kiefer* (London, 2013), p. 85, but in the Royal Academy retrospective, 2014 (no. 62, 1–3) the date is given as 1987/2014. Private collection.

66 No. 97 in the Royal Academy retrospective, 1987/2014. Both the works discussed here are listed as in a private collection, presumably that of the artist. Bachmann was an Austrian poet (1926–1973). Another version of *For Ingeborg Bachmann: The Renowned Orders of the Night*, with the addition of the figure of the artist prostrate on the ground under the starry sky and without the diamonds (1997, acrylic and emulsion) is in the Guggenheim Museum, Bilbao. I am unable to reproduce Kiefer's works incorporating diamonds as, despite repeated requests by his agent on my behalf, no response was received.

FOUR   A Girl's Best Friend? Diamonds as Luxury and Necessity

1   'Elizabeth Taylor Jewellery Auction Fetches $116m', www.bbc.co.uk, 14 December 2011.

2   'Duchess of Windsor Jewel Auction, London, United Kingdom', www.thejewellery editor.com, 30 November 2010.

3   Madeleine Albright interviewed for the *Smithsonian* magazine in June 2010, at the time of an exhibition of her jewellery at the Smithsonian Museum: www. smithsonianmag.com.

4   Mrs Pendarves to Mrs Anne Granville, 4 March 1728–9, in *The Autobiography and Correspondence of Mary Granville, Mrs Delany*, ed. Lady Llanover (London, 1861), vol. I, p. 191.

5   Hannah Greig describes how the new Lady Scarborough toured her husband's regional estate draped with over £10,000 worth of diamonds, to the great satisfaction of the onlookers, in Hannah Greig, *The Beau Monde: Fashionable Society in Georgian London* (Oxford, 2013), p. 48.

6   Georg Simmel, *Philosophie der Mode* [1905], in vol. x of *Gesamtausgabe* (Frankfurt am Main, 1995).

7   E. Cannan, ed. *Lectures on Justice, Police, Revenue and Arms, Delivered in the University of Glasgow by Adam Smith, Reported by a Student in 1763* (Oxford, 1896), pp. 157, 178.

8   Adam Smith, 'Of the Imitative Arts', in *Adam Smith: Essays on Philosophical Subjects*, ed. W.P.D. Wightman and J. P. Bryce (Oxford, 1980), pp. 182–3.

9   C. G. Bapst, *Histoire des Joyaux de la Couronne de France* (Paris, 1889), vol. II, p. 440.

10   George Hardinge to Horace Walpole, 13 April 1775, *The Yale Edition of Horace Walpole's Correspondence*, ed. W. S. Lewis, vol. XXXV (London and New Haven, CT, 1973), p. 577.

11   W. C. Oulton, *Authentic and Impartial Memoirs of her Late Majesty, Charlotte . . .* (London, 1819), p. 135.

12   Quoted in Amanda Foreman, *Georgiana, Duchess of Devonshire* (London, 1999), p. 223.

13   The adaptation was in the first place a Broadway production of 1949.

14   There is a considerable literature on eighteenth-century attitudes to luxury. See, for example, Maxine Berg, *Luxury and Pleasure in Eighteenth-century Britain* (Oxford, 2005).

15   Edward Jay Epstein, 'Have You Ever Tried to Sell a Diamond?', *The Atlantic* (February 1982).

16   In Jule Styne and Leo Robin, 'Diamonds Are a Girl's Best Friend' (1949); lyrics at www.metrolyrics.com.

17   Amanda Lear, 'Diamonds' (1979); lyrics at www.elyrics.net.

18   Anita Loos, *Gentlemen Prefer Blondes* [1925] (Harmondsworth, 1992), p. 25.

19   London, 18 September 1735, Strafford Papers, BM Add. MS 22, 256 (36).

20   See in particular Northumberland County Record Office (hereafter NCRO), MS. 2DE 31/10/7, a tiny piece of paper on which are inscribed a series of pieces of jewellery (earrings, pins, knots, a necklace) for which the total value is calculated as £1,862.

21   James Fog to Sir John Delaval, 23 June 1772, NCRO, MS. 2DE 34/2/65. At the sale of Queen Charlotte's personal jewellery at Christie's in London on 17–19 May, on the first day a number of lots were purchased by someone called 'Fogg'; see annotated copy of the sale catalogue, Christie's Library.

22 Lady Delaval had been a widow; she married John Hussey Delaval in 1750 and the couple had seven children but their only son predeceased his father. Her husband was elevated to a baronetcy in 1760 and the peerage in 1786, three years after her death.

23 Diana Scarisbrick describes an esclavage as clusters of diamonds strung in rows or rivières with the centre emphasized in some way with a large stone or a cross. Sometimes this pendant was linked to the band encircling the neck by another band, also called an esclavage, which hung down over the breasts. See Diana Scarisbrick, *Jewellery in Britain, 1066–1837* (Wilby, 1994), p. 284.

24 NCRO, MS. 2DE 28/1/128. Receipt dated 2 March 1754.

25 Scarisbrick, *Jewellery in Britain*, p. 283; there are further orders to Belliard at NCRO, MS. 2DE 31/10 20 a and b; 2DE 31/10/23.

26 Sir John Hussey Delaval 'bought of James Cox', London, 11 June 1772, NCRO, MS. 2DE 31/10/ 24. On James Cox see Marcia Pointon, *Brilliant Effects: A Cultural History of Gem Stones and Jewellery* (London and New Haven, CT, 2009), chap. 7.

27 Ambrose Heal, *The London Goldsmiths, 1200–1800* (Cambridge, 1935), gives these dates. Thomas Mortimer's *The Universal Director* (London, 1763), lists Charles Belliard, Pall Mall as 'Jeweller to His Royal Highness the Duke of York'. The Duke, second son of George III, was born in August 1763.

28 Invoices 1750–51, James Dormer archive, Antwerp Stadsarchief, 1171/1.

29 London Metropolitan Archive Sun Insurance register, 1775–87, MS. 11936/342, no. 529365.

30 I have relied here on the summary provided by the Record Office, www.experience woodhorn.com, 2DE, accessed 10 March 2016.

31 *Holden's Triennial Directory* (London, 1799).

32 Lord Delaval had ordered earrings of oriental topaz but this had proved difficult to source and the jewellers had made them of very nice Brazilian topaz while expressing a willingness to search further and change them if necessary; Rundell & Bridge to Lord Delaval, 28 January 1803, NCRO, MS. 2DE 34/3/14.

33 Rundell & Bridge to Lord Delaval, 31 January 1803, NCRO, MS. 2DE 34/3/12.

34 Rundell & Bridge to Lord Delaval, 12 February 1806, NCRO, MS. 2DE 34/3/46. There are no invoices or receipts for these items.

35 Rundell & Bridge to Lord Delaval, 10 January 1807 and 3 February 1807, NCRO, MS. 2DE 34/3/55 and 58.

36 See Marcia Pointon, 'Material Manoeuvres: Sarah Churchill, Duchess of Marlborough, and the Power of Artefacts', *Art History*, XXXII/3 (June 2009), pp. 485–515; Hannah Greig, 'Leading the Fashion: The Material Culture of London's

Beau Monde', in *Gender, Taste and Material Culture in Britain and North America, 1700–1830*, ed. J. Styles and A. Vickery (New Haven, CT, 2007).

37 Greig, *The Beau Monde*, p. 48.

38 Fanny Burney, *Camilla* [1796] (Oxford, 1999), p. 250.

39 Guy de Maupassant, *La Parure*, first published in *Le Gaulois* (Paris, 1884).

40 Interview with Gerald Ratner, *Financial Times Magazine*, 4 May 2011, p. 39. See also Angela Levin's article for 'This Is Money', Mail Online, www.thisismoney.com, published 22:35 on 20 July 2013 and updated 22 July 2013.

41 Ethel Frey Cushing, *Culture and Good Manners* (Memphis, TN, 1926), quoted in Karen Levi, *The Power of Love: Six Centuries of Diamond Betrothal Rings* (London, 1988), p. 1.

42 Epstein, 'Have You Ever Tried to Sell a Diamond?', p. 4. This article is a summary of the material in Epstein's book *The Diamond Invention* (London, 1982), where on p. 223 he states that A. J. Ayer noted in 1953, "'Diamonds do not wear out and are not consumed. New diamonds add to the existing supply in trade channels and in the possession of the public. In our opinion old diamonds are in 'safe hands' only when widely dispersed and held by individuals as cherished possessions far above their market price." Epstein published a number of books with different titles which are basically the same content. See also *The Rise and Fall of Diamonds: The Shattering of a Brilliant Illusion* (New York, 1982) and *The Death of the Diamond: The Coming Collapse in Diamond Prices* (London, 1983).

43 Shirley M. Ogletree, 'With This Ring I Thee Wed: Relating Gender Roles and Love Styles to Attitudes towards Engagement Rings and Weddings', *Gender Issues*, XXVII (June 2010), pp. 68, 70, 74.

44 Edith Wharton, *The Custom of the Country* [1913] (Oxford, 2008), chap. VII, p. 54.

45 Ibid., chap. XIV, p. 134.

46 *The Dundee Courier and Argus and Northern Warder*, 20 July 1880, p.3.

47 'A Lovers' Quarrel', *The Huddersfield Chronicle* (9 August 1880), p. 4.

48 Heiman v. Parrish, 942 P. 2d 631, quoted in Brooke A. Blecher, 'Broken Engagements: Who Is Entitled to the Engagement Ring?', in *Family Law Quarterly*, XXXIV/3 (Fall 2000), pp. 588–9.

49 Lindh v. Surman, no. 39, W.D. Appeal Docket, 1998, 1999 WL 1073639 (Pa. Nov. 23 1999), reported in Jennifer L. Reichert, 'No-fault Principles Govern Return of Engagement Ring', *Trial: Journal of the Association of Trial Lawyers of America*, XXXVI/3 (March 2000), pp. 107–8.

50 Ogletree, 'With This Ring I Thee Wed', p. 74.

51   *North Eastern Daily Gazette*, 9 May 1885, unpaginated.

52   Meghan O'Rourke at Slate.com, 11 June 2007; *The Groom-to-be's Handbook: The Ultimate Guide to a Fabulous Ring, a Memorable Proposal, and a Perfect Wedding* (New York, 2007), p. 11.

53   John Lewis Partnership Archive, 2847/j Memo from R. M. Hadden to General Manager (Merchandise), July 1973.

54   *The Engagement Ring* (1912), Biograph Company, dir. Mack Sennett, starring Mabel Normand, downloaded from Archive.org through Creative Commons, www.archive.org. Vintage silent slapstick clips on the web suggest that car crashes became a feature of films made from the 1920s and 1930s: www.youtube.com/watch?v=SfxkFJrNm1g.

55   See Pointon, *Brilliant Effects*, pp. 64–5.

56   Edward Jay Epstein, 'Have You Ever Tried to Sell a Diamond?'

57   *San Francisco Call*, 21 March 1909, p. 10, Library of Congress: Chronicling America, image 10.

58   Classic CBS sitcom, episode aired 13 March 1952, https://archive.org/details/GracieRing, downloaded under Creative Commons.

59   Quoted in Epstein, 'Have You Ever Tried to Sell a Diamond?'

60   N. W. Ayer produced a study that claimed to find that 'the semi-passive role played by women receiving diamonds seemed to resemble closely the sex relations in a Victorian novel'. Quoted ibid.

61   Anthony Thwaite interviewed by Sarah O'Reilly, 2008, Millennium Memory Bank, British Library, C1276/15.

62   Carroll Sullivan speaking to anonymous interviewer, BBC Radio Humberside, 1999, Millennium Memory Bank, British Library, C900/07098C1.

63   Gladys Ellis interviewed by Evelyn Draper for BBC Radio Merseyside, 1999, Millennium Memory Bank, British Library, C900/10069.

64   Rev. John Ayling interviewed by Chris Eldon for BBC Radio Shropshire, 1998, Millennium Memory Bank, British Library, C900/15002C1.

65   Harold Crowe interviewed by John Watson for BBC Radio Cumbria, 1999, Millennium Memory Bank, British Library, C900/02589.

66   Patricia Fern interviewed by Lucy Ashwell for BBC Radio Humberside, 1999, Millennium Memory Bank, British Library, C900/07098C1.

67   Derek Moore interviewed by Clare Jenkins for BBC Radio Sheffield, 1999, Millennium Memory Bank, British Library, C900/14627C1.

68   'More Londoners are Faking It to Keep Hold of Their Jewellery', *London Evening Standard*, 24 October 2011.

69 David Solomon interviewed by Evelyn Draper for BBC Radio Mersey, 1998, Millennium Memory Bank, British Library, C900/1009.

FIVE **Theft**

1 Mark Koba, 'Copper Theft "Like an Epidemic" Sweeping U.S.', www.cnbc.com, 30 July 2015.
2 Wilkie Collins, *The Moonstone* (London, 1868); *Rififi* (1955), dir. Jules Dassin.
3 Robert Parrot of the Parish of St James Westminster. The value of the earrings was assessed at £40. Court Proceedings of the Old Bailey, www.oldbaileyonline.org.
4 See Ian Balfour, *Famous Diamonds*, 3rd edn (London, 1997), pp. 154–72.
5 Ibid., pp. 186–91, 205–9.
6 The property of De Beers, this, and other diamonds on display, were replaced by replicas on the night before the attempted theft. For the timeline of the theft see 'Timeline: Dome Diamond Heist', http://news.bbc.co.uk, 18 February 2002.
7 See www.oldbaileyonline.org, 14 January 1702.
8 There are considerable difficulties attached to calculating average historical wages but see Gregory Clark, 'Farm Wages and Living Standards in the Industrial Revolution: England, 1670–1850', www.econ.ucdavis.edu, accessed 11 March 2016, and J. F. Field, 'Service, Gender and Wages in England, c. 1700–1860', www.ehs.org.uk, 2010. Wages varied regionally and between domestic service and rural labour, but by any measure £80 would have been more than the annual income of all but the most privileged household servant.
9 See www.oldbaileyonline.org, 13 October 1703.
10 See www.oldbailey.org, 7 December 1743.
11 See www.oldbailey.org, 29 June 1785. The text states Bailey found the things missing after his return *to* India but this does not make sense given the rest of the account, in which Bailey refers to returning from India in 1784, and given the date of the trial a year later. It is more likely to be an error in the transcript of proceedings.
12 The £32 million worth of rough diamonds was seized in 2013 by robbers who held up a passenger plane at Brussels airport onto which a case of gems was being loaded for transport to India: Ian Traynor, '31 Arrested over £32m Diamond Robbery at Brussels Airport', www.theguardian.com, 8 May 2013.
13 On trade routes see Tijl Vanneste, *Global Trade and Commercial Networks: Eighteenth-century Diamond Merchants* (London, 2011), and for an excellent account of the changing patterns of production, movement and processing of diamonds see Karin Hofmeester, 'Shifting Trajectories of Diamond Processing:

From India to Europe and Back, From the Fifteenth Century to the Twentieth', *Journal of Global History*, VIII/1 (March 2013), pp. 25–49.

14 'fra di esse una pietra con un diamante di gran valore che tutti essi valevano piu di venti milla ducati . . . una pietra grande puntaquadrata . . . che erano molti anni che non era uscito dall'India un altro simile . . .': Archivio di Stato, Tribunale Criminale del Governatore, Processo 1620–1631, 265 Bis, ff. 1197r–1197v and f. 1212r–1214r (hereafter Proceedings). My account here draws on three sources: the original transcriptions of court proceedings in the Archivio di Stato di Roma; the account published by A. Bertolotti entitled 'P. P. Rubens, Corneille de Wael, Jean Roos, Antoine van Dyck: Lettres et Rensignement Inédits', *Rubens-Bulletijn Jaarboeken* (Brussels, 1888), pp. 197–213; Jane Costello, 'The Twelve Pictures "Ordered by Velasquez" and the Trial of Valguarnera', *Journal of the Warburg and Courtauld Institutes*, XIII/3/4 (1950), pp. 237–84, which includes partial transcripts of documents in the appendices. It should be pointed out that Bertolotti and Costello have little or no interest in the diamonds per se and focus on the fact that a number of artists were called to give evidence at the trial of the accused who had dealt in paintings. Ducats were the gold coins of Venice; their value varied according to the price of gold.

15 R. Baetens lists Balthazar de Groot, Hendrik and Jacomo de Groot and Caesar Volpi as established in 1619 and merging into the firm of Jacomo, Balthasar & Ferdinand de Groot, and Jan Fourment, Jeronimo & Nicolaas Volpi by 1632. Later the firm became the well-known one of Van Colen & De Groot; see R. Baetens, 'Een Antwerps Handelshuis uit de XVIIe eeuw, de Firma Van Colen', in *Tijdschrift voor Geschiedenis*, LXXIII (1960), pp. 198–214.

16 Testimony of Domenico Fernandez, muleteer of Lisbon, Madrid, 11 November 1629: 'certi panni di lino alcuni d'essi sigillati'. The words used for the bulses are 'sachetti' and 'bisagli', Proceedings f.1213 v. On muleteers and merchants see Peter N. Miller, *Peiresc's Mediterranean World* (Cambridge, MA, 2015), ch. 27.

17 'milla ducati in sedici sagottini Che d'altre nome si chiamano bisagli di diamanti e colgarmenti detti diamanti bruti', Proceedings, 1212r.

18 See Hofmeester, 'Shifting Trajectories of Diamond Processing', p. 33.

19 A further good example is the cut-cornered rectangular portrait-cut diamond in the Al Thani Collection, recently displayed at the Victoria and Albert Museum, London; see Susan Stronge, ed., *Bejewelled: Treasures from the Al Thani Collection* (London, 2015), cat. no. 9.

20 Named as Louis de Freytas [sic] Pinto, he was cited as creditor in a case brought in Antwerp in 1634 by Diego Texera des Sanpayo, in which he is described as former

captain of a company of cuirassiers and part of a War Council of His Majesty of the Netherlands; Antwerp Stadsarchief, MS.7 #6238.

21 The names of the key players in the affair and their origins are given in the formal accusation, Proceedings, MSS.265 bis, ff. ii97r–f. ii98r. More detail is given in the deposition to the court in Madrid that is translated into Italian, ff. i212r–i230v, which includes the testimonies of the muleteers. Valguarnera claimed that Carapetto had squandered most of the diamonds on the way back to Rome.

22 Proceedings, ii60v.

23 Proceedings, i309v., letter dated November 1629.

24 See Costello, 'The Twelve Pictures "Ordered by Velasquez" and the Trial of Valguarnera', and Stefano Pierguidi, 'Marcello Sacchetti, Francesco Valguarnera e il ratto delle sabine di Pietro da Cortona', *Bollettino dei Musei Comunali di Roma* (2009), pp. 65–76.

25 See Costello, 'The Twelve Pictures "Ordered by Velasquez" and the Trial of Valguarnera', p. 260, who points out that speculation in works of art and precious objects was commonplace among gentlemen, diplomats and members of the clergy.

26 Proceedings, ff. ii61v.–ii65r., transcribed by Costello, ibid., pp. 274–5.

27 'ad faccette fatto à core [a cuore] legato in un anello d'oro'. Proceedings, f. ii6iv.

28 Proceedings, f. i384r., dated 12 May 1631.

29 Proceedings, unnumbered page following i246r.

30 The jewellers' names are spelt in various ways in the legal documents and narrative accounts of the affair. For the sake of consistency I have adopted the spelling used in one of the original depositions though it varies in others (Paris, Bibliothèque Nationale, MS Joly de Fleury 2088, f. 15; hereafter BN). Bassange was 44 in 1786 and resided with Bohmer in rue Vendôme; see Émile Campardon, *Marie-Antoinette et le Procès du Collier* (Paris, 1963), pp. 72–3.

31 Jeanne-Louise Genet, Mme Campan, *Mémoires sur la vie privée de Marie-Antoinette . . . suivis de souvenirs et anecdotes historiques sur les Règnes de Louis XIV, de Louis XV et de Louis XVI*, 6th edn (Paris, 1826), vol. I, p. 6; ibid., vol. II, p. 4. Carlyle points out in 'The Diamond Necklace' (in Thomas Carlyle, *Critical and Miscellaneous Essays Republished* (London, 1869), p. 12 n.) that there is no evidence of the date of manufacture of the necklace apart from Campan's statement that it was intended for Du Barry.

32 A standardized metric carat is now 0.2 g or 3.08467 grains, but this has not always been the case. According to Ian Balfour a number of different systems have been used to calculate the weight of diamonds at different times and in different places.

In the seventeenth century diamonds were not measured in decimals as now but in fractions from a quarter to a sixty-fourth. The grain was 3.1783 of a carat and 480 carats made a troy ounce. I have used this measure as a rough guide. In 1907 the French decided to rationalize gem weight and introduced the metric carat, which is exactly ⅕ g; the UK and the USA followed suit in 1914 (see Balfour, *Famous Diamonds*, p. 307). See also 'Hope Diamond: Carats, French Carats, and Grains', http://mineralsciences.si.edu, accessed 11 March 2016.

33 Carlyle, *Critical and Miscellaneous Essays Republished*, p. 12.

34 'Un grand collier en brillants comme une collection unique et rare en ce genre.' The official valuation by Dögny and Mailliard appears in MS. Paris, BN Joly de Fleury 2088, f. 15. The conversion from livres/francs to sterling is made via www.pierre-marteau.com/currency/converter/fra-eng.html. The calculation for historic currencies for 1790 given on www.nationalarchives.gov.uk for 2005 is £12,102,480. Any such estimate must of necessity be approximate but a comparison might be made with the necklace made by Fog for the Empress of Russia in 1772 which cost £2,200; see Chapter Four, p. 147.

35 Jonathan Beckman, *How to Ruin a Queen: Marie Antoinette, the Stolen Diamonds and the Scandal That Shook the French Throne* (London, 2014).

36 See, however, my own chap. 5 in *Brilliant Effects: A Cultural History of Gem Stones and Jewellery* (New Haven, CT, and London, 2009).

37 My account here is based on many primary and secondary sources, details of which can be found in *Brilliant Effects*. See also the bibliography in Beckman, *How to Ruin a Queen*.

38 Sarah Maza, *Private Lives and Public Affairs: The Causes Célèbres of Pre-revolutionary France* (Berkeley, CA, and Los Angeles, CA, 1993), p. 173.

39 Mary Sheriff, who makes this point in 'The Portrait of the Queen', in *Marie-Antoinette: Writings on the Body of a Queen*, ed. D. Goodman (London, 2003), wrongly asserts that it was Mme de la Motte who impersonated the queen. In fact it was Nicole le Guay who acted the part without, she subsequently claimed, knowing at all what was going on. The portrait is now in Hessische Hausstiftung, Darmstadt.

40 Carlyle, *Critical and Miscellaneous Essays Republished*, p.13.

41 Ibid., p. 96.

42 Campan, *Mémoires sur la vie privée de Marie-Antoinette*, vol. II, p. 285.

43 'Nous n'avons pu voir sans une juste indignation que l'on ait osé emprunter un nom auguste & qui nous est cher à tant de titres, & violer avec une témérité aussi inouïe le respect dû à la Majesté Royale', Lettres-Patentes du Roi Données à St-Cloud

le 5 Septembre au Parlement de Paris . . ., in *Collection Complette* [sic] *de tous les mémoires qui ont paru dans la fameuse affaire du collier avec toutes les pièces secrètes qui y ont rapport, & qui ont pas paru* (Paris, 1786).

44 Sylvan Paul Audebert, *L'Affaire du collier de la reine d'après La correspondance inédite du chevalier de Pujol* (Rouen, 1901), p. 28.

45 See Bibliothèque Historique de la Ville de Paris (hereafter BHVP), MS. 690 Target, f. 276.

46 Only eight items purchased in exchange for diamonds are listed, statement of 16 December 1785, transcribed by Émile Campardon in *Marie-Antoinette et le procès du collier*, pp. 94–5.

47 'Les pierres, que je reçus de M. de Valois, ressemblent à quelques égards si exactement, et à tous égards d'une manière si approchante, aux pierres d'un collier fait dernièrement à Paris (collier qui m'est connu par un dessin et d'un détail qui m'ont été récemment confiés) que je n'eus pas le moindre doute que les pierres n'ayant été enlevées de ce collier . . . Tous ces diamans étoient démontés, lorsque M. de Valois me les apporta, et les tailles [cut/surface] en étoient si endommagées que je comprends qu'on les aura détachés de leurs montures avec un couteau ou quelque'autre instrument semblable.' MS Paris, Archives diplomatiques, Mémoires et Documents, vol. 1399, f.293–4, official translation of a lost English original. An inaccurate transcript is given in Campardon, *Marie-Antoinette et le procès du collier*, pp. 85–92.

48 Depositions of jewellers, quoted in Campardon, *Marie-Antoinette et le procès du collier*, p. 73.

49 Ibid., p. 98, quoting *Mémoire pour le Cardinal de Rohan*, evidence from the court case.

50 Criminal proceedings against the de la Mottes, Archives Nationales, X2B/1417, no. 3.

51 BHVP Target MS. 691, f. 319; Faillite Bassenge et Bohmer 31 mars 1790, MS. Archives de Paris D4B6 cart 109/7761.

52 Wilkie Collins, *The Moonstone* [1868], ed. J.I.M. Stewart (Harmondsworth, 1986), pp. 231–2.

53 John Meade Falkner, *Moonfleet* [1898] (Harmondsworth, 1994), p. 179. Film by Fritz Lang, 1955, with substantial changes to the text, and several television adaptations, most recently by Sky 1 in 2013.

54 Falkner, *Moonfleet*, p. 274.

55 Most recently seen in Europe in March 2015.

56 Peter Ackroyd, *Wilkie Collins* (London, 2012), pp. 126, 131.

57 This was C. W. King's *The Natural History, Ancient and Modern, of Precious Stones and Gems* (1865). The *locus classicus* for understanding the importance of gems and jewellery in Victorian fiction is Kurt Tetzeli von Rosador, 'Gems and Jewellery in Victorian Fiction', *REAL*, vol. 11 (1984), pp. 275–300. On Collins's reading see Ackroyd, *Wilkie Collins*, p. 122.

58 Ackroyd, *Wilkie Collins*, p. 130.

59 National Gallery of Scotland, 348.50 x 267.90 cm.

60 The history of the cutting of this stone both before and after its sale are discussed by François Farges in 'Les grands diamants de la Couronne de François 1er à Louis XVI', *Versalia: Revue de la Société des Amis de Versailles* (2014), pp. 69–71. The Regent diamond now belongs to the French state and is on display in the Louvre.

61 Collins, *The Moonstone*, p. 71.

62 Ibid., p. 97.

63 Ibid., p. 67.

64 Falkner, *Moonfleet*, p. 197.

65 Ibid.

66 Ibid., p. 220.

67 Until Sergeant Manby invented his apparatus in 1808, which fired a mortar with a rope attached to the stricken vessel, enabling sailors to secure the rope and thus pass along it to the beach and safety, thousands died in storms along England's coasts. J.M.W. Turner's 1831 painting now in the Victoria and Albert Museum, *Lifeboat and Manby Apparatus Going Off to a Stranded Vessel Making Signal (Blue Lights) of Distress*, is a reminder of how important this invention was.

FURTHER READING

Antwerp Diamond Bourse, company website, www.diamondbourseantwerp.com

Arfe y Villafañe, Juan de, *Quiltador, de la plata, oro, y piedras, conforme a las leyes reales, y para declaracion de ellas* [1572] (Madrid, 1598)

Armstrong, Isobel, *Victorian Glassworlds: Glass Culture and the Imagination, 1830–1880* (Oxford, 2008)

Baer, Eva, *Islamic Ornament* (Edinburgh, 1998)

Balfour, Ian, *Famous Diamonds*, 3rd edn (London, 1997)

Bapst, C. G., *Histoire des joyaux de la couronne de France* (Paris, 1889)

Barber, E.J.W., 'On the Antiquity of East European Bridal Clothing', in *Folk Dress*, ed. Linda Welters (Oxford, 1999)

Bari, Hubert, *Diamants: au coeur de la terre, au coeur des étoiles, au coeur du pouvoir* (Paris, 2001)

Belleau, Remy de, *Les Amours et nouveaux eschanges des pierres précieuses: vertus et propriétés d'icelles* (Paris, 1576)

Berg, Maxine, *Luxury and Pleasure in Eighteenth-century Britain* (Oxford, 2005)

Bhagat, Dipti, 'Buying More Than a Diamond: South Africa at the Colonial and Indian Exhibition, 1886', MA dissertation, V&A/RCA, May 1996

Bieri, Franziska, *From Blood Diamonds to the Kimberley Process: How NGOs Cleaned Up the Global Diamond Industry* (Farnham, 2010)

Blair, Claude, ed., *The Crown Jewels: The History of the Coronation Regalia in the Jewel House of the Tower of London* (London, 1998)

Bowden, Rosalind, 'The Letter Books of John and Nathaniel Cholmley, Diamond Merchants', North Yorkshire County Record Office Publication no. 67, *Review 2001* (Northallerton, 2002)

Bycroft, Michael, 'Wonders in the Academy: The Value of Strange Facts in the

Experimental Research of Charles Dufay', *Historical Studies in the Natural Sciences*, XLIII/3 (June 2013)

Chardin, Jean, *Journal du voyage du Chevalier Chardin en Perse et aux Indes Orientales...* (London, 1686)

Chayes, Evelien, *L'Éloquence des pierres précieuses de Marbode de Rennes à Alard d'Amsterdam et Remy Belleau, sur quelques lapidaires du XVIe siècle* (Paris, 2010)

'Conflict Diamonds', campaign page, www.globalwitness.org

Cruysse, Dirk Van der, *Chardin le Persan* (Paris, 1998)

Cunningham, DeeDee, *The Diamond Compendium* (London, 2011)

Daelen, Veerle Vanden, 'Negotiating the Return of the Diamond Sector and Its Jews: The Belgian Government during the Second World War and the Immediate Post-war Period', *Holocaust Studies: A Journal of Culture and History*, 18 (Autumn/Winter 2012)

Diamond, company website, www.diamond.ac.uk

Dickinson, Joan Younger, *The Book of Diamonds* (New York, 1965)

The Engagement Ring (1912), dir. Mack Sennett. Available to watch at www.archive.org

Epstein, Edward Jay, 'Have You Ever Tried to Sell a Diamond?', www.theatlantic.com, February 1982

—, *The Diamond Invention* (London, 1982)

Farges, François, 'Les grands diamants de la Couronne de François Ier à Louis XVI', *Versalia: Revue de la Société des Amis de Versailles* (2014), pp. 55–78

Forsyth, Hazel, *London's Lost Jewels: The Cheapside Hoard* (London, 2013)

Gambino, Megan, 'Madeleine Albright on Her Life in Pins', www.smithsonianmag.com, June 2010

Greenfield, Jeanette, *The Return of Cultural Treasures* (Cambridge, 1989)

Greig, Hannah, *The Beau Monde: Fashionable Society in Georgian London* (Oxford, 2013)

The Groom-to-be's Handbook: The Ultimate Guide to a Fabulous Ring, a Memorable Proposal, and a Perfect Wedding (New York, 2007)

Hofmeester, Karin, 'Shifting Trajectories of Diamond Processing: From India to Europe and Back, from the Fifteenth Century to the Twentieth', *Journal of Global History*, VIII/1 (March 2013)

Howarth, Stephen, *The Koh-i-noor Diamond: The History and the Legend* (London, 1980)

Jeffries, David, *A Treatise on Diamonds and Pearls: In Which Their Importance is Considered: And Plain Rules are Exhibited for Ascertaining the Value of Both: and the True Method of Manufacturing Diamonds* [1750], 2nd edn with large improvements (London, 1751)

Kanfer, Stefan, *The Last Empire: De Beers, Diamonds, and the World* (London, Sydney and Auckland, 1993)

Kiefer, Anselm, 'Art Will Survive its Ruins', www.college-de-france.fr, 2010–11

'The Kimberley Process', www.globalwitness.org, 1 April 2013

The Kimberley Process, organization website, www.kimberleyprocess.com

King James Bible, www.biblehub.com/KJ2000

Kockelbergh, Iris, Eddy Vleeschdrager and Jan Walgrave, *The Brilliant Story of Antwerp Diamonds*, trans. Gilberte Lenaerts (Antwerp, 1992)

Kreitman, Esther, *Diamonds* [1944], trans. Heather Valencia (London, 2010)

Kunz, George Frederick, *The Curious Lore of Precious Stones* [1913] (New York, 1971)

Lear, Amanda, 'Diamonds' (1979), song lyrics, www.elyrics.net

Lenzen, Godehard, *The History of Diamond Production and the Diamond Trade* [1966], trans. F. Bradley (London, 1970)

Leonardus, Camillus, *The Mirror of Stones . . . Now Translated into English* (London, 1750)

Levi, Karen, *The Power of Love: Six Centuries of Diamond Betrothal Rings* (London, 1988)

Loos, Anita, *Gentlemen Prefer Blondes* [1925] (Harmondsworth, 1992)

'Making Diamonds with a Blowtorch', www.bbc.co.uk, 15 August 2011

Mander, Karel Van, *Het Schilder-boeck* (Haarlem, 1604)

Maupassant, Guy de, *La Parure*, first published in *Le Gaulois* (Paris, 1884)

Mawe, John, *Travels in the Gold and Diamond Districts of Brazil* [1812], revd edn (London, 1821)

May, Paul W., 'Diamond Thin Films: A 21st-century Material', *Philosophical Transactions of the Royal Society of London*, Series A (2000), 358, pp. 473–95

Meisenberg, Simon, 'The Final Judgement in the Trial of Charles Taylor', http://blog.oup.com, 23 September 2013

Meredith, Martin, *Diamonds, Gold and War: The Making of South Africa* [2007] (London, 2008)

Nechtman, Tillman W., 'A Jewel in the Crown? Indian Wealth in Domestic Britain in the Late Eighteenth Century', *Eighteenth-century Studies*, XLI/1 (2007)

Ogletree, Shirley M., 'With This Ring, I Thee Wed: Relating Gender Roles and Love Styles to Attitudes towards Engagement Rings and Weddings', *Gender Issues*, XXVII (June 2010)

Opačić, Zoë, *Diamond Vaults: Innovation and Geometry in Medieval Architecture* (London, 2005)

Partnership Africa Canada, organization website, www.pacweb.org

Pointon, Marcia, *Brilliant Effects: A Cultural History of Gem Stones and Jewellery* (New Haven, CT, and London, 2009)

—, 'Material Manoeuvres: Sarah Churchill, Duchess of Marlborough, and the Power of Artefacts', *Art History*, XXXII/3 (June 2009), pp. 485–515

Prieto, Carlos, *Mining in the New World* (New York, 1973)

Proctor, R. N., 'Anti-agate: The Great Diamond Hoax and the Semiprecious Stone Scam', *Configurations*, IX/3 (2001)

O'Reilley, Jennifer, 'Patristic and Insular Traditions of the Evangelists: Exegesis and Iconography', in *Le Isole Britanniche e Roma in età Romanicobarbarica*, ed. A. M. Luiselli Fadda and É. Ó. Carragáin (Roma, 1998)

Roberts, Janine, *Glitter and Greed: The Secret World of the Diamond Cartel* [2003] (New York, 2007)

Rudoe, Judy, 'Jewellery at the Great Exhibition', in *The Great Exhibition and Its Legacy*, ed. Franz Bosbach and John R. Davis (Munich, 2002)

Scarisbrick, Diana, 'Seventeenth-century Diamond Jewellery and the Ornamental Print', *Een Eeuw van Schittering: diamantjuwelen uit de 17 de eeuw* (Antwerp, 1993)

—, *Jewellery in Britain, 1066–1837* (Wilby, 1994)

Séguin, Jean-Pierre, *Le Jeu de carte* (Paris, 1968)

Sen, N. B., *Glorious History of Koh-i-noor* (Delhi, 1974)

Serlio, Sebastiano, *The First Book of Architecture* (London, 1611)

Smalberger, John M., 'I.D.B. [illicit diamond buying] and the Mining Compound System in the 1880s', *South African Journal of Economics*, XLII/4 (December 1974), pp. 398–414

Smith, Adam, 'Of the Imitative Arts', in *Adam Smith: Essays on Philosophical Subjects*, ed. W.P.D. Wightman and J. P. Bryce (Oxford, 1980)

Streeter, Edwin E., *Precious Stones and Gems* (London, 1898)

Tavernier, Jean-Baptiste, *Les Six voyages de Jean-Baptiste Tavernier, ecuyer Baron d'Aubonne en Turquie, en Perse et aux Indes* (Paris, 1676)

Teresa of Avila, *The Interior Castle* in *The Collected Works of St Teresa of Avila*, 2nd revd edn, ed. Kieran Kavanagh and Otilio Rodriguez (Washington, DC, 1987)

Theophrastus On Stones, trans. and ed. Earle R. Caley and John F. C. Richards (Columbus, OH, 1956)

Tillander, Herbert, *Diamond Cuts in Historic Jewellery, 1381–1910* (London, 1995)

Timmermans, Bert, *Patronen van patronage in het zeventiende-eeuwse Antwerpen* (Amsterdam, 2008)

Tolansky, S., *The History and Use of Diamond* (London, 1962)

Vai, Gian Battista, and W. Glen Caldwell, eds, *The Origins of Geology in Italy*, Geological Society of America, Special Paper 411 (Boulder, CO, 2006)

Vanneste, Tijl, *Global Trade and Commercial Networks: Eighteenth-century Diamond Merchants* (London, 2011)

Vries, David De, *Diamonds and War: State, Capital, and Labor in British-ruled Palestine* (New York and Oxford, 2010)

WG [William Gaspey] *Tallis's Description of the Crystal Palace: Illustrated* (London and New York, 1851)

Woolf, Maurice, 'Joseph Salvador, 1716–1786', *Transactions and Miscellanies of the Jewish Historical Society of England*, 21 (1962–7)

World Diamond Council, organization website, www.worlddiamondcouncil.com

World Federation of Diamond Bourses, organization website, www.wfdb.com

Yogev, Gedalia, *Diamonds and Coral: Anglo-Dutch Jews and Eighteenth-century Trade* (Leicester, 1978)

Young, Paul, '"Carbon, Mere Carbon": The Kohinoor, the Crystal Palace, and the Mission to Make Sense of British India', *Nineteenth-century Contexts: An Interdisciplinary Journal*, XXIX/4 (December 2007)

http://www.debeersgroup.com/sustainability/ethics/conflict-diamonds

https://archive.org/details/GracieRing, 1950s television series

ACKNOWLEDGEMENTS

Many librarians, curators and archivists have assisted me in the preparation of this book; they are too numerous to name but for their patience and expertise I am truly grateful. Many friends, colleagues and relatives have advised and encouraged me. I would like to thank the following for their invaluable help and advice: Audrey Aquilina, Michael Bycroft, Tarnya Cooper, Veerle Vanden Daelen, Barbara Descheemaecker, Carol Dyhouse, Sam Eden, Tamar Garb, Lucy Gent, Susan Lambert, Graham McCallum, Paul May, Alisa Miller, James Miller, John Mitchell, Victoria Mitchell, Daniel Myelemans, Lyn Nead, Didier Nectoux, Jack Ogden, Peter Pomerantsev, Carlo Scaletti, Kerrie Smith, Lindsay Smith, Christine Stevenson, Susan Stronge, Mark Taylor, Paul Taylor, Grenville Turner, Elke Verhoeven, Cordelia Warr, Bert Watteeuw and Michael Willis.

Special gratitude is due to Marc De la Ruelle for his scholarly advice, for help with the index and for his hospitality; to Vladimir Rzhebdev for endeavouring to secure access to material in Russia; and to Tijl Vanneste for generously making time to read the introduction and first two chapters of this book. I am deeply grateful to Michael Leaman of Reaktion Books for encouraging me to write 'off piste', to Harry Gilonis for his exacting standards and to Martha Jay for her patience and courtesy in seeing my text through to print. The Leverhulme Trust generously awarded me a Senior Research Fellowship which allowed me to wander creatively on the road to completing my text and assembling my images. Any lacunae or infelicities are my own.

My conversations with Professor Gisela Ecker began when we met at the University of Sussex in 1982 and have continued, at many times and in many places, to illuminate, instruct and entertain me ever since. It is to her this book is dedicated.

London and Motrone 2016

PHOTO ACKNOWLEDGEMENTS

The author and publishers wish to express their thanks to the following sources of illustrative material and/or permission to reproduce it. Some locations are also supplied here for reasons of brevity. Every effort has been made to contact copyright holders; any copyright holders we have been unable to reach or to whom inaccurate acknowledgements have been made should contact the publisher.

Courtesy The Advertising Archive: 84; Africana Library, Kimberley: 17; Amgueddfa Genedlaethol Cymru/National Museum of Wales, Cardiff: 62; photo © James L. Amos/ Corbis (RM): 9; Antwerp City Archives: 96 (MS. IB 166), 98 (MS. GA 4477 [36]); Archivio di Stato, Rome (courtesy of the Italian Ministry of Cultural Property and Activities): 95; from Juan de Arfe y Villafañe, *Quilatador, de la plata, oro, y piedras, conforme a las leyes reales, y para declaracion de ellas . . .* ([1572] Madrid, 1598): 7; from Juan de Arfe y Villafañe, *De varia Commensuracion para la Esculptura y Architectura . . .* (Seville, 1585): 65; Ashmolean Museum, University of Oxford (photo © Ashmolean Museum): 37; photo James Austin (© The Conway Library, Courtauld Institute of Art, London): 64; photo author: 8, 28, 29, 30, 31, 38, 39, 41, 42, 43, 61, 67, 75, 76, 86, 90, 92, 93; The Barnes Foundation, Philadelphia, Pennsylvania (image © The Barnes Foundation): 74; Bibliothèque Nationale de France (MS Latin 1, f. 329 v) – photo © Bibliothèque Nationale: 54; Boston Museum of Fine Arts (Frank B. Bemis Fund, John H. and Ernestine A. Payne Fund, Elizabeth M. and John F. Paramino Fund in memory of John F. Paramino, Boston Sculptor, Helen B. Sweeney Fund, Mary L. Smith Fund, Textile Income Purchase Fund, Joyce Arnold Rusoff Fund, and Alice J. Morse Fund – photo © 2017 Boston Museum of Fine Arts): 50; The British Library, London (photo © The British Library Board): 52, 53; photos © The British Library Board: 15, 25, 57, 60; The British Museum, London (photo © The Trustees of the British Museum): 3; photos © The Trustees of the British Museum, London: 45, 47; California

Digital Newspaper Collection, Center for Bibliographic Studies and Research, University of California, Riverside http://cdnc.ucr.edu: 91; photo © Marcel Clemens/Shutterstock: 49; from Wilkie Collins, *The Moonstone* (London, 1894), photo courtesy of the University of St Andrews Library: 102; photo Corbis: 48; © Erfgoedbank Kempens Karakter: 19, 40, 44; photo © Serguei Fomine/Global Look/Corbis: 1; photo GIock/Shutterstock.com: 56; courtesy of GIA: 20, 34; from *Harper's and Queen* (May 1977): 78; photo © Blaine Harrington III/Corbis: 16; Damien Hirst and Science Ltd – all rights reserved, © DACS 2016 – photo © Tate London 2015: 77; photo Dazzini Macchine: 5; from *The Illustrated London News* (7 May 1851): 25; from Henri Jacobs et Nicolas Chatrian, *Le Diamant* (Paris, 1884): 15; Kunsthistorisches Museum, Vienna (photo KHM-Museumsverband): 81; © Alicja Kwade (courtesy of the artist and König Galerie, photo Matthias Kolb): 2; photo © Liszt Collection/ Bridgeman Library: 13; photo Patrik Ljungman: 63; by kind permission of Professor Paul May: 8; courtesy Meylemans and Somers, Antwerp: 28, 29, 30, 31; Musée de la Minéralogie, Paris (photo Jean-Michel LE CLEAC'H MINES Paristech): 4; photos National Art Library, Victoria and Albert Museum, London: 7, 51, 65, 83, 88; The National Gallery, London: 71, 72; National Portrait Gallery, London (photo © National Portrait Gallery): 32, 33; N. W. Ayer Advertising Agency Records, Archives Center, National Museum of American History, Smithsonian Institution, Washington, DC: 82; photo © Suzanne Plunkett/Reuters/Corbis (RM): 79; from George Puttenham, *The Arte of English Poesie . . .* (London, 1589) – photo © The British Library Board: 60; from *Recueil des Planches, sur les sciences, les arts liberaux et les arts méchaniques . . .* (Paris, 1793): 36; photo © Roger Ressmeyer/Corbis: 101; RIBA Collections: 46; from Louis Rousselet, *L'Inde des Rajahs: Voyage dans l'Inde Centrale* (Paris: Hachette, 1877) – photo © The British Library Board: 14; Royal Collection Trust © Her Majesty Queen Elizabeth II 2015: 23, 26, 27; courtesy Royal Geographical Society (with IBG): 18; photo © Joel Sartore/ National Geographic Creative / Corbis (RM): 11; from *Les Six voyages de Jean-Baptiste Tavernier, Ecuyer Baron d'Aubonne en Turquie, en Perse et aux Indes*, II (Paris, 1676) – photo © The British Library Board: 10, 12; St John's College, Oxford (MS. 17) – reproduced by permission of the President and Fellows of St John's College, Oxford: 55; from Sebastiano Serlio, *Regole generali d'architetura . . . sopra le cinque maniere de gli edifici . . .* (Venice, 1537) – photo © The British Library Board: 69; © Richard Serra – photography by Rob McKeever – courtesy of the artist and Gagosian Gallery, © ARS, NY, and DACS, London, 2016: 73; photo © Keren Su/China Span/Alamy: 59; from Joannes Antonides van der Goes, *Menschelyke beezigheeden* (Amsterdam, 1695): 35; photo © Victoria and Albert Museum, London: 70; from Hans Vredeman de Vries, *Architectura oder bauung der Antiquen auss dem Vitruvius . . .* ([1577], Antwerp: 1581) – photo © Getty Research Institute, Los Angeles: 68; image from www.ferraraincantesimo.com: 66; Yale University Library, New Haven, CT (South Africa Historical Collection [MS 1556]): 21.

INDEX